CHANNELED
MESSAGES
OF HOPE

Published by Lisa Hagan Books 2024

www.lisahaganbooks.com

Copyright © Carolyn Thomas 2024

ISBN: 978-1-945962-61-5

Author and Interviewer: Carolyn Thomas
Channeler: Sam Larkin
Co-Interviewer: John Thomas

Cover and interior layout by Simon Hartshorne

CHANNELED MESSAGES OF HOPE

Conversations with History's Most
Prominent Souls on the Other Side on Global
Warming and Climate Change

| CAROLYN THOMAS | JOHN THOMAS | WITH SAM LARKIN |

Praise for Channeled Messages of Hope

"Enlightening conversations with historical icons that will fill your soul with optimism for the future of our planet while bringing comfort to those seeking answers about crossing over into the spirit world. A compelling read..."

—**James Van Praagh**, Spiritual Medium/
NY Times Bestselling Author

"*Channeled Messages of Hope* is an inspirational read that feels like a warm, comforting blanket on a cold, stormy day. The reader will feel a sense of hope and optimism in a time of great uncertainty. The overriding message is Love. Love for each other, the animals, all living things, including Mother Earth. Fascinating words from some of the world's most fascinating souls. I could not put this book down..."

—**Holly Coleman**, intuitive consultant

"This is an important book; it lifts our limited human perspective into the higher wisdom of the divine realms. By communicating with sacred beings who once walked the earth we receive vast expansive ideas and solutions to the challenges humans face today. In Unity teachings, we call this "Divine Mind" where the God force supplies us with all we need on earth. This book captures the frequency of Divine Mind and provides an enlightening perspective on our earthly 'unsolvable' problems."

— **Rev Sue Frederick**, author of *Through a Divine Lens*

"The very concept of this book is a wonderful mix of the scientific and the spiritual. The interviews are fascinating and eye-opening. It's heartening to know that these individuals, who contributed so much in their lifetimes, don't stop caring about what happens to the people and the planet after they transition, but are actively helping to improve life on Earth through their intuitive guidance and support. I was left with a great feeling of hope that with their assistance, and our own deliberate intention to open our hearts to more love for each other and our beautiful planet, we can come together to create a better world."

—**Mary Ursettie**, teacher and spiritual advisor,
Have a Better Day™

"In this wonderfully profound book, the author provides us with an insider's channeled view of brilliant men and women from science and politics on our current state of the environment. Beautifully written in an interview format, you will not want to put it down."

—**Chris Bledsoe**, author of *UFO of GOD:*
The Extraordinary True Story of Chris Bledsoe

"Love, knowledge and wisdom learned by those who have gone before us is eternal and this book presents us with the everlasting gift of it. Through messages from brilliant creators, explorers and thought leaders, readers receive guidance knowing that those who cared deeply about humanity and the planet still do care and are still very much with us."

—**Elaine Clayton,** author of *The Way of the Empath*

Contents

A Message from The Council

Dear Ones,

We greet you with love and support from the higher realms. We are here to help you create a bridge to an awakening and a transformation. Your loving presence is all that we seek to serve and assist you. But we cannot interfere as you have free will that allows you the freedom to choose any reality and experience and expression of all that you are.

Know that the Earth is magical, miraculous, and divinely orchestrated, and we are all connected as One. We encourage you to step into the light and navigate our changing world with a new level of consciousness and go beyond your thinking mind toward manifestation to create a limitless, abundant heaven on Earth.

Let us support you in coming together in a magnificent light of Love, Harmony, and Unity to embrace the beautiful, blissful magic and higher wisdom that we know as home.

-The Council, February 2023

Preface

Channeled Messages of Hope is a compilation of channeled conversations obtained through a free-flowing interview format that took place from October 2022 through March 2023 with nineteen prominent souls. From their unique vantage point on the other side, the souls impart messages of hope for all of us on Earth during a time of human-induced global warming that has been accelerating at an unprecedented rate, causing extreme weather and environmental events, rising sea levels, ocean acidification, biodiversity loss, diminished food security, increased health risks, and poverty and displacement.

Taking a comprehensive approach, we interviewed souls who had been political leaders, scientists, marine biologists, oceanographers, climate change researchers, physicists, inventors, conservationists, spiritual leaders, a self-help author, and even a saint. These souls had been very influential while in a physical body, and most acted on behalf of the planet. They were asked to draw upon knowledge gained from their time on Earth as well as their perspective now on the other side.

The souls provide insights into what the future holds along with upcoming technological innovations and breakthroughs; meaningful actions that each of us on Earth can take, why this crisis is happening from a higher perspective, what we are to learn; and tools that we can employ for self-care. The souls also share surprising revelations from their time on Earth, such as what their experience was like when crossing over, who they are guides for and how they help them, collaborations with souls on the other side, and if they have plans for another incarnation.

The souls felt so honored and excited to participate in this endeavor, and it is my honor and privilege to relay their messages of hope to you.

-Carolyn Thomas

Introduction

Carolyn (Author and Interviewer)

Why did I create this book? I have an agreement with a group of souls known as The Council to put forth messages of hope from inspirational beings on the other side to people on Earth. The Council sends me nudges and ideas that pop into my head, and they facilitate the interviews that I conduct through a channeler. For this first book, The Council led me to the topic of global warming and climate change. They are aware that as the climate crisis intensifies, it is leaving many with a sense of despair for the world and their future. People are searching for a sense of safety, comfort, and hope during this unprecedented time. This is The Council's project, and I am the messenger.

Allow me to back up a bit. While I have been on a spiritual path since the late 1980s and feel very comfortable with, and am open to, channeled information, I never imagined that I would be talking one-on-one with souls on the other side, and extremely notable ones, no less. I worked for many years at high-tech companies and venture capital firms in Silicon Valley and exited the workforce in 2007 to address health issues that had progressively worsened.

How did this all come about? I first met Sam in 2013 when I was having behavioral issues with one of my cats. Sam is clairvoyant and highly clairsentient with many psychic gifts, including the ability to communicate with animals. With no words spoken, she could converse with my cat and provide valuable feedback. Over time, Sam and I developed a close friendship.

In 2021, Sam began to receive messages from what she could feel was a high-vibrational, very powerful soul on the other side, and the messages were for me. During this period, Sam attempted something that she had never tried before: channeling a soul from the other side. Sam "stepped away" from her body, surrendered control, and allowed the essence of this soul to inhabit her body, utilize her vocal cords, and talk one-on-one with me. This highly evolved soul had been a Hindu guru and spiritual master for many people during his previous life on Earth and wished to have a connection with me.

Speaking in English with a Hindi accent through Sam, the guru explained that we had shared many lifetimes together and that he had been looking after me since I was a child. I recalled a childhood bicycle accident in which I became airborne and inexplicably kind of floated back down to the asphalt, gently landing on my feet. I knew that I should have been injured, and I also knew that despite my young age, something very special had just happened. There were also several close calls in my early adulthood that almost felt like divine intervention, where I got through some very dangerous situations completely unscathed. The soul confirmed he'd had a hand in each case.

This soul also told me that in 2009, from the other side, he could see that I was subconsciously getting ready to cross over, and he stepped in to intervene because it was not my time. I recalled that I had been in a lot of unrelenting physical pain and exhaustion in 2008, stemming from a chronic illness. I was in bed for most of this period, and I had thought to myself that I no longer wanted to be in this body if things didn't turn around within one year. To circumvent an unplanned and early exit, this soul had guided and assisted in various ways, unbeknownst to me, and brought the perfect beings into my life so that I would feel more comfortable in my body and want to stick around on the Earth plane. I refer to him as Baba and continue to maintain regular contact through Sam and another channeler.

While taking a shower in August 2022, an idea popped into my head to take this experience a step further and explore channeling other souls through Sam while I ask the questions in a conversational style interview format. After several successful test interviews, including one with British singer David Bowie—an artist that both Sam and I love, a flash of inspiration to create a messages of hope book based on such interviews came to me, and the project began immediately.

Through Sam, I shared my idea about the project with Baba, the Hindu guru on the other side. Baba then began to fill in the gaps. "Well, I am on a council . . . The Council. I am with other souls, and we are talking about your project because we want to send hope—messages of hope. We want the people to know that we are witnessing their struggles, but we see that Mother Earth is struggling most of all. We are looking forward to giving information to you."

Further, it was revealed that The Council were the ones that had downloaded the idea of the project to me in the first place. As Baba told me, "We do that because we know that you are susceptible to what we want to do, and you and Sam are here to help. It's our project, and we are giving you the responsibility of helping with this project. But it originated with The Council." For those unfamiliar with The Council, it is a group of ascended master beings on the other side who prefer to remain anonymous, which is why I am unable to disclose Baba's name. While we can't be certain, we have been led to conclude that souls such as Saint Francis, Jesus Christ, and other enlightened beings are members of The Council.

For this book, I had knowledge that The Council was initiating contact with the souls to be interviewed, paving the way for access that otherwise would likely not have been possible. When asked how he knew that I wanted to speak with him, John McCain directly said that it was The Council. "I was called into a meeting, and I was told that I would be meeting with all of you," McCain explained.

It was Sam's and my desire to retain our privacy and use pseudonyms for the book along with my husband, John, who is the co-interviewer. The decision was also made not to disclose what was happening with most of our friends and family. In all fairness, how could they possibly understand? Further, I share things of a personal nature in the book that I would not feel so inclined to do if I were forthcoming with my name. Some of my stories make me feel a little vulnerable. In the end, my name is not important. Again, I am the messenger.

How do these conversations take place? Sam channels the souls and I conduct the interviews, along with help from John. Leading up to the interviews, I handle the research and preparation of questions, and Sam sees nothing in advance except a photo of the soul that she will soon be channeling. Sam channels from her home, an hour away from where I live. The interviews are conducted over the phone, recorded, and later transcribed.

What was it like to interact with these souls? Early on, I would feel extremely anxious right before an interview and, honestly, quite intimidated. Not only was I about to talk with a distinguished and well-known soul that I held in high regard in most cases, but I was also keenly aware that The Council would be watching, and I did not want to let them down. This was their project, after all. Thankfully, I would find most of the souls to be very approachable, forthcoming, and kind, which helped put me at ease. Over time, pre-interview jitters were replaced with anticipation, and I absolutely loved doing the interviews.

The souls who had been on the planet during my time, expressed themselves through Sam, much as they had on television or how they had been described in biographies. Some were friendly and easygoing, while others were stronger and more direct. I experienced the souls to be reflective, without ego, and softer around the edges than how I had remembered them on Earth. Some of the souls displayed a sense of humor, while others were more serious. Mohandas Gandhi was, of course, very wise and very profound, but he surprised us with his playfulness and quick wit. And I was able to get George H. W. Bush involved in delivering an inside joke back to his friend Gandhi for us.

While spoken in English, I heard accents from around the world that were channeled through Sam, including Italian (Saint Francis of Assisi), German (Albert Einstein), Eastern Indian (Gandhi), Serbian (Nikola Tesla), French (Jacques Cousteau), Southern US (Samuel Clemens / Mark Twain), Portuguese (Chico Mendes), and a hint of Scottish (John Muir). The responses from the souls have not been edited and, for the most part, appear as stated. For some, English was not their first language, so brackets were added for clarification purposes. On occasion, unnecessary words were omitted for clarity and concision, and these omissions are marked with ellipses.

At times, it was difficult for Sam to hold a channel for longer than one hour, so several interviews were sometimes necessary. Because of this, I started to form, what felt like, friendly relationships with some of the souls, and the conversations could get light and jokey at the end of the interviews. Some of these souls would share things off-record, such as big political news that would soon be forthcoming or information of a helpful nature personally.

John led some of the more technical interviews. He has an engineering background, so the preparation came much more easily to him. John was particularly interested in talking with the inventors and physicists, and these souls appreciated speaking with a person who had a greater understanding of and exposure to science and technology.

The souls have the sincerest of desires to provide you, the reader, with the much-needed hope that life on Earth really will get better, along with specific actions that each of us can take to help reach this objective. As Theodore Roosevelt said, "We can do this. We can come together and save this beautiful land. I believe with all my heart that it will be done." Or, in the words of Samuel Clemens, "I truly know and believe the world is going to be a better, happier place in about twenty years. But it doesn't mean y'all need to get lazy."

And it is my sincere hope that you will find comfort and inspiration in their messages.

John (Co-interviewer)

I could not believe what I was hearing. Richard Nixon was coming through! And Carolyn was talking directly with him. So, why would Carolyn want to talk to Nixon if this is a book about messages of hope for our planet?

This is the magic, in my opinion, of this effort. Nixon, of course, had a very checkered past and a negative public perception based on the Watergate scandal. But at the same time, he was a Republican president of the United States who seemingly had some conscience around the environment. Part of the intention of this book is to explore not just the technical potential for the future but also to understand the mindset of policymakers from the past and illicit guidance on how to influence current elected officials and move forward in a direction that will help our planet. But back to Nixon. Carolyn was very apprehensive about this interview. She had been told by several souls that Nixon was deep in self-isolation and reflecting on his lessons. Because of this, we did not think he would surface when asked. But he did. Do not underestimate the power of The Council, is my takeaway. Carolyn was initially terrified upon hearing Nixon's voice through Sam. I, however, as simply an observer, was fascinated. And I appreciated Nixon showing up.

So, who am I, and why am I involved? I am Carolyn's husband. I am very fortunate to be Carolyn's husband! I graduated with a degree in chemical engineering, and my background is classic corporate technology. I went down the typical Silicon Valley tech company path but soon diverted to marketing, sales, and business development. I've tried my hand at big companies and cofounded several start-ups. I've had some successes, some failures, and lots of interesting experiences.

My involvement with the book began several months in, after Carolyn had already interviewed four souls. The opportunity emerged when Carolyn was preparing for the Nikola Tesla interview. Without an engineering background, she was having difficulty formulating the more technical questions fitting for such a soul and asked for my help. I ended up leading the interview with Tesla, as well as the interviews with Albert Einstein and his first wife, Mileva, who revealed that she co-authored Einstein's paper on relativity, along with four other papers filed in 1905. I also felt drawn to speak with Ronald Reagan and Samuel Clemens, and would go on to participate in the remaining interviews with Carolyn. We felt that having the two of us interview a soul made for more interesting conversation as well as follow-on questions.

I must say, I was blown away to have had the opportunity to interact directly with these souls. And in three unexpected instances, we found ourselves talking with the soul's higher self on the other side. This was because the soul was back in a body on Earth, as was the case with John Muir. Yes, right now, today, John Muir is incarnated on our planet, and is a young Canadian lad who loves to snowboard. We also discovered that Theodore Roosevelt is currently a Franciscan monk in Kenya, and Mileva Einstein is a psychotherapist in India. This is blow-away material, as far as I'm concerned.

Along with their perspectives on the future of our planet, the souls share what it was like when crossing over and what they are now doing on the other side. The souls are not just resting on their laurels. They are assigned to or chosen for certain areas of interest to them, to help others both on the other side and on Earth. Or, they are in a state of deep reflection, with the intent to learn from their past life and evolve.

I know that our connection to those in spirit form is very real and very close. I have also learned that it is all about Love. The souls on the other side love and care for us deeply and want the best for our planet. Prior to this book, I intellectually knew and believed that we were all connected. But now, I *feel* it. And this includes all things, even what we might say are "inanimate" things. Our Earth has a soul and needs to be treated as a loved one. This is clear to me, and I thank the souls for imparting this knowledge and helping to raise my awareness.

I believe the readers will feel inspired and enlightened by the information contained within this book. While each of us still has a responsibility to love and honor our planet and try to make this place better for future generations, it is my hope that readers will feel deeply touched and comforted by the souls' words and optimistic about this beautiful place we presently call home.

Sam (Channeler)

Whenever I'm asked, "How was your weekend?" I answer with, "Great! How was yours?" and quickly flip the question back to my colleagues at the investment firm where I work. I would never tell them that I spent my past Saturday channeling Albert Einstein or Nikola Tesla, because (1) That would be crazy; and (2) Is that even possible? I'll admit that it's kind of crazy. But it's also entirely possible.

Although channeling is somewhat new for me, I've always been intuitive. In fact, until I was eleven, it never occurred to me that this was not the norm, as I assumed that everyone was intuitive. So, I just took it for granted. But when my family bought a farm that eleventh summer and I was surrounded by various types of farm animals, I realized that my mom and dad did not share in my awareness in knowing that a cow was ill before exhibiting physical symptoms or that one of our horses was not just "skittish" but fearful of plastic bags in the wind. Much later, I learned that the animals were telepathically communicating this information to me in pictures, and I was interpreting the pictures. This is called clairvoyance, which literally means "clear seeing." Along the way, I also discovered that I am highly clairsentient, which is the ability to feel an innate emotional awareness of psychic information.

As I got older and began working in the corporate world, I also started sharing my animal communication and psychic work with others by offering "readings" on the weekends while I held down my day job in financial services. This is how I met Carolyn, who was one of my clients, and before long, we became close friends. Eventually, I decided to stop doing my readings because the experience felt "complete" to me. I knew I wanted to use my intuitive gifts in other ways, and I decided to look for a "next step." Little did I know that next step would include channeling notable spirits and working on a book project with Carolyn!

So, you're probably wondering how a person with a master's degree working in such a "serious" day job ends up channeling Albert Einstein or Nikola Tesla—or anyone for that matter. Well, as you've probably guessed, having an open mind is essential! Also, having a sense of play while also being fully committed to the prospect of unlimited possibilities is a crucial element. And as you can imagine, it's very important that I fully prepare myself before each session.

Before I begin to channel, I meditate, which includes grounding and running my energy with the intent of bringing in only the spirit that Carolyn and I have agreed upon (I've found that it also helps to have a photo of the spirit that I wish to connect with, close by). I imagine roses on the outside of my aura (an invisible bubble of energy that surrounds my body) that I refer to as "protection roses." I then cleanse my chakras and proceed to close down my first chakra (root) to 10 percent, my second chakra (sacral) to 10 percent, and lastly, my third chakra (solar plexus) to 50 percent.

Once I've prepared my body, I go into a light trance and envision the spirit we wish to bring in that day (almost always, I see the spirit in the wings of a theatre, waiting for their "entrance"), while Carolyn says an invocation prayer, beckoning the spirit to enter. From there, I imagine the top of my head (crown chakra) opening, and I proceed to watch myself rise up out of my body as the invoked spirit enters through the top of my head and takes my place.

Although they all share a sense of urgency in their approach, each spirit has their own distinct and creative way of entering my body. For example, climbing a ladder up to the top of my head, "flying" into the top of my head suited up as an astronaut, captaining a tiny submarine (bonjour, Captain Cousteau!), riding an escalator to the top of my head, nervously approaching with notes in hand, or simply strolling in from the "wings." I had expected Samuel Clemens to move slowly, but he was very quick and super springy right up the ladder. An especially memorable entrance, however, was Theodore Roosevelt galloping in on a beloved horse.

Once the spirit has taken their place in my body, I imagine the top of my head closing. All these elements help me to surrender control and allow the essence of the spirit to channel through me. After the spirit inhabits my body and the interview begins, I feel like I'm in the back seat of a car, watching the driver and front-seat passenger having a conversation. Afterward, I seldom remember anything that has been said by the spirit or even Carolyn's and John's questions, but I very clearly feel the unique energy of each soul. For example, Albert Einstein had a pragmatic steadiness and accommodating energy, whereas Nikola Tesla had a light, kind-hearted, and well-meaning, conscientious energy.

When the interview is over, I imagine the crown chakra at the top of my head opening once more; I trade places with the spirit and close the "lid" on the top of my head. One time, I hadn't opened the top of my head fast enough, and the poor soul banged his head on the inside of my head! Finally, after a successful exit, he then playfully walked around my office as though he were drunk! Another time, I was touched to have John McCain thank me after he exited. A true gentleman, indeed. And Wayne Dyer sweetly gave me a hug and a kiss on the cheek after his interview.

I found out that I could channel because I was willing to try. If I had not had a sense of play, a willingness, and a belief that it was possible, I would never have known that a meeting with Samuel

Clemens is much more fun than sitting in a meeting with a group of portfolio managers. There's a quote from artist Pablo Picasso that I love: "I am always doing things I can't do, that's how I get to do them." Well said, Pablo. And with Carolyn's undeniable support, encouragement, meticulous research, and thoughtful interviews, we were off. And that's exactly how this book began.

CHAPTER 1:

Soul Invocation / Global Warming & Climate Change Summary

Soul Invocation

Every channeled interview began in the same way. Contact with the soul was made through an invocation, where they were invited to come forth to be channeled. After the soul arrived and was welcomed, introductions were made, and the topic and purpose of the book were explained. The soul was then asked to participate in an interview to discuss the crisis from their unique perspective on the other side.

The below summary was then read to the soul before the start of the interview. While the circumstances described may sound grim, please be assured there will be many reasons to feel hopeful and optimistic about the future of our planet in the chapters that follow.

Global Warming and Climate Change Summary

Earth's global temperature has increased an average of 1.1 degrees Celsius since the preindustrial period between 1850 and 1900 to present day, and since 1975, it has been increasing at a rate of 0.15 to 0.20 degrees Celsius per decade. From the time global temperature recordkeeping began in 1880, the ten warmest years have occurred since 2010. According to the Intergovernmental Panel on Climate Change (IPCC) in 2022, the world is now warming faster than at any point in recorded history.

The scientific community is in consensus that global warming and climate change are human-caused from greenhouse gas emissions—primarily carbon dioxide, but also methane, nitrous oxide, and fluorinated gases—and there is an abundance of scientific evidence to support this assertion. The existential threat to humanity is no longer something we read about that is far off in the future. The time has arrived, and human beings around the world are personally witnessing the devastating effects of a rapidly changing climate. Along with temperature increases that are causing ice loss at the poles and mountain glaciers leading to rising sea levels, people are experiencing an increase in the intensity and frequency of extreme weather events such as heatwaves, droughts, and wildfires, along with hurricanes, heavy precipitation, and flooding.

The burning of fossil fuels, deforestation, and livestock farming are the primary drivers influencing the global temperature and climate. In 2022, fossil fuels—coal, oil, and gas—were the largest contributors to climate change, accounting for over 75 percent of global greenhouse gas emissions in the atmosphere, which trap the sun's heat. Fossil fuels supplied 80 percent of the world's energy—electricity, transport, and heat—with renewables such as solar, wind turbines, and hydropower picking up the balance, along with zero-emission nuclear power.

There are many global climate coalitions, all with a common goal to reach net-zero carbon emissions and limit warming to no more than 1.5 degrees Celsius above preindustrial levels by 2050. The largest and most prominent of these coalitions, the Paris Agreement, is comprised of 193 countries, in addition to the European Union, which have all pledged to adopt this common goal.

In 2022, the United Nations Environment Programme (UNEP) reported that commitments made by governments to cut emissions fell far short of what is required, and there was no credible plan in place to limit warming to 1.5 degrees Celsius unless countries immediately transitioned from fossil fuels to clean energy sources. Also in 2022, the IPCC forecasted that, on the current trajectory, Earth's temperature could rise 2.8 degrees Celsius above preindustrial levels by the end of the century, creating a global catastrophe.

Even a rise of 2 degrees Celsius would be dire. Nearly 40 percent of the population would face severe heatwaves at least once every five years, and up to three billion people could experience chronic water scarcity. Category 4 and 5 storms would be more common, and 36 percent of land would be exposed to extreme precipitation. Millions would be impacted by a rise in sea level, forcing many to escape coastal communities. A 34 percent loss of plant and animal species and an 8 percent loss of vertebrates by 2100 would be seen, and more than 99 percent of coral reefs would be destroyed. Health impacts from increased vector-borne disease would occur, along with increased crop failures that lead to a steep rise in hunger and famine.

Most emissions come from just a few countries. According to the 2022 UNEP Emissions Gap Report, the top seven emitters—China, the US, India, the European Union, Indonesia, Russia, and Brazil—accounted for about half of global greenhouse gas emissions in 2020. The group of twenty—Argentina, Australia, Brazil, Canada, China, France, Germany, India, Indonesia, Italy, Japan, Republic of Korea, Mexico, Russia, Saudi Arabia, South Africa, Turkey, the United Kingdom, the United States, and the European Union—are responsible for about 75 percent of global greenhouse gas emissions.

To reach the Paris Agreement goal of limiting warming to 1.5 degrees Celsius by 2050, emissions would need to be reduced by 45 percent by 2030 and reach net-zero by 2050. The world's nations must drastically, and immediately, reduce reliance on fossil fuels and deploy the clean energy resources that are already available, along with upcoming innovations and breakthrough technologies that will help take us the rest of the way. Global cooperation, especially from the top emitters, will be imperative if we are to avoid a climate disaster.

CHAPTER 2:

Senator John McCain (1936–2018)

Interview dates: January 13, 2023, and January 15, 2023

John McCain served in the US Navy, flew fighter jets in the Vietnam War, and was a tortured prisoner of war in Vietnam for five and a half years. He went on to serve as a Republican Representative, followed by six terms in the US Senate until his passing. McCain was a favorite of reporters who admired his directness and saw him as a straight shooter, and he developed a reputation as a political maverick, unafraid to cross party lines.

McCain took stands on many issues that distanced him from the conservative Republican mainstream in Washington and was outspoken about the climate during his last two decades in office. In 2017, he cast the deciding vote against a motion to proceed with the repeal of the Obama administration's regulations on the greenhouse gas methane, a notable source of global warming. His surprise vote kept the regulations in place.

McCain introduced the bipartisan Climate Stewardship Acts along with then Democratic Senator, Joe Lieberman and other cosponsors. Unfortunately, all three acts failed to gain enough votes to pass through the Senate. But his efforts provided an example of how collaboration can influence policy on issues of global significance, such as the environment.

McCain also brought climate science to Capitol Hill, chairing hearings and inviting top climate scientists to testify about issues such as melting ice shelves in Antarctica and dying coral reefs, in an effort to help educate his Republican colleagues on the impact of climate change.

Part One: January 13, 2023

Carolyn: First of all, do you agree with my global warming and climate change summary? And what are your thoughts right now, given your perspective on the other side, with respect to the current state of the planet?

McCain: I agree with your summary. This is something that has been at the forefront of my mind and something that I was working to change while I was in a body. I would like to say that I have always been direct and straightforward, and I've always been honest. And I am happy to be here and answer your questions as best I can.

I feel that we are getting closer to educating people and accepting the fact that this is real—that this is a fact, not a hunch. I am in agreement with this, and I feel that we are on track to make the goal, but I feel that we have a lot of work ahead of us. It's a leadership approach that I was hoping for in addressing climate change as a nation and as a global concern. I would like to say, though, that I feel that we are becoming more accepting of this, and it's very much like the denial of smoking being cancerous. Now we are accepting that cigarette smoking does cause cancer, but it took a long time because commerce and a lot of money are involved. And this is something that is very much like the warning about cigarettes and cancer. But I feel that people are starting to accept, embrace, and be proactive about climate change.

John: Relations between China and the United States have been more than frosty until recently. President Joe Biden and President Xi Jinping are finally back on speaking terms, and the White House recently announced that the two countries would resume their climate talks. We know these superpower relations go up and down, but do you see China; currently the world's largest emitter, taking tangible, meaningful steps in the very near future to finally get on board with meeting their Paris Agreement commitments? Or is it going to take cheaper-than-fossil fuel innovations becoming available for China's leadership to finally take action? Or is it something else?

McCain: Well, I feel, John, that you are correct in that it's going to take innovations that are more affordable for China to fully get on board. They are behind in their way of thinking and accepting the global change. They continue to pour huge amounts of carbon emissions into the environment, and they continue to pollute their country and the planet. So, I feel that, for them to fully get on board, there needs to be cheaper innovations for them to curb their manufacturing and for them to actually commit 100 percent. It is a bit of a precarious situation at this time. Joe [Biden] feels that this is something that he needs to be careful about pressing at this time. But it is something that he is trying to be strategic about, and all of those who are in agreement with the Paris Agreement realize that China is holding us back in their full commitment to this cause.

Carolyn: If you were still in the Senate, are there actions you would propose to encourage China to honor their commitments, at least until these cheaper innovations can be made available?

McCain: I agree with Joe [Biden] that you need to be tenderfooted around this situation. But I feel that opening talks and getting back into the talks, again treading lightly, is going to be helpful in making steps toward getting China to collaborate with those in the Paris Agreement. It's not only going to be Joe. It's going to be world leaders that also need to do their part. But China is the problem child that we are all worried about.

John: Does everything go through President Xi, or are there other paths?

McCain: That's an excellent question, and yes, it does go through Xi. There are other advisers in China that are actually working to persuade Xi at this time. It's all about getting someone who is very strong-willed and very stubborn to see that there is another way because his main concern is the economy of his country. To make that change at this time, he sees it as his economy going belly-up, and he does not see that there could be support for that. If China goes, we all go, as far as the economy. We have to be very careful about this subject. But yes, it does primarily go through President Xi. Again, he does have advisers trying to get him to see another way. However, the Paris Agreement is buying them some time to figure out how they are going to fix this, and it is also buying them time to make changes of mind as well as changes to their contribution to global warming, which is significant.

Carolyn: Do you believe that President Xi understands his contribution to global warming is significant?

McCain: Yes, he is aware. I support Joe Biden in his efforts, and I'd like to say that this is a time when we can make progress with Biden in office. I think from the American citizens' point of view that he may be reticent to have these kinds of conversations and to take these kinds of actions to heart . . . I don't see that. I see him making a significant contribution toward improvements and also toward our talks about climate change. I also see him making progress with President Xi.

Carolyn: Excellent.

McCain: Carolyn, if I may say one more thing.

Carolyn: Of course.

McCain: 2023 is going to be a year where our former president, Donald Trump, definitely gets his due.

Carolyn: [Quietly.] Thank God.

McCain: [Laughs.] There are many people saying that under their breath right now with you.

[Note: McCain also shared some positive news on the personal front that would soon be forthcoming for John and me. We eventually got back to the topic at hand.]

Carolyn: In 2022, President Biden signed the largest climate legislation in United States history. This new law basically provides all sorts of incentives, tax breaks, rebates, and a huge investment in growing our renewable energy infrastructure, such as solar panels and wind turbines, all for the transition to renewable energy that will put us on track to meet our Paris Agreement commitment. It is also expected to encourage a cycle of innovation that would ultimately reduce costs, with the intention of helping to make the transition to a low-carbon future more affordable worldwide. Do you see this legislation acting as a major catalyst to spur technological innovations and breakthroughs in the private sector to help the world meet the Paris Agreement goals of net-zero emissions by 2050 and limiting warming to no more than 1.5 degrees Celsius?

McCain: Carolyn, I do. I feel this. I have to tell you that government cannot make progress without creating incentives to cut carbon emissions. What Joe [Biden] is doing . . . this is part of the progress I was talking about. I feel that this is a huge stride forward. We are still educating so many politicians about climate change, and there are so many who refuse to accept this. But I feel that this will truly be the catalyst to move us forward.

Carolyn: Wonderful. Is there something more the government should be doing to stimulate innovations and advancements in the private sector?

McCain: In the private sector, there are incentives in the market that are still on the side of carbon-based energy. The incentives need to tilt more toward decreasing carbon-based energy and fossil fuel usage. So, I feel that there is still more that can be done.

Carolyn: Okay. Thank you.

McCain: There is always more, Carolyn. I don't know if you were aware of that. Especially to get people to get their minds off of money. There is always more that can be done.

Carolyn: Yes, I can imagine. Not a single Republican in the US House or Senate voted for Biden's climate bill, although some do see climate danger. Republicans argued that the bill was packed with unnecessary spending and would not address rising inflation. Although many conservatives still don't accept that burning fossil fuels is the primary cause of global warming, a majority of voters do, with extreme flooding, massive wildfires, and other climate impacts visible across the country. Republicans in Congress are out of step with the American public on climate. Do Republicans simply not see the future risk? Do they not believe the science? Is it just a matter of the fossil fuel industry driving policy? Or a little of all the above?

McCain: Yes. It's all of the above. The Republican Party as we know it today is not a party that I would want to represent at this time. I would not want to be part of the Republican Party as we know it today. There are people who are accepting [of climate change] and wanting to move forward in the Republican Party, but it is a hard sell when the majority are confused about what the party stands for—what America stands for. And confused about what they stand for as individuals. There is a lack of education about the environment and global warming and a lack of acceptance, often for no reason, just because. And that is the only way I can say that. It's black or white, and the party, at this time is in complete disarray. They have to have a major reset within the Republican Party, or I see a lot of this discussion and voting being in vain. I feel that it will move forward, but there are so many people who are trying to block this at this time. The party has to reset itself. And it's not just about global warming; it's about everything. When I was a member of the party, I brought in scientists to educate the Senate about what was happening. I brought in scientists with facts, and there were still people who said, "You know, I don't know."

There's not a sense of urgency . . . Since then—and that was a number of years ago—we are in a much more urgent situation. And in 2000, the Senate voted closer than the Republicans did this time on climate change. There has to be a come-to-Jesus moment here. I feel that we can do it, but there are many members of the party that are not serving the party. And that's the only way that I can say it. If those who stand for what the Republican Party is about and stand for America and our country . . . if those people were to become more adamant and more aggressive about what they are there to take care of, then we can save the party, we can save the initiatives, and we can save the direction of the incentives in climate change. I see that they are on the precipice of that happening, but I feel like it will be in time. And I know that's a lot of talking around the subject, but it is a big obstacle right now.

Carolyn: So, Senator, other than the threat of getting voted out of office, how do we, the American public, appeal to Republicans to see global warming and climate change not as a partisan issue or contest between interest groups but as a clear and present threat to our way of life?

McCain: Yes, there needs to be an upsurge. It needs to be shoved in their faces by the American public, and they need to speak their mind. They need to write to their congressmen, and there needs to be an upsurgence. They are very good at protesting climate change, but what needs to happen is they need to protest those voting against climate change even being a thing.

Carolyn: What actions would get your attention if you were still in the House or Senate, to advance climate legislation?

McCain: Well, when I worked toward educating the Senate, I had pictures of the Arctic from one hundred years ago and pictures from 2000. The difference was shocking. Shocking. That is something that I know affected the votes, to see the differences. Those who say, "Oh, that's a natural progression of the environment," those are the ones who need to be educated the most. I think that we are at a point now where those politicians need to be shocked. It may even be that there's another education summit that they attend, and they have to see the grisly pictures. And then, if they are still denying it, then that is . . . the party just wanting to be opposed to anything that can move Biden's plan forward.

Carolyn: The House is now led by Republicans, with a Speaker largely beholden to the Freedom Caucus, which will likely prevent future legislation to address climate change. From your vantage point, do you see any climate legislation being passed before the 2024 election?

McCain: I do see that. And I'm not sure how that's going to happen, Carolyn, to tell you the truth. It may not be as much as we'd like, but I do see that happening. You are correct. He [Speaker Kevin McCarthy] has dug himself into a hole, and he's given them the power to designate how everything will go down at this point according to their whims. I do see action going forward, but I don't know how that's going to happen, to be completely honest.

Carolyn: From your perspective, do you see a shift or improvement in how Congress as a whole addresses climate change legislation following the 2024 presidential election? Or will it take longer to see more substantial climate legislation?

McCain: Carolyn, I don't know why I'm such an optimist, but I think it's going to happen. How can we continue to ignore this? I mean, as I was saying, cigarettes being the cause of cancer was denied for what was that, fifty, seventy-five years? And we finally got there. But I see this being more imminent. I see this happening, actually sooner, as climate change continues to affect people on a personal level.

Carolyn: Do you see a change in the Speaker of the House soon, where perhaps it's more of a moderate Republican?

McCain: Yes, I don't think he'll [Speaker McCarthy] be in place very long. I'm an optimist. I think this is why I see some change happening because I don't see him being the Speaker for very long.

John: I noticed that your second Climate Stewardship Act called for the federal government to play a lead role in researching and commercializing new energy technologies, particularly nuclear plant designs. A major nuclear fusion energy breakthrough was recently announced that could lead to a source of safe, unlimited, carbon-free energy in the future with no meltdowns or nuclear waste. While there is still much work to be done, when do you see widespread use of this new fusion technology?

McCain: Well, I still feel there are breakthroughs that need to happen. As far as putting a timeline on it, I feel that we could be talking up to twenty years from now, but I also feel that the announcement that was made was not in vain. They didn't need to pat themselves on the back. They feel they are getting closer. My trust is in the scientists that are working on this. They feel they are getting closer and closer, and all their energies are being put into this. I know that they are hoping that this will take as little as ten years from now, at the maximum. I feel that we cannot move forward in a significant way without nuclear clean energy. From what I'm seeing in the strides we will be making, I feel that nuclear fusion will play a significant part in that. I have faith that they will deliver sooner than later. I know that's not very specific, but I know that all their energies are going to this, and they are hoping to complete this before the ten-year mark is up.

John: Well, that's really good news. So, in your opinion, should we also be working on more widely deploying current generation fission nuclear plants until we can get up to speed with the new fusion technology?

McCain: I think the goal is to wait, but I also see that it may begin to take place. It's quite costly to deal with that radioactivity [waste], so the goal is to make it not only perform but also to make it affordable so it can be widely used. So, yes, that is an option.

John: What message would you like to give to the public who may fear nuclear power after witnessing the Three Mile Island, Chernobyl, and Fukushima meltdowns?

McCain: The public needs to have more education. That is something that could not only come from the government but also from the media. The public needs more education and more information, and they simply don't have it. They have access to it, but they are fearful sometimes of getting that access. It needs to come in a soft, kind way so they want to learn more about the progress we are making. People still have "fear pictures" around meltdowns in their minds, and that is something where education could come from the government and media as well. But it needs to be presented in a clear, concise, not-over-your-head type of way, and it needs to be presented in a very optimistic way—that these are good things that are happening.

John: It sounds like nuclear fusion would be a good place to start.

McCain: I agree.

John: Drought conditions are a problem in many places, including the Southwest. The Colorado River provides water and electricity to about forty million people in seven states, including your home state of Arizona. The Colorado River system as a whole was at 34 percent of its peak capacity in 2022, down from 40 percent last year. Mandatory water cuts are now in place, but they're not going to solve the problem. It looks like a major emergency is about to happen anywhere there is dependence on Colorado River water. What do you see happening to this part of the country over the next one to two years or however many years it takes for the river to run below levels that sustain society in the region? How will the region react? Or, more basic, will this region become America's next "Dust Bowl?"

McCain: Well, that is something that I would never want to see. I know that we have plenty of sun in Arizona, but the water is another issue. It does continue to become a drier and drier and drier environment. Something significant needs to happen because I don't see it improving. I do see the weather changing in the Southwest and the West, but I don't see the Arizona climate and the water situation improving. So, that is something that is an urgent matter and needs to be addressed.

John: Do you see water-sourcing technologies that can replenish water without generating carbon emissions coming forth in the near future to save the Colorado River system?

McCain: Well, it has to be saved. I mean, we can't just turn away from that. I know that scientists are looking into restoring the water, and they are also looking into other ways, such as geothermal energy and types of hydropower. The thing is, though, it's going to take several of those modalities to restore a complete Colorado River system. I feel that nuclear energy will be playing a part in that as well. Scientifically, I don't know how that occurs or how that happens, but I feel that it will be something that will be addressed. You cannot allow something to go toward the way of a dust bowl, as you say. We have the technology that is on the verge of becoming a reality, so I feel this will be addressed in a large way, and in a way that saves the river system, but it will take some time—a lot of time.

Carolyn: Senator, we've been going for almost an hour now, and Sam has got to be feeling very tired at this point. But we've still got some really great questions for you, so we'd like to reconnect in the next couple of days and pick up where we left off.

McCain: And you know, Carolyn and John, I am not a scientist. I never tried to be, but if this is helping in some way, I'm more than happy to try and address your questions.

Carolyn: Oh no, this is great. I was interested in your perspective since you have spent so much of your life in the Senate, and I wanted to have a better understanding of how we can make that shift with the current elected officials. It's really important for us to get that perspective. The other topics that we want to address are more about the things that you're doing now, on the other side. I think that's going to be very interesting, for us and for the readers.

John: If I might add, yes, the topics have been more technical in nature, but your perspective as a policymaker and as a leader is instrumental in our messages of hope. Your perspective is extremely important.

McCain: Well, thank you, John. Thank you, Carolyn. It's an honor for me to participate, and I look forward to hearing from you soon.

Carolyn: And that you will, sir.

Part Two: January 15, 2023

McCain: Hello again.

Carolyn: Hello, Senator. How are you doing today?

McCain: I'm doing fine, thank you. It's a wonderful opportunity to be here today.

Carolyn: Well, thank you for joining us again today for the second part of our interview. John is going to ask the first set of questions in terms of the kinds of things you might be doing on the other side. And then I've got some questions before we wrap things up.

John: Senator, it's certainly a pleasure to be speaking with you again. The first thing I want to do is thank you for dealing with us [all laugh], for all the questions on global warming and the technical questions. You were very helpful on that. Very helpful.

McCain: Well, surprise, surprise. I'm happy that I could be helpful. It's a little out of my ballpark, but however I can be of service, I want to be there for you two.

John: Today we're going to switch gears, and we'd like to ask about the kinds of things you might be doing on the other side. Are you active with respect to helping or influencing things happening on Earth?

McCain: Well, uh, John, I am a patriot, and I believe in this country with all my heart. And I am telling you that . . . I am so proud of the Constitution and what it stands for. And I am doing my damnedest to protect the Constitution at this time. Myself, Franklin Roosevelt, and George Washington—a few of us—we are doing our damnedest to protect our Constitution at this vulnerable time. That is something that we believe in and something that we will give it our all to. It may seem in jeopardy at times, of course, but we want to make sure that it holds in place. We are doing what we can from this place, and we're doing what we can from afar. A lot of influence, we hope, on those that are in a position to carry our Constitution through and to fight for our democracy.

John: That is just wonderful to hear. How do you exert that influence? How is that done?

McCain: Well, you know that saying, "There are no new ideas"? Well, that is something that we do. We transfer thoughts, a lot of times to people, and we also believe in our country, and we believe in the passion and the integrity of the souls of our country. We do come through dreams. And how do I say this? There is an influence involved, but we also do everything we can to keep that Constitution in place, and sometimes that just means adding a bit of luck to the mixture, the formula, the recipe. And we know that without the Constitution in place, our democracy and our country have no future with integrity. So, we do influence. We come through in dreams, and we also sometimes—I hope I'm not giving anything away here—sometimes we do influence with a bit of luck thrown in. You know how sometimes people say, "Well, that was lucky," or "How did that happen?" A lot of times we are behind that, because we want to see the patriots of the country follow this Constitution through. If there are times when it seems more in jeopardy than ever, we definitely do our best to see that karma comes through and do our best to see that the patriots that we believe in are in significant seats of power to see that Constitution through.

John: That is fascinating. You mentioned Franklin Roosevelt, George Washington, and others that you are working with. How are those associations made? Do you select them? Do you come together because there is a common interest?

McCain: Sometimes roles are assigned. You see, when we cross over, we keep our true essence. We keep our true selves, and it's just an extension of the life we were living on Earth. So, those who have the interest and the passion, and those who feel the calling are usually assigned in that way. It's not so much that people need to learn more lessons, and of course, we all need to learn. There's a school on Earth, and there's a school where we are at, at this time. They are very good at matching the right people with the right passion to oversee these types of endeavors.

John: Do you enjoy yourself on the other side?

McCain: I do. I am here with my family. I am so proud of my family. I am here with my mother, my father, and my grandmother. And I am just so—I guess you would say—I am feeling blissful. I am just so happy to be reunited with my family. I think that's something we often don't really think is a possibility, but it is if you desire it. I am very happy, and enjoying everything I'm doing. Again, it's just an extension of everything I was doing on Earth. My soul is still intact. I'm still me. As I was leaving my body, I felt like I was losing myself, but that is not the reality.

John: When you were on Earth before you transitioned, did you have a strong idea that you would arrive at something such as what we call the other side? What were your thoughts, as an earthly being as you approached your transition, on where you would end up?

McCain: Right. Well, I just believed that I would manifest what my idea of it was, and I had hoped for a sense of unity, and I had hoped for a feeling of reuniting with my family and my friends. And that is what I manifested . . . I had many people who came to see me before I left my body, and they were very disturbed because I didn't seem to be me. But I never left. I was still me. But they were concerned about my forgetfulness and other things I was going through with the headaches and the pain. I tried to present myself in my best way for them, but my body was dying, and I was in a lot of pain. But when I crossed over I found that the pain was completely relieved, and I was still who I had always been. I was still the same person I'd always been, with my family there to meet me. So, that is something that I had wanted and something that I received, and I feel that you manifest your beliefs.

John: When you said that you felt like you had left yourself before you transitioned, were you meaning in the weeks and months when you were going through a really tough time?

McCain: Yes, that is correct. When I was in a lot of pain and struggling with my mind and struggling with my cancer, my illness.

John: Is it fair to say that you remember your earthly experience vividly?

McCain: I do. I do remember my earthly experience. I remember the pain that I went through as a POW (prisoner of war). I went through that pain, and I can tap into that pain any time I wish, which I don't wish. But I know that it is there for me if I need to reexperience that type of body memory.

John: We have been told by yourself, and many other souls, that after a person transitions, it's a very beautiful experience. The comfort this could bring people on Earth who have so much sorrow and grief after a loved one passes or those who have so much fear around their own impending transition—this information could help so many.

McCain: Well, yes. There is a lot of fear around the idea of leaving the body. We are so attached to the body. But I want to tell you that, yes, it would be comforting for people to realize that . . . The human experience is so short, and so vulnerable, and so fragile, and it is so precious. The opportunities and the choices that we make while in a body—we see that from here, that there is no script. There is no predestined script. It is about choices. It is about how you navigate through the human experience. And when you cross over it is a beautiful feeling of accomplishment; it is a beautiful feeling of peace and a beautiful feeling of comfort—reviewing your life in a way that gives you an opportunity to see how much you truly accomplished in such a short time. There is no fear. No fear.

John: Senator, your time on Earth is certainly an inspiration to me and many others. I thank you for all the things you did, how you stood up for what you believed in, and how you were honest and straightforward. It was clear that you were passionate about our country and what you were trying to do. For a guy who never met you, I saw that, and I admired that. And I thank you. You also inspire me with what you are telling me about the transition process and how life is a series of choices. And how important it is for us to really make the most of it.

McCain: Indeed. Thank you, John. Thank you.

John: Let me turn things over now to Carolyn.

Carolyn: Senator, while this is not a climate question, it goes back to your war hero days. I'd like to ask about your time as a prisoner of war, if you're willing to talk about it. As you look back on this, was this experience part of some sort of higher-order contract? Or were you led to this experience for specific reasons?

McCain: Carolyn, it's not my favorite part to revisit, but I will do that for you in order to educate. This was something that my soul chose, which I know seems like a ridiculous idea. But my soul chose this, and I wanted the full experience. You know, they called me "the maverick". They did that when I was a politician. Yes, I was a maverick, but I was also quite "the maverick" in my early days before I was taken as a prisoner of war. I had not known true adversity. I was very good at most things that I tried because I had passion.

I don't mean to brag, but I had not had a lot of adversity in my life. My soul chose this course. And my soul was like, "Let's just do it. Let's just go for it." And I chose to take most of the hits all at once rather than in increments. What I remember most was feeling pain and feeling cold, but I will tell you that my beliefs and my faith told me—and I mean that in a hopeful way—that something could break through for me, and I could find freedom again and eventually be released. That was my faith. My belief and my faith are what got me through. I believe in hope; that is my God. And that is what got me through it. But I do remember being very much in pain when I was taken into the prison. I was already injured. Of course, those were things that were not addressed as a POW—my injuries. It was an experience where I had to try and transcend what my body was experiencing and try to separate my mind and my body and transcend that experience. And it was something that I perhaps—and I know this may sound crazy—something that I'm most proud of—being able to transcend that experience.

Carolyn: That really is incredible, and I'm so sorry you had to go through that experience. Thank you for sharing that, Senator. Have you seen the people who mistreated you—no, it went beyond mistreatment—since you've been on the other side? If so, has there been remorse on their part? Have you been able to forgive them?

McCain: Yes, which has been the most beautiful experience in healing. We know that we are all souls in search of an experience, and we know that we are souls that have karma with each other, as you would say, Carolyn. This is all about healing by forgiveness. That is one of the most important tools that we have as souls on Earth and souls that are not on Earth. We have forgiveness. And without forgiveness, we could remain stuck for a very long time. But it has to be completely genuine, and it has to be completely authentic.

Carolyn: We are looking to do a book on the power of forgiveness, and if you'd be willing, I'd very much like the opportunity to talk with you about your process. I wouldn't want you to have to drudge up your experience again, but your ability to forgive and the healing that you received by doing so, I think would be very helpful for many people.

McCain: Understood. I'm happy to help.

Carolyn: Thank you, thank you. I'm sure the readers would like to know if you have plans to incarnate again, and if so, what would you like to accomplish or experience?

McCain: Well, I am not ready. Every once in a while, I will be asked if I'm ready. And I am not ready to come back yet. When I do come back, I want to do something different, in a different way. And I want to be more of a servant to my country. I know that I served for my country, and I know it appears to be something that I've already done, but I want to truly experience it in a different way and in all facets . . . that are possible. And that is really all that I know at this time. That is what my goal is to accomplish. And I cannot tell you how that goal will be accomplished because I don't have that information. I am not ready. I am still doing what I need to do, and I promise you though, that when I am ready, I am actually looking forward to it. It's a new start. It's a new beginning. And then we start again. And it goes on and on and on.

Carolyn: Well, it's only been four and a half years since you crossed over.

McCain: It's not about time. Some people go right back into a body. It's about just knowing when you're ready to go back and do it again. But it truly is much shorter than we think. When seen from our point of view, it is really a short time that we have on Earth, and it's something that you need to prepare for, and I am still preparing.

Carolyn: I always like to ask this question to the souls we've been speaking with—

McCain: Carolyn, may I interrupt for a moment?

Carolyn: Sure, sure.

McCain: Carolyn, I just want to tell you, you have a lovely voice—like an angel.

Carolyn: [Stunned] Okay, I'm blushing now . . .

John: I have to agree, Senator.

Carolyn: Aww, thank you! So, I'd like to know, Senator, how did you find out that we would like to talk with you? Can you share how this came about?

McCain: Well, I can only tell you that I was called into a meeting, and I was told that I would be meeting with all of you. I did not know when, but when it was time for me to meet with you—and I thought it would just be one time, but this has been a pleasure to meet with you again, like a bonus—I received a message.

Carolyn: And that message was from a soul or a group of souls?

McCain: You know, the meeting was with a group of souls, and they are people who we refer to as The Council. But the message just appears.

Carolyn: Have you seen any of the other interviews, and if so, what are your thoughts so far?

McCain: I caught a little bit of the one with Theodore Roosevelt, and I thought it was incredibly interesting. I thought it was absolutely astonishing how it worked, and I couldn't wait to be a part of it.

Carolyn: What questions am I missing, do you think? What would be interesting and hopeful for the readers on the topic of global warming and climate change?

McCain: Oh, Carolyn, I think you're covering it. You've got it covered. You're looking at what can be done and what might be happening with inventors and scientists. You're looking at all points of view. I don't feel that you've left a stone uncovered. I feel that you have been very thorough.

Carolyn: Thank you. Who else would you recommend on the other side, that we speak with on our topic of global warming and climate change?

McCain: I'm very impressed with your list of souls that you've been speaking with. I have seen your list. I don't feel that there's anyone else to add. Everyone has an opinion, and you could go on and on until infinity. I feel that your list is quite thorough.

Carolyn: Wonderful. Yeah, we would like to wrap this book up so we can move on to the next one. Lastly, and while this is not climate related—I know this topic is very important to you—I was wondering if you would like to pass on messages of hope to Vladimir Kara-Murza and Alexei Navalny.

But first, I wanted to provide a summary for the readers of these two very brave men. Kara-Murza and Navalny are Russian citizens, and vocal critics of President Vladimir Putin, who found the courage to speak up against the war on Ukraine and corruption in Russia. Putin views opposition leaders and activists like these as threats to his grip on power, and as a result, they were poisoned. Navalny shocked the world with his courage to return to Russia following the poisoning, and both are now political prisoners sitting in Russian prisons.

In 2022, Navalny accepted the International Republican Institute's John S. McCain Freedom Award from behind bars. Through his lawyers on social media, he encouraged fellow democracy seekers in Russia to stand up against the corrupt regime in Moscow and fight for freedom. And Kara-Murza, a pallbearer at Senator McCain's funeral in 2018, continues to write from prison, offering glimmers of hope in the fight against Putin's regime and for free speech in Russia. [Note: Shortly before the publication of this book, Navalny died in prison under suspicious circumstances, with widespread speculation that it was a political assassination.]

Senator, from the other side, are you somehow helping in some way, Navalny and Kara-Murza?

McCain: Well, yes. This is something that I have great interest in, of course. And these men are patriots. They are dear to my heart because of their patriotism. Their souls chose this experience. They are influencing so many souls through their actions and through their patriotism. Their hearts are true. They are very close to me in communication, and they are very close to my heart as well. I do not know the outcome because, again, their souls have chosen this experience. But I want to say that they have the type of integrity that will be rewarded in some way. They are, again, very close to me in communication, and I feel that their release will eventually come, but I don't know the duration of their imprisonment.

Carolyn: While I can't send letters to Navalny, I might be able to reach Mrs. Kara-Murza through the Free Russia Foundation. I was wondering, is there something you would like for me to pass on to Mrs. Kara-Murza from you for Vladimir, where they would know the message is legitimate? If so, I would be more than happy to send a letter.

McCain: Thank you, Carolyn. Thank you. I would like to. Please send my love and support and encouragement, and please, if you have the opportunity to, reference the red pocket scarf.

Carolyn: The red pocket scarf. Got it. Oh, my. Okay, I've got goose bumps. Before we part, is there anything you would like to add?

McCain: Oh, I would just like to thank you for this experience, and I would like to thank you for what you are doing for the people of the world and what you're doing for humanity. This is very, very important. And you have the integrity that I was speaking about, and you have the passion, and you are a patriot. Both of you are patriots. And I thank you for everything you are doing today and moving forward.

Carolyn: Oh, thank you so much, Senator. Before we part, would you be open to us contacting you again? I would like to discuss protecting the American democracy, unifying a polarized country, as well as the power of forgiveness, and transcending pain from your POW days. I'd also like to talk about Russia.

McCain: Oh, just a few trivial topics. [Laughs.] Yes, I would look forward to the opportunity.

Carolyn: Thank you for coming in today. And thank you for all that you did on behalf of, not only the United States, but also the world. Your life of public service and your service defending our country, including in the most trying times, has been such an inspiration to us and to many others. It's been such an honor to speak with you today, and I look forward to the next time.

McCain: Thank you, Carolyn. Thank you, John. And it's been an honor to speak with you as well. I appreciate this opportunity.

CHAPTER 3:

Nikola Tesla (1856–1943)

Interview date: December 1, 2022

Nikola Tesla was a Serbian American who is recognized as one of history's most important and prolific inventors, holding approximately 300 patents across twenty-seven countries in electrical technology, wireless transmission of energy, remote control, and many other areas. His inventions are behind major technologies that we continue to enjoy today, including electricity generation and delivery systems around the globe.

Tesla's name is on everything from a major American automotive and clean energy company to basic units of measure of magnetic force. A firm believer in green energy, Tesla supported hydroelectric, geothermal, and solar power more than one hundred years ago. He cocreated the world's first hydroelectric power plant at Niagara Falls in 1895, changing the way we look at powerful natural forces. As of 2020, hydropower was responsible for 17 percent of global electricity generation.

Tesla's most famous contribution was the development of AC (alternating current) electricity generation and transmission, which is still in use today. Despite this, Tesla saw the dangers of burning fossil fuels to generate electricity and was in pursuit of energy methods that could meet the needs of society while also being safe for the environment—one of which was wireless electricity.

Carolyn: Welcome, Mr. Tesla. Thank you so much for joining us today.

Tesla: Hello, Carolyn. Please call me Nikola.

John: Hello, Nikola. I'm John. Thank you again for being here today. Before we get started with questions, I thought I'd open it up to what your thoughts are on the current state of the planet. Do you agree with the situation as Carolyn described it, and can you give us your thoughts and perspective on how you see our world today and going forward?

Tesla: I do not disagree. Yes, I feel that in the present and the future . . . I see them simultaneously. I am always looking to the future and how this can be and how we can benefit from this. I will tell you that the electric companies . . . that industry is a monopolized industry. It is very rigid and has not helped with the production of energy and for all to have energy, and this has been to the detriment as to what is happening today with the climate. I would like to talk about what I foresee happening.

John: Let's talk about clean energy technologies that we know about now. We are in the process of a clean energy transition, as agreed to in the Paris Agreement. The top three renewable energy sources are solar, wind turbines, and hydropower. And then there is nuclear energy.

Many experts agree that nuclear energy will need to play an important role in our transition to clean energy. Progress in nuclear power technologies is leading to next-generation reactor designs that can help make nuclear power a more efficient, affordable, safe, and attractive option for decarbonization. It has been reported that you were a pioneer in the application of nuclear fission for power generation. From your perspective, as a man who was very concerned with energy sources and the environment, what is your opinion about nuclear energy, as we know it now, as an option?

Tesla: Yes, it is an option. It is more than an option. It is a very viable way to make change and accelerate change that we need to have . . . for us to reach the goal. So, I will say that nuclear energy is being studied and worked on by many teams and many laboratories, and being studied by the United States government. And it is something that I feel is very positive, very doable. It is all about preventing the saturation of uranium, and that must be addressed.

I am advising many people from my place—I am advising many people on Earth at this time. It is something we can do and is not far off. It is a matter of convincing those who are hesitant that this is a new way to look at renewable energy and nuclear power plants, a new way to bring this to fruition and make this invention a reality.

John: Do you think nuclear energy is necessary to help us reach the 2050 net-zero carbon goal?

Tesla: That, I am not sure about that. I see other ways that are being studied and worked on at this time that are also very positive. I cannot say that nuclear energy is the only way to get us to achieve this goal. I feel that there are patents that I created for bladeless wind energy. Those are being studied.

John: Let's talk about another known technology that you are also associated with. In 1900, you were already contemplating what, today, we call geothermal energy. Currently, geothermal accounts for less than 1 percent of net electricity generation in the United States due to lack of suitable locations and cost. As you well know, geothermal energy is always on; it is not intermittent. From your experience and your vantage point, are we missing a big opportunity with geothermal in terms of scaling a viable clean energy source? If so, what can be done, in your opinion, to harness this underutilized energy source on a widespread and cost-effective scale?

Tesla: Hmmm, I like your question. This is something that is breaking down between my vision and bringing this to reality. My vision was to—I feel that the Earth and the world are in abundance of vibration and frequencies, and the Earth has a layer of energetic field. The energy can be condensed and transformed into electric current. This is a way to provide renewable energy. I don't understand where there is a breakdown from my vision to reality. Why is it not happening? I have seen this happen. I have seen people bring this to a reality, but perhaps it is, as you say, the inability to provide a station to capture that energy—as you say, "harness" that energy. I think that is the problem—where the breakdown is.

John: Let's switch gears a bit and talk about some very futuristic topics. You theorized and experimented with the concept that electricity could be transmitted wirelessly through the air at long distances, but your ambitions for a wireless global electricity supply were never realized. This is obviously a globally transformative technology. If we could make it work on a large-scale basis, it would completely change our world. Wireless power is still a major engineering challenge, and many engineers are working on this across the world, but the actual status and progress are not well understood. From your perspective, do you believe that this technology is viable on a global scale? If so, does our society have the talent, skill, and, most importantly, the will to make this happen? Or is this technology somehow being downplayed by either governments or other forces?

Tesla: Thank you for this. These are really good questions. I have seen this in my own hands; I have seen it work. I know this invention works. What the problem is, is that when I died, the United States government—they seized a lot of my records, my papers. They have information, and they are afraid it will get into the wrong hands. That is truly what is preventing this from taking place. This is not about talent or skill. It is about being controlled. In those papers, there was information as to how to transmit beams to take warships out—weapons of war out—and the government is frightened this will get into the wrong hands. I feel that people know this technology already, but it is being prevented because of other ways this technology can be used.

John: Let me now go to the topic of the work you did while you were here. You worked on an amazing volume of technologies and concepts, and your inventions and innovations are behind so many things we enjoy today. But do we know all the things you worked on? This brings us to the topic of your documents, the transcripts that we refer to as the Tesla papers.

Are there important innovations in your documented works that contain breakthroughs that could be helping us today—especially in clean energy—and for whatever reason, we simply do not have access to this information? If so, are these documents in existence but hidden, or somehow not available to technologists?

If so, do you see any possible way that your work can be made public so that it can be used to further the good of mankind?

Tesla: This is a very difficult question because . . . there is information in there that they have around the tower beam that I created to transmit beams and to end war as we know it—to end weaponry in war. This is mostly what they are frightened of and what they have in their possession. I was always working, so focused, so motivated to discover. That is what makes everything such a joy and how to better humanity. I have realized that some things were better not to be known. Do I feel it will become public? Not in your lifetime, John, I don't. I see people trying to work past this, but I'm not certain it could be manifested with the protection around it.

John: I understand. Is the protection around all your works coming from the United States and/or other governments?

Tesla: There are other governments involved. Serbia. Croatia. They have information but are not sharing. They inherited this through what I left behind. There is a lot of protection on both sides, and I feel like there has been an agreement to not disclose information for mankind to protect itself. They are protecting mankind from this information. Do I feel they need protection from this? At this time, I would say I would agree. Something that I thought was idealistic; I could see how it could be a detriment in many ways because not everyone who walks this earth has the intention to make it a positive thing for the betterment of humanity.

John: Is there a technology that the world is missing with respect to clean energy?

Tesla: No. From my place, I see there is technology that is being invented and worked on using a lot of my information and patents, and there are a lot of amazing things that are happening. And I will say, there are a lot of people working toward this goal right now. Don't forget that. That is very important. That is your message of hope. There are hundreds, if not thousands, working on this goal. There are inventors in isolation working to ... see their inventions become a reality. Laboratory teams are working toward this goal, too. There are many things that are happening that are coming through and will break through soon.

There are machines working to capture air filled with pollutants and release the carbon dioxide that has been cleaned. There is a way to use a fuel that actually is better than fossil fuel, but it has an additive in it, and it is better for emissions. They are reduced greatly. There is also a way to use automatons to ... go through food waste and take out particular pollutants, and then put the remaining food waste into the earth. Very helpful for farmers. So many people working toward this goal.

John: And maybe this is related, but let me please ask about any interaction you might be having with people here on Earth. Specifically, can you tell us if you are now part of a scientific working group or a think tank where you are collaborating with other inventors and scientists?

Tesla: Yes, I am. That is part of what I do. I want to help. It's not that every idea comes from me. Please do not misunderstand. But I was always very good at going into dreams when I was in a body—daydreams and night dreams—meeting new people and traveling to new places. I am basically doing the same thing now, going into their dreams and giving them pictures and lots of encouragement. That's how it works, a picture. And then they say, "Aha! I know what this means now!" And that is how I work.

John: Are you helping in this way with hundreds or thousands of inventors? Any names?

Tesla: It is difficult because I don't want these people to—I don't want it misunderstood that all information comes from me, and I don't want to give names because I do not want you to know who I work with. I want their ideas to come from them. I am just simply showing them pictures and helping and guiding them. You have a curiosity, John.

John: [Laughs.] People on Earth, knowing that you're active—this is going to be a big message of hope.

Tesla: Thank you for telling me.

John: Let me ask you about a company that is a major global supplier of electric vehicles. The world's largest electric vehicle manufacturer is a company called Tesla, Inc., founded in 2003. The company's name is a tribute to you, and the logo is the cross section of an electric motor first designed by you. Tesla, Inc. is also accelerating the world's transition to sustainable energy with solar and integrated renewable solutions for homes. It should also be noted that, to this day, your patented AC induction motor system is used in the majority of electric motors, not just Tesla vehicles. Is this company that bears your name operating in a way that you feel moves your interests and agenda forward around clean, responsible energy?

Tesla: I am in disagreement with some of the things that they are doing. Their emissions are higher than they are disclosing.

John: In carbon footprint?

Tesla: Yes.

John: Is this about emissions solely with Tesla or with all electric vehicles?

Tesla: Tesla, the company. They are working toward the goal, though, to bring us this renewable energy. Another way I'm hopeful is that they will use this for the betterment of humanity and not be immersed in profit. They can do this, and I want them to do this because that is the whole reason to be an inventor—to be working and focused on how to make things better for the world. I am hopeful they will do the right thing.

John: Do you ever provide technology "nudges" or "downloads" to Tesla CEO Elon Musk? And does he make use of these "downloads" or "nudges?"

Tesla: Well, John, Mr. Musk is an investor. He is not what I would call an inventor. And, yes, I worked through the founders of Tesla to rediscover some of my inventions. But I do not work personally with Mr. Musk. I work 100 percent with some members of his Tesla company but not with him.

John: Let me now switch gears to a new topic. We have a fast-growing trend to replace gas-powered cars with electric cars. This is somewhat ironic given the very first cars were, in fact, electric-powered. But the move to electric vehicles is global, and it is happening fast. Most electric vehicles use lithium-ion batteries. Global supplies of batteries and materials for batteries are under strain because of the rising electric vehicle demand, and the battery production resources are concentrated in only a few areas, with over half of today's production in areas with high water stress. There is much work being done to create new battery chemistries that are lighter and more durable. Especially in the United States, we have many start-up companies working on new and better battery technologies. Are we doing the right thing with batteries, and do you see the battery aspect as one of the big problems?

Tesla: Yes, it is still a big problem that needs to be solved. This is something that I do not have information on how to solve at this time, but I know people are working to solve this and I am working with them. I am continuously working with them. With the batteries, you are trading one deficit for another. Do you understand?

John: I do understand. I'm curious as to how you discovered that Carolyn and I would like to talk with you today. Can you share how that came about?

Tesla: Yes, I'm happy to share. The communication works in that you put your thoughts out into the air, and then we are all with you on this. We feel we are all working with you on this. When we hear you and see you with the motivation to speak with us, we become very excited.

John: Are there many souls aware of our messages of hope effort?

Tesla: Yes. It is not a matter of how many. It is more of a large group of support. Even though you will not be talking to all of us, there are so many souls who are supporting this work, just being part of the inspiration, feeling love, and sending love and support.

John: Do you have any plans to incarnate soon, and if so, would it be for the advancement of clean energy innovations?

Tesla: Well, at this point, I do not know when I will incarnate, but I know that I will. I also know that there are many things I need to learn. My life on Earth was lonely. I had friends, but not many. I focused on my work, and my life was very lonely without true love and people in my life. I left my family and went to America and really didn't have time for people in my life except for very few friends. There is more for me to learn about human relationships. A man sees in the world what he carries in his heart. I just wanted to make the world better.

John: Is there anyone else from the other side that you might recommend that we speak with?

Tesla: Samuel Clemens (Mark Twain). He would be a very good person to speak with for hope. He sees the flaws and foibles in human beings and is able to find hope and humor.

John: Lastly, what message of hope would you like to give to the people?

Tesla: Thank you, John. I feel that you have given me such questions to be able to express myself. I would like to say that without hope, we are nothing. And that I embrace, support, and find inspiration in what you are doing—you and your partners—and I want you to know that we all know that this is going to be a very positive thing. You and the readers of the book will receive great joy from this. This will be going on and on for quite some time. I am very pleased with your sensibilities and who you are ethically.

John: Well, thank you so much, Nikola. And thank you for your incredible inventions, which have made such an important contribution to our society. Thank you so much.

Tesla: Things are going to be very exciting for you!

CHAPTER 4:

Samuel Clemens aka Mark Twain (1835–1910)

Interview date: January 26, 2023

Nikola Tesla suggested that we also speak with his friend Samuel Clemens, and we were puzzled as to how Clemens, the author of such books as *The Adventures of Tom Sawyer* and *Adventures of Huckleberry Finn*, could fit into a global warming and climate change discussion. But, the following month, we went forth with the interview and were greeted by a friendly voice with a heavy southern US accent.

Clemens: Hello?

John: Mr. Clemens?

Clemens: Yes.

John: Welcome! Thank you so much for joining us today. How are you?

Clemens: Thank you, I am well. How are you?

John: I am doing well. Let me introduce myself. My name is John, and Sam is the person who is channeling you. And I am also joined on the call by my wife, Carolyn.

Carolyn: Hello, Mr. Clemens!

Clemens: Hello, hello, Carolyn! How are you?

Carolyn: I'm doing just fine, thank you!

John: We are currently working on a book and have been speaking with souls on the other side who have made meaningful contributions to the planet during their time on Earth. The focus of the book is on global warming and climate change, and the intention is to provide messages of hope to the masses at a very challenging time when many feel a sense of hopelessness, even despair.

We recently spoke with your friend Nikola Tesla about this topic, and he recommended that we also speak with you. Mr. Tesla said that you would be a very good person to speak with because, and I quote, "Samuel sees the flaws and foibles in human beings and is able to find hope and humor." And I think the readers here would all very much appreciate some hope and humor coming from you at this time.

Clemens: [Laughs.] Oh well, I'm happy to be here, happy to help.

John: I would like to begin by providing a brief biography for the readers, with some special attention given to your friendship with Mr. Tesla. Known by your pen name, Mark Twain, you were a writer of classic novels, and you were also a humorist, entrepreneur, publisher, and lecturer. Extremely interested in technology and electricity, you became friends with Mr. Tesla while visiting New York in the 1890s. Mr. Tesla had an interest in meeting Mark Twain, having read some of your early works while recovering from a serious illness in the 1870s. The books were instrumental to Mr. Tesla's recovery; he said the stories were, and I quote, "So captivating as to make me utterly forget my hopeless state." Mr. Tesla was able to share this when you eventually met, reportedly bringing you to tears.

We know that you were a very active investor, particularly interested in new technologies. This interest in investing is what, as we understand, drew you and Mr. Tesla together. You were an investor; he was an inventor. There are some famous stories, such as one where Mr. Tesla's invention of the electro-mechanical oscillator cured your constipation. [All laugh.] In fact, cured it so quickly that it sent you running off to the restroom in—I guess we might say—an emergency. [More laughter.] Is this story true?

Clemens: It is a true story. It worked too damn well. Shook it all up. [All laugh.] It makes for a good story, and that's what life is all about.

John: And you are a good storyteller.

Clemens: Why, thank you.

John: And, of course, you are very famous worldwide for all your literary accomplishments, including *The Adventures of Tom Sawyer* and *Adventures of Huckleberry Finn*. I read those in school, and Tom and Huck are American icons. But you also published on a variety of topics, everything from travel experiences to political views to historical novels about people and events. We are very interested in many aspects of your life and your perspective on the world that we are in today. So, thank you so much, again, Mr. Clemens, for being here today.

Clemens: My pleasure.

John: I would now like to . . .

Clemens: John, I'd just like to interrupt you for a second. I was also an inventor. Did you know that?

John: Yes, there were several inventions that I noted in my research. Did you do the oscillator?

Clemens: No, no, no, no, no, no . . .

John: Oh, you had the scrapbooks.

Clemens: I had the scrapbook, which did pretty well, and I had a patent on that. And I had a garment fastener—another patent—and I also had a history trivia game with a patent. So, just wanted to say that because I didn't know if you knew.

John: Well, I did read about the scrapbook and the garment fastener, but now I'm interested in the history trivia game. I'll have to do more reading on that. There are many trivia games that we like to play, so that could be very interesting.

Clemens: Well, there you go. I don't know if you could answer all of these because they were before your time, but I guess that is what history is, right?

John: We have this thing now, called Google. Are you familiar with that?

Clemens: Yeah, I heard about the Google. [All laugh.] Yeah, I've heard about it. You could probably Google everything in my game. That didn't do so well . . . anyway, go on, I'm sorry.

John: Did you see our interview with Mr. Tesla?

Clemens: Yes, I did. I was very impressed with that. Nikola is a very fine, fine man. He is so humble and so kind and well-meaning and a very special, special, special soul.

John: Yeah, we really enjoyed our conversation with him. Have you had an opportunity to meet with him about what was discussed?

Clemens: Yes, I did. I saw your interview and thought you did a fine job.

John: Carolyn does the research on this, and she's doing a lot of work.

Clemens: Yes, I know you're both working long hours on this.

Carolyn: Well, it's a labor of love; it truly is.

Clemens: That will keep it going. That will keep it in a lovely place then because everything needs to be a labor of love.

John: When you met with Mr. Tesla, were there any topics that he recommended that you talk with us about?

Clemens: Well, I guess that he thought I would be good to bounce some things off of. I'm no scientist. I invented a few things. I used to hang out in his lab quite a bit because he was fascinating, and I was just fascinated by what he was doing. But I would like to say what's happening with the climate and the global warming . . . I would like to say that nature knows no indecencies. Man invents them. And that's sort of where we're at today. Nature is pure, and *Man* has brought this on. But I think it can be turned around because Man is also highly intelligent. If Man had created Man, he would be ashamed of his performance so far with what's been going on with the climate and the temperatures and nature.

I'd like to say that I think that what you're doing is so special because people need this hope, and people need to move forward and know that it can be turned around. And I think that we need to be honest about what's going on. Well, I always say, I don't think we become honest until we're dead, but people oughta start dead, and then they'd be honest much earlier. [All laugh.] We just gotta face this and work on this diligently and come together. I think that humor is always important, and even when it's something like this that is so concerning, we need to have a light heart.

You know, I used to say, "Buy land because they're not making it anymore." But now, I say, "Preserve land because they're not making it anymore." But I think that mankind is also highly special and highly intelligent, and this is about coming together, being humble, facing it head-on, and having some belief in our scientists and inventors like Nikola and all that's going on to turn this around. I can tell you right now, I'm pretty sure this is gonna be turned around.

John: Well, you know our goal is to find these kinds of messages of hope, to keep people optimistic, to keep them trying. Man created this problem, but Man can also solve this problem.

Clemens: That's right, John, that's exactly right. Man is capable of many great things, and they have the wisdom to fix this, and I surely do think that we will.

John: Do you view global warming as an urgent situation, or, in your opinion, are other issues as important or even more important?

Clemens: Well, I know that in America, you have a serious, serious problem with shootings. That's a serious problem, and it's becoming a normal thing. And it can't go on. It's not fair to people growing up in the world. They need to have a fair chance. They don't need to be frightened to go to school. They need to be able to concentrate and focus and not be concerned about someone breaking into their classroom or one of their classmates carrying a gun. It's the wild, wild west. I thought that was fixed a long time ago.

John: This is an especially disturbing trend. We try to stay neutral for the book, but there are political realities in our world now that are very disturbing. And the fact that we cannot seem to have people come together responsibly to solve this issue of gun violence . . . it may be a whole other book in this series.

Clemens: You know, everyone deserves a fair chance to grow up in a world where they're not constantly feeling like a target. And I know it's getting off subject, but it's just something I wanted to say.

John: It doesn't inspire us to go out in large public settings, which is highly disappointing. You never know what might happen, and it's very disturbing.

Clemens: It is highly disturbing. Boy, it's a tough one.

John: Let's switch gears now and talk about nuclear energy. We know that nuclear power has promise to be a very clean approach to creating energy. But there are two issues. First, most of the population fears nuclear, as they have seen disasters such as Chernobyl, Fukushima, and others. And the second issue is the problem of nuclear waste.

There was a major nuclear fusion energy breakthrough that was recently announced that could lead to a source of safe, unlimited, carbon-free energy in the future, with no meltdowns or nuclear waste. But this technology is still very early. I know you were not a scientist, but from your vantage point, as an investor, would you look at nuclear fusion technology as something promising that the world's governments and emerging technology private companies should be investing in?

Clemens: My opinion is yes, yes, we should all invest. Anyone who has the funds to invest should invest in this, and those who don't should invest in learning more about it. I just think this is just going to be phenomenal. I am very excited about this technology, and I see this coming to fruition. I see this happening for our world, and I see that once people get on board, as you say, and excited about it, and see all that can be done and changed, there's not going to be any problem with people being afraid of this. They're going to be so excited by what can be done.

I just want to say that I see the world being a much better, happier place in the next twenty years. I'm real excited about what they are doing. And I'm real excited because I see people embracing this, seeing how things can change for the better, and starting to see obvious improvements once this hits. I am telling you, the world is going to be a better place in twenty years.

John: That's reassuring to hear you say that.

Clemens: I'm telling you, it's going to be a happier place, and it's really going to be a good time to be alive.

John: What kind of impact do you see nuclear fusion technology having on the planet, once available, in terms of our being able to meet the agreed-upon goal of limiting warming to no more than 1.5 degrees Celsius with net-zero emissions by 2050?

Clemens: I think that we're going to land somewhere in there. I don't know if it's a little above that marker or a little below, but I think it's going to land somewhere around there.

John: Even if we're above, do you think there's a chance we can reverse the trend and come back below?

Clemens: Yes, I do. Yes, I do.

John: Let me switch topics and ask some questions related to what you are doing on the other side. As a famous author and a man who was well-known globally, you touched many people. Can you share what types of activities you are doing on the other side?

Clemens: Well, I can tell you a little bit about that, um, not a great deal. I work with a group of souls, and we are very concerned about mankind. We're very concerned about what's happening in the world. I'd just like to say that you have our support in what you are doing.

John: Are you working on topics of importance to the Earth, or maybe focused on your own personal growth work? Can you share anything about your activities?

Clemens: This is my job; this is my role; this is helping me continue to grow; and so being with this group of souls and overseeing ways to help mankind is what I am working on, you see.

John: Are you a guide for people here on Earth, and if so, are there particular types of people you are drawn to or are in alignment with, such as authors or other people trying to get their opinions and voices heard?

Clemens: Yeah. Well, this may surprise you, but I work with people who have encountered great loss in their lives. Any type of loss—of family, loss in their self, human life—I work with people in that way. You know, you are never the same when you go through loss in a way that's unnatural, when someone in their life passes before they have lived their life, or dies at a young age, or is not really given a chance to expand in their life. So, that's primarily what I work with people on.

John: Would it be fair to say you might be a guide for some of these gun violence victims? Would those be the kind of souls you help?

Clemens: Well, exactly. There are many souls that don't get a chance, just for whatever reason, and yes, of course, gun violence is part of that. Especially poor, innocent kids that are just trying to walk home and they're shot. Most of the souls I work for arrive pretty confused because they were just walking to school or they were just swimming in the river, and then their physical body expires. So, it's a great shock.

John: Are you there to meet them when they cross over?

Clemens: Yes, I am. It's important. I had family members that died at a very young age, and, you know, I just felt a hole in my heart around that, and it's something where I wanted to be of help.

John: Meeting the souls that come over that may be confused . . . there are families that are left behind. Are you acting as a guide for them as well?

Clemens: Yes, that is right. You know, sometimes it's just temporary, sometimes it's longer. And some people never recover from that type of loss. They feel bereft and abandoned. So much guilt, many times when there was nothing they could have done. So yes, great loss where people need comforting, whether they were the one whose life expired or the one who lost them.

John: If I knew of someone on Earth who had gone through great loss as you are describing, and if I meditated and asked you on their behalf if you would somehow work with them or connect with them, is that a reasonable thing to ask?

Clemens: Yes, it is, of course. We don't have to have certain forms filled out. [All laugh.]

John: As we speak with you now, are you also in a body on Earth?

Clemens: No, no, no I am not.

John: Do you have plans to incarnate again?

Clemens: I actually graduated, and I'm done.

John: You're done? Wow.

Clemens: Pretty good, huh?

John: Here on Earth, some might refer to you as an ascended master. Is that the right nomenclature for you?

Clemens: Look at you, John Thomas! [All laugh.] Well, I don't know . . . I mean, if you need to get fussy about it, I really just like to go by Samuel or Sam. I'm fine.

John: You are a very experienced author, and I was worried about messages of hope from these prominent souls, and that people wouldn't believe the source was credible. But then, I was corrected to think about it a different way: appeal to those who are already believers. Still, we're going to have to find a way to get these messages of hope to the people who need them. You had great reach . . . do you have any advice in terms of how to reach these people?

Clemens: Well, I'll tell ya, I wrote things that I found interesting. That's why I wrote, and I wanted to tell the stories. Being somebody who can reach, as you say, that means that you need to have information or a good story that people want to latch onto.

John, you have quite the story here—quite the story. And now, if people need convincing, I agree, that's of no concern to you. Just write the messages that you're getting, and let us take it from there. It's going to be fine because you will reach people.

Do you have any idea how many people are searching for something right now to believe in, that there can be a change in this world? There are people who are very depressed right now about this. Let me ask you this . . . would you buy this book?

John: Yes, I would buy this book. I absolutely would buy this book.

Clemens: And Miss Carolyn, would you buy this book?

Carolyn: Without question, yes.

Clemens: There are many people out there who would love to plunk down their money for this book. They need this, they want this, and those that question it, who cares? You know, do you think that everything I wrote was absolutely 100 percent true and accurate? No, because I'm a storyteller. And that's what you are, too. But you are telling stories from the souls that you are interviewing.

There is no way to prove this, and that doesn't matter. What matters is that people need this right now. They need this hope, and they need to know there is more in their future and that things are going to turn around. They need something to believe in.

John: That's exactly what we're trying to do, and we want to reach those people and give them hope.

Clemens: I just want to say, what you're doing, it's going to be very comforting for a lot of people out there. There's nothing like it, is there?

John: I don't think so. It's unique.

Carolyn: Can I please ask a question, Mr. Clemens? Going back to gun violence in America, I would like to be able to find a little nugget of hope for the people. And with that said, when do you see our government, our political leaders, finally changing their stance and passing meaningful gun legislation, and banning these weapons of war to keep kids safe? When do you see this change starting?

Clemens: Well, Miss Carolyn, I'd like to give you a good answer on that. This is something that we're working on, and I can't tell you. I can't tell you *when* this is going to change, and I can't tell you *if* it's going to change. But I know we are working toward that to involve people like you and John who can help us with that. I sometimes think it's something more complex than what you are working on right now.

Carolyn: Mr. Clemens, what can John and I do, as well as the readers? What can we do as individuals?

Clemens: At this point, it seems you can write till you're blue in the face, but it's in a state of paralysis right now. We've got some people working on this, like you and John. We're trying to gauge what can be done about this because it's very locked in place. We're scratching our heads on this because we actually feel much more positive about climate change and reversing climate change than we do right now on this gun issue.

So, I'd like to fill your heart with this and say everything is going to be great, but I'm a little stuck on this one right now, and so are the souls we are working with. But you can trust we will continue working on this and do everything possible that we can do, and we've got some good people working on this. I think it's maybe something where I'd like to contact you again when I have some updates.

Carolyn: Yes, we'd very much like that. In the meantime, would it help if John and I, and the readers, sent all of you love for all the work that you are doing on the other side to try and help the situation? Would that help?

Clemens: Oh, I would not say no to that at any time. That is a beautiful, beautiful sentiment. Thank you, Miss Carolyn.

Carolyn: My pleasure.

John: You know, Samuel, in your day, were there also incidents of gun violence?

Clemens: Yeah, John, there were, but it seemed like people, I don't know, people used them, people didn't go crazy just shooting up places for the heck of it. They usually just used the guns for a purpose, and they had a definite reason. Right now, everything just seems so random.

John: Yes, that's how it feels to us, too. I'm really hoping we can speak with you on this topic again. How would you get a hold of us when you've got updates?

Clemens: Oh, I'd let you know. I'd nudge you in some way and let you know that you need to contact me, or I'd just send you a message.

John: That's fabulous; thank you, Samuel. We're kind of near the end, and we were wondering if you might have a message of hope to leave with the readers.

Clemens: I'd just like to say that my parting comments would be . . . to reiterate what I was saying before, that I truly believe and know the world is going to be a better, happier place in about twenty years. Doesn't mean y'all need to get lazy. It's going to be a much happier place, a better place. I'd like to think it has to do with preserving the world and nature, and let's hope, for goodness' sake, that gun violence comes to an end. But I can tell you it's going to be a much happier place.

John: That's so good to hear. And thank you so much for talking with us today, and thank you for all the work you did in your lifetime. Your books entertained and touched many, and I know you inspired people then, and you still do today. And we're very much looking forward to talking with you again.

Clemens: Well, thank you very much. And, Carolyn, I am going to hold you to that; send the love.

Carolyn: Oh, I will. I look forward to that.

Clemens: Alrighty!

CHAPTER 5:

Jacques Cousteau (1910–1997)

Interview dates: February 4, 2023, and February 6, 2023

Jacques Cousteau was an undersea explorer, oceanographer, photographer, filmmaker, author, and environmental activist. He also co-invented the Aqua-Lung, an extremely popular apparatus that allows divers to breathe for long periods for undersea exploration, enabling Cousteau to produce some of his first underwater documentaries. Cousteau would go on to create award-winning underwater documentaries and television shows, educating viewers on the importance of oceans and sea life and inspiring conservation. He established The Cousteau Society to save and protect marine life, spearheaded a successful campaign to prevent France's government from dumping nuclear waste into the Mediterranean Sea, and spent much of his later years appealing to political leaders to address climate change.

Part One: February 4, 2023

John: Captain Cousteau, this is certainly an honor. Thank you for being here today.

Cousteau: Hello, hello! It is so good to be here.

John: Do you agree with the global warming and climate change summary as read by Carolyn, and what are your thoughts now, given your perspective on the other side, with respect to the current state of the planet?

Cousteau: Oui, yes, I agree. I would say that, yes, it is something that we are working on and addressing. I have grandchildren today who are carrying on the work that I began. It is an ongoing process. I began to notice in my explorations that the sea was starting to decay, and it was not looking so good. I noticed a decrease in marine life biodiversity. Yes, I agree with what Carolyn is saying. I know that this is something that is paramount right now to mankind: to save this planet while we still have time.

John: What do you think people need to hear now, and what should we all be doing to take better care of our planet in general, and our oceans in particular?

Cousteau: I would ask that they continue to cut down on waste and to reuse plastics. I would ask that they continue to be aware that everything on Earth gravitates towards the water, towards the ocean, [and] to please be aware of garbage and litter that is in the streets. Please be aware to clean this up so it does not go into the ocean. The ocean is so vulnerable. And the ocean is, right now, going through a lot of dramatic changes caused by global warming. In the coral reef, there is a problem with coral bleaching, which simply means the heat—the sun—is hotter than normal and it is bleaching the coral, which causes it to lose its nutrients.

Please be aware of all of these things because they do not just go away: the garbage, the litter. It goes into our oceans, and it is affecting everything. This is very important as a recommendation and also to continue to support those organizations that are working towards studying the ocean and cleaning up the ocean and, of course, the planet. That is basically what I would offer at this time.

Carolyn: Are there any organizations that you can recommend?

Cousteau: Thank you for asking that. There is Oceans 2050, which is run by my granddaughter.

Carolyn: The oceans have absorbed about 90 percent of the heat generated by rising emissions, and they absorb a third or more of the carbon dioxide that enters the atmosphere, which makes the oceans more acidic over time. Rising ocean temperatures can cause coral to eject the algae that live harmoniously with them, in a process known as bleaching, which you mentioned. Bleached coral is more likely to die. Coral reefs protect coastlines from storms and erosion, provide jobs for local communities, and offer opportunities for recreation. And over half a billion people depend on reefs for food, income, and protection.

Scientists say that just 1.5 degrees Celsius of warming could destroy up to 90 percent of tropical coral reefs, which are home to an incredible diversity of organisms and form the basis of many fisheries. With that said, the Paris Agreement goal of limiting warming to no more than 1.5 degrees Celsius is still catastrophic for the coral reefs. From your vantage point, will there be technological advancements soon that can help save the coral reefs?

Cousteau: Yes, we are working with replanting coral reefs. This is harvesting and regrowing [coral] in labs and then replanting into the ocean. There is an entire elaborate ecosystem that is dependent on the coral reefs to exist. Without the coral reefs and algae, all of those ecosystems will die off. That is something that is already in progress and is being addressed and worked on with the growth of coral reefs.

Carolyn: We know that coral reefs are home to many species, and if the reefs fail, many of these species may not survive. Can you tell us why the viability of the coral reefs is so important and why every single person should take this very seriously?

Cousteau: I don't think that people understand that when our environment starts to die off, then we are next. They do not see that. They see it as something that is happening someplace else. The ocean is still very new to people. When I started my exploring, people had never seen the sea life that vividly. They had no idea. They just thought of the ocean as a place to dump trash. I was able to introduce people to what is going on in this wondrous, wondrous world.

John: We recently spoke with Dr. Charles Keeling, and he talked about deacidification of the oceans through a type of mineralization process, which could help save the coral reefs. From the other side, do you have more information on this?

Cousteau: This is something that I am not as reliable with, this information, as Dr. Keeling. But this is about replanting coral reefs. You see, as the bleaching occurs, it acidifies the reefs, and they actually become like skeletons without their nutrients.

Carolyn: From what I'm hearing, coral is being regrown in labs and then replanted in the reefs. How do we prevent coral bleaching from happening again after it has been replanted?

Cousteau: It could very well happen again. And we replant again until we can get the warming under control because that is what is causing the reefs to die off.

John: Is this deacidification something you believe will work, and is possible in our lifetime, on a large scale?

Cousteau: I believe that is the future; that is the goal. I believe it is our best alternative at this point. But also, I would say that preserving the coral reefs as sanctuaries without human interaction will be important. Until we can get a handle on things, the diving needs to be on a much smaller scale. There are too many divers encroaching on the reefs.

Carolyn: Just 9.7 percent of the world's oceans are protected, but there is some good news. In late 2022, the United Nations COP15 Biodiversity Conference struck a historic deal on protecting and restoring nature. To help safeguard plant and animal species and ensure natural resources are used sustainably, almost 200 countries have signed on to protect 30 percent of the planet's land and 30 percent of the oceans or marine areas by 2030. Marine protected areas are seen by many as essential to protect marine habitats and the life they support. Can you please give us your thoughts on this landmark deal, how you see it helping our oceans and marine areas from your vantage point, and if you think it goes far enough?

Cousteau: I think it is a fantastic agreement. And I feel that, yes, there is always more that can be done, but I feel that this is very positive. I am very excited to see that this is taking place. I feel that we are on our way. We can do this and turn this around. With this agreement, with over 200 countries, I feel that we truly can begin to give the oceans the respect that they require and need.

Carolyn: Do you see this percentage of protected areas increasing soon, perhaps in the next decade?

Cousteau: Oh, oui, yes, most definitely. I do see it. There is more awareness, and there is more participation. Yes, I agree.

Carolyn: Wonderful! I wanted to talk about plastics now. Approximately 60 to 95 percent of the waste currently in the ocean is plastics, and there are around 50 to 75 trillion pieces of these plastics. Every year, over one million seabirds die from plastic pollution, and sea turtles are also frequent victims of plastic. Around 33 percent of all fish captured for consumption by humans contain some form of plastic.

Some statistics show that less than 10 percent of plastic products produced have ever been recycled. Most plastics take between 500 to 1,000 years to degrade; even then, they break down into microplastics that do not fully degrade and are consumed by sea life and then human life. Other than limiting the use of plastics, especially single-use plastics, what would you like the readers here to do about this other than reusing items, recycling them, and volunteering to help clean up beaches and rivers that lead to oceans?

Cousteau: I want to tell you that they are harvesting seaweed and kelp to create reusable plastic, and it's something that is happening as we speak. This will reduce the manufacturing of plastics greatly. A very simple thing for people to do is please be aware of the refuse at the beaches. Please pick up anything you see, but most especially, pick up the plastic. I know there are individuals and some small companies that are working on ways to remove plastic from the oceans, but I do not think there is anything that is newsbreaking at this time.

Carolyn: This is just fantastic. When do you see this kind of reusable plastic becoming readily available?

Cousteau: Time frame is not so easy for me, but I know that as we speak, it is happening, and there is something called aquaculture. It is seaweed and kelp bonding, and it is sustainable renewable plastics. Also, the seaweed kelp can be used for feeding cattle and creating biofuel. It also regenerates the marine ecosystems. So, there is great progress here, but timelines, I'm not so good at. But it is something that is forming an industry of its own and also giving people much-needed income from this type of harvesting. And it is actually good for the ocean.

Carolyn: Captain, I think we're going to exhaust our channeler, so it might be best if we stop for today and reconnect in a few days. It can be difficult for Sam to hold a channel for longer than an hour, and there's much more we'd like to talk with you about. Next week, we will look to reconnect if that might work?

Cousteau: Oh, yes, yes, yes, I would definitely be available for you.

Part Two: February 6, 2023

Carolyn: Thank you so much for coming back today, Captain. First of all, we had a chance to look into your granddaughter, Alexandra's organization, Oceans 2050, and you must be immensely proud of her efforts. For the readers, instead of working to conserve and sustain the limited marine resources that remain, this organization is seeking to *restore* ocean abundance by the year 2050. In 2021, Oceans 2050 received funding from the World Wildlife Fund to help support their work to demonstrate the role of seaweed aquaculture as a climate mitigation solution by storing carbon. And this is just one area of their focus. It's all very exciting and hopeful.

Cousteau: I would like to say that my entire family is working on conservation in some way, whether it is filming as an oceanographer or, as my grandson is doing, ocean flooring analysis. We are all very invested, and I am immensely proud, as you say.

Carolyn: Well, I can certainly see why. In your first interview we spoke a bit about regrowing and replanting coral reefs, and the need to designate more coral reefs as sanctuaries. With that said, I was wondering if, from your vantage point, do you have an overall message of hope about the coral reefs for the readers?

Cousteau: I do. I would say that there was a time when I was making films to show people the ocean and the marine life. And that was my mission, to introduce people to that. But I started to get very pessimistic about the environment after twenty or twenty-five years because I saw what was happening to the ocean.

I became very cynical or too dark for my television show, and I became angry.

But my message of hope is that I believe that we are in good hands, and I'm optimistic. I have great faith in mankind, and it is amazing to see all of these young people so passionate about the sea and preserving the coral reefs. It is up to them to carry on, and I feel that they will, as you can see with my family. And I feel that diving does not have to be completely off limits, just until we can get a handle on our coral reefs.

Carolyn: Thank you for that. Between the years 1751 and 1996, the average pH value of the ocean surface decreased from approximately 8.25 to 8.14. The root cause of ocean acidification is carbon dioxide emissions from human activities, and the oceans absorb carbon dioxide from the atmosphere. Decreased ocean pH has a range of potentially harmful effects on marine organisms, and the effects of ocean acidification affect some one billion people who are wholly or partially dependent on fishing and tourism provided by coral reefs. From your vantage point, can you please tell us about any carbon removal technologies that you are aware of which add alkalinity, thereby increasing the pH balance?

Cousteau: It is happening through the aquaculture of the seaweed and kelp. I am not a scientist, but I hope I can answer your question. The seaweed will remove carbon emissions. And the pH balance can be restored through more of the replanting that I spoke about before. But I am probably not the best person to describe this to you.

Carolyn: Okay, I understand. Here's another question: . . . The effects of human activity, from climate change to pollution, are devastating marine life, with nearly a tenth of underwater plants and animals threatened with extinction. If humanity's greenhouse gas emissions continue to increase, studies have warned that roughly a third of all marine animals could vanish within 300 years. From your perspective on the other side, do you see the world being able to meet the Paris Agreement goal of limiting warming to no more than 1.5 degrees Celsius by 2050 with net-zero emissions?

Cousteau: Well, we have many countries that are part of the Paris Agreement, and we have more education now, and more awareness. I can only say, from my vantage point, that I see the belief system is in place, that we can do it. That is our goal, of course, and that is what we are hoping for. It may be that we may not make it, but we are passionate about making it. The people who are working so hard are passionate about educating more and more people to make these goals, and are working all the time. From my point of view, I do not see a number; I see that it is only possible because we are working so hard to achieve that goal.

I will say that Antarctica needs to be focused on primarily at this time, and should not be touched until 2030. It cannot be touched for mining, for any type of fishing, for any type of drilling, or for anything else. Antarctica is a cold source for the world, and the sun is our heat source. If we can keep Antarctica in place, if we can keep soaking in all the research, all the funding, we can make that goal. But Antarctica has to be our primary focus.

John: Do you see nuclear fusion energy as a critical technology?

Cousteau: I do. I feel that improvements are being made all the time, and I feel it is extremely important in making the goal.

Carolyn: Another huge threat to the oceans today is overfishing. Too many fish are caught at once, so the breeding population becomes too depleted to recover. As a result of prolonged and widespread overfishing, nearly one-third of the world's fisheries are now in deep trouble—and that's likely an underestimate. Overfishing is endangering ocean ecosystems and the billions of people who rely on seafood as a key source of protein. From your perspective on the other side, what can we do here to improve fishing management or fishing rights so that we can reverse the incentives that lead to overfishing?

Cousteau: We need to be more conscientious about the way we are fishing. Sea life is being caught in the fisheries' nets, as well as the primary fish they are aiming for. There needs to be a more conscientious way to do this. I do know it may not sound very appealing to a lot of people, but there is substitute fish, and it will be much more palatable in fifteen to twenty years.

John: Are you talking about plant-based seafood substitutes?

Cousteau: Yes. Can you imagine the difference it would make in the oceans? It would be bountiful, and it would be preserved. Now it is very reckless, the way overfishing is taking place. Even if overfishing were just fishing, it is still destroying a lot of biodiversity.

Carolyn: What would you like the readers here to do? Look into plant-based seafood substitutes?

Cousteau: There's much improvement that needs to be made on the taste, so it's probably not an easy answer at this point. Please support Greenpeace because they are very active in overfishing. And continue to support other conservation groups that are also active in this area. Protest and write.

John: Now, let's talk about nuclear waste dumping. In 1960, you spearheaded a campaign to oppose France's plan to dump nuclear waste into the Mediterranean Sea, and in 1992, you spoke very passionately at a United Nations conference on this issue. Thanks in part to your efforts, since 1993, the disposal of high-level radioactive waste in the ocean has been banned.

Unfortunately, low-level radioactive waste dumping is still permitted. And currently, Japan is trying to move forward to release 1.3 million tons of radioactive water from the defunct Fukushima nuclear power plant. Whether or not this happens remains to be seen. Can you please give us your perspective on low-level nuclear waste dumping? Is any nuclear waste dumping a disaster?

Cousteau: When I first started my expeditions, different governments were dumping radioactive waste into the ocean. I protested to stop them from doing that, which they did. I feel that even a low level has toxicity. The ocean is not where you put low-level radioactive waste. It does not belong there.

Carolyn: What actions do you suggest the readers here take regarding Fukushima?

Cousteau: Write to their government in active support of protesting this.

John: Are your grandchildren specifically working on this?

Cousteau: I am not aware, but I know that it should be part of what they are working on, and I would hope they would be. They are not involved with what is happening in other countries because when they look at the oceans, they look at the entire world. But it sounds like something that both of my grandchildren would be working on, Fabien and Alexandra.

John: Captain, I'd now like to get your thoughts on what the role of the oceans are in our world. How would you describe to today's society the importance of oceans in our world as it affects us and future generations? What do people need to know or understand about our oceans?

Cousteau: The oceans are life. Without the oceans and without the sea life, we have no future. It is part of the planet. It is not a separate entity. Our future depends on the future of the species. You cannot expect to lose species and not lose the human race as well. It is all connected.

As a human race, though, we have come very far. When I first started my expeditions, people did not even know what was going on in the water. They had only heard stories but they did not really understand the world that is in the ocean and how each species is dependent on the other. And that is what we have to recognize, as human beings, that each species on our planet is dependent on each other. We will turn into sand without our marine life. We are all connected.

Carolyn: You were a strong advocate for the oceans, making films, writing books, speaking before the United Nations, etc. What can you recommend to the readers, in terms of advocacy efforts, that they can undertake to raise more awareness to elevate what is happening in the oceans so these issues are as apparent and visible as what people see on land?

Cousteau: Single-use plastic is at an all-time high. That is something that we need to be more vocal about: the future of plastics. We can be more vocal, and we can be more proactive in our use of plastic and how we use it. Recycle and remove it from our surfaces, especially near the water. The future of plastics will not be what it is now. It will be about reusable plastics and sustainability.

John: I'd now like to talk about what you are doing on the other side. Can you tell us if you are part of a scientific working group or a think tank on the other side where you are collaborating with others?

Cousteau: What I am doing is working with people in a body on Earth. I am supporting them as a guide, and I am supporting them in their research. Sometimes, I am part of their think tank, [where they are] learning more and more about how we can make improvements and also be able to provide information [to the public]. I know that my family feels me with them. There are others who are doing this type of work, and I am helping them as well. So, that is what I am focusing on at this time.

I am amazed by what this younger generation is doing. I believe in this generation. And as I was saying, there was a time when I thought it was too late. In the late 1960s and 1970s I saw so much damage. But I feel more hopeful than ever. There is so much happening, and there are so many improvements and [so much] research. We know that we are in a race with time for our existence, and I am amazed by what the young people are doing. And the kids are so excited. They are learning about this all the time in school, and they have more information in their hands than their parents ever did.

John: We understand you are collaborating with your grandchildren, and there are others that you are acting as a guide for. When we were talking with Dr. Keeling, he mentioned that you have been a guide for his son, Ralph Keeling, at Scripps. Is that still the case?

Cousteau: Yes, that is what my role is since crossing over. I work with Dr. Keeling's son, and I work with many, many, many conservationists and scientists. And I'm also working with oceanographers. It is like I never left in many ways.

John: Do you have plans to incarnate again? If so, what would you like to accomplish?

Cousteau: I do not feel it will be long before I come back, and I will take over where I left when I was in a body. I want to be part of a new generation that is working towards preserving the ocean and conservation. But I also want to work towards preserving [outer] space and the conservation of space to prevent damage, like what has happened to our oceans.

Carolyn: Do you think that we could channel the essence of the ocean?

Cousteau: Of course, absolutely. The ocean has a soul; the ocean has a vibration. Everything is energy.

Carolyn: Have you seen any of the other interviews, and if so, what are your thoughts so far?

Cousteau: Yes, I have seen Dr. Keeling and I have seen Mrs. Einstein. I think what you are doing is fantastic. It is another way of doing conservation. It's doing conservation work by providing this information and by providing our thoughts and viewpoints to the public. This is conservation and education.

Carolyn: That's a great way of looking at this. I hadn't thought of it that way, thank you. As we wrap things up here, and I know you've given us quite a bit, but is there anything you would like to add before we part?

Cousteau: I believe in the human race. I believe in meeting the goal, and I hope that is the reality. I know we are doing everything we can to do that, and I think that mankind is fascinating in everything they are able to do. There are two sides: a destruction side and a creation side. And I am happy to say that I see more and more creation and using that towards making our world a cleaner, better place.

Carolyn: Thank you so much for talking with us again today, and thank you, thank you for all the work that you did to educate society on the wonders of the oceans and all your efforts then and now to protect this incredible living, breathing part of our Earth. Thank you so much. And lastly, I just want to say how much I enjoyed your television show when I was a child, *The Undersea World of Jacques Cousteau*. It was truly the highlight of each and every Sunday night.

Cousteau: Oh, thank you so much, thank you!

CHAPTER 6:

Albert Einstein &
Mileva Maric-Einstein

Part One: Albert Einstein (1879–1955)

Interview date: January 7, 2023

Albert Einstein is widely acknowledged as the greatest physicist of all time, and he is best known for his contributions to quantum mechanics and famous discoveries and theories such as the existence of atoms, the photoelectric effect, special relativity, and the theory of general relativity. He developed the world's most famous equation, $E=mc^2$, which quantifies that mass can be converted into energy and energy can be converted into mass. It is also used to explain how nuclear fusion occurs, when atoms combine to produce heavier elements, resulting in the release of large amounts of energy.

During the 1930s, physicists began to consider whether $E=mc^2$ could be used as a basis to create atomic bombs that could ultimately destroy the world. Einstein warned President Franklin Delano Roosevelt that the Nazis might be developing atomic weapons, and Einstein was acknowledged as the driver that propelled American nuclear arms development programs to ensure the United States did not get left in a vulnerable world position.

From nuclear energy production to common consumer products, many inventions have been derived from Einstein's discoveries. His fundamental works explain how the universe functions and serves as a theoretical and scientific basis to help us reconcile and explain, at the atomic and energy level, phenomena we see in the physical world. And a famous Einstein quote, "We cannot solve our problems with the same level of thinking that created them," seems especially relevant when applied to the global warming and climate change crisis.

John: Do you agree with our global warming and climate change summary, and can you share your thoughts and perspective on how you see the world today, moving forward with respect to the environment?

Einstein: Yes. What I want to say is that this is all man-made. We see this evidence in the carbon emissions that are in the air. We see that this is something that must be addressed. Carbon emissions are causing global warming. They are causing the Earth to get warmer and warmer until it will be impossible to continue to exist on this Earth. I would like to say this is the main issue that needs to be addressed with climate change at this time because it is affecting everything. It is affecting hurricanes and the erratic weather from the warming of the oceans. It is affecting so much. It's a cycle, and it must be addressed. This is the core issue.

John: Unfortunately, many people do not see climate change as human-caused and will say it is "just the weather." Do you think that humankind only sees what they see from the snapshot of time while they are on Earth? Which perspective is correct, the long view that these things have a way of working themselves out, or is it the short view that says we've created a very serious problem, one that we may not be able to fix naturally?

Einstein: It is the short view. Because first of all, Man will always think primarily of himself as coming first and what his needs are. That will always be in existence because we are human. But there are many people, enough people, who are working toward this issue. There are enough people who are going to make a difference. When you say, "How much time will this take?" Well, it was not created overnight, and it will take time. But there are many, many, many scientists and physicists working toward this issue. It is something that people may continue to deny, but there will be enough people—and there are enough people—that are working toward and accepting this issue.

John: That is a message of hope. Eighty percent of global energy still comes from fossil fuels, and many experts agree that nuclear energy will need to play an important role in the transition to clean energy. As you look at nuclear as a clean energy technology, do you think it is necessary to help us reach the 2050 net-zero carbon goal?

Einstein: My opinion is that it is paramount. However, I feel that many strategies must be in place, not just one and not just nuclear energy. But nuclear energy, right now, is on the precipice of creating a new way to release energy that is not radioactive. Nuclear fission has been established. But nuclear fusion is still being established, which is when you have more energy from fusion—as you receive more energy from fusion than is put into the act of fusion. So, if you have two hydrogen atoms that become one, they become helium, which is nonradioactive-releasing energy. That is what scientists are working on.

On your timeline, it may feel like a very long time, but it will accelerate the damage being renewed and repaired. I am working very closely with scientists and physicists on this project. I feel that on your timeline, we are looking at possibly twenty-five years of putting this into a reality. But once it's put into reality, it will be able to address this damage at an accelerated rate. I do feel it is highly paramount and necessary for reversing climate change.

John: Well, that's very interesting. Is it fair to say that fission technology will not get us to where we need to go, but we absolutely need this fusion technology for us to reach net-zero carbon?

Einstein: That is my feeling because fission still creates many small pieces of radioactive energy, which is hard to break down and transport. We want it to be completely clean. I am looking toward fusion, and I am working toward fusion. That is, in my opinion, the way to obtain this.

John: Do you think that humankind will be able to work with other countries to bring this fusion technology to a highly scalable energy source? Do you believe that we will be able to do it?

Einstein: I do believe. When I was on Earth, I received many ideas—my peers called it daydreaming—but they were always in pictures and thoughts. These were coming to me from Sir Isaac Newton. I didn't realize it at the time, but now I do know that he was helping me from the other side, the other realm. I did not have that information at the time. I just knew that I kept receiving thoughts and ideas.

This is something that I work with at this time to help them— many scientists and physicists—to have these "daydreams" and pictures. I feel that there is definitely a resounding cry for this. Countries that may be behind in their thoughts toward moving forward with reversing climate change—we will get them on board. I don't mean just America. There are many countries that are working toward this. We will get them involved. This is about survival. They will be on board. I promise you.

John: But on the topic of survival, is there a threat about rogue nations that could use these nuclear advancements, such as fusion, to create weapons? Do we have a risk that this new technology will be detrimental to humankind?

Einstein: Well, I do think there is always a possibility of a human choosing to use something for good, for bad, or for evil. But part of the reason why this is something that we are working on so urgently is to eliminate that being an option. That is actually the most complex part. We can't control all the thoughts of mankind. There is always an opportunity for mankind to make the wrong choice. But my feeling is that the greater good will prevail, and that will not be an issue.

John: Do you have any guidance on what we could do to influence people to make the best choices that will prevail for the greater good?

Einstein: I would say that the greater good is the path that we are moving toward. We have been so—as a people, as a country, as the world—we have been so focused on our own needs. We put them first. I see mankind—the human race—moving toward a place where we are thinking and acting collectively for the greater good and not putting our needs first, which has separated us and alienated us from each other.

At this moment in time, this is presenting an opportunity for us all to stop thinking of ourselves and think of the world, the collective, coming together. I feel, and others feel with me, that this is a choice mankind will make, and will move toward a place, move toward a path where we will take the higher good, and move toward the higher good. This is a time of transition. It is a time when we can all come together, or there will not be success. I feel we will come together, and others are with me on this, that we will come together.

John: Let's talk about some other technologies, the first being geothermal energy. Currently, geothermal accounts for less than 1 percent of net electricity generation in the United States due to lack of suitable locations and cost. Geothermal energy is always on; it is not intermittent. I'm wondering if you have done any work with technology like this and if you have any opinions on this clean energy approach.

Einstein: I have not been working on geothermal, but I have an opinion that it can be greatly improved. There are many modalities and strategies that can be in place all at once. I don't feel that one way is the best way. There are many ways we can do this to be less demanding of the environment and to be less expensive. And there is good in most of these ways. I feel that nuclear fusion is paramount, and I think nuclear fusion is the fastest way to get to where we need to be. But I also feel that geothermal energy is also an aspect of where we need to go and it has its place.

John: A very famous inventor that we spoke with, Nikola Tesla, was well-known for his belief that electricity could be transmitted wirelessly through the air at long distances, but this has never been proven on a large-scale basis. If this concept is, in fact, possible, and if we could make it work on a large-scale basis, it would completely change our world. Have you looked at this or even collaborated with Mr. Tesla on this type of concept?

Einstein: Yes, we have collaborated. And it is something that is still being tested, something that is still "untestable" to a great deal. We are still collaborating to see how this can advance. It seems to be at a point where many people have surrendered that this cannot be measured. It is untestable, but Mr. Tesla feels this is something that can still be accomplished and advanced, and it is something that many, including us, are still working to move forward. It is a very complex idea. No, it is a very simple idea, but putting it into effect is very complex. We have ideas. Sometimes our ideas are so simple that testing them and proving them becomes extremely complex.

John: And I should point out that Mr. Tesla also feels that this technology, in the wrong hands, could result in harmful weapons.

Einstein: Yes.

John: Moving to a new topic, we have a fast-growing trend to replace gas-powered cars with electric vehicles. This is somewhat ironic given the very first cars were, in fact, electric-powered.

Do you see moving to electric vehicles as being a key point to limiting the negative effects of greenhouse gas emissions? Is going to electric vehicles the right move for our society, or do we need either more or different solutions? Maybe it is planes and trains, too? And are there downsides to this transition to electric vehicles that we simply do not understand today, but will become apparent when electric vehicles are deployed on a global scale?

Einstein: Well, I feel that it's the only way that we can move forward. We can't keep putting fossil fuel emissions into the air, and we can't continue to work to take them out. It is cyclical, and that is not to our advantage. Electric vehicles are something that we need to continue to refine and make affordable for all. That is the only way that they can be successful. A car is a very big investment. You can't have people deciding to go to college or buy a car. You must have it not become—have it not be such a handicap financially. But I do feel electric vehicles will be of great importance to us to move forward because we cannot afford to keep polluting the air with emissions from fossil fuels.

I feel trains becoming electric is definitely something we need to move toward to eliminate coal. There will be problems. There will be. These are problems about a new industry, fairly new to us at this time. And there will be problems with longevity. There will be problems with just basic management. But it will be such a long stride toward correcting the fossil fuel emissions that are in our air at this time that we must move forward with, and it must be something that all can utilize.

John: Part of this transition is the batteries. Are you involved in any collaboration around the technology of batteries?

Einstein: This is not something I am working on at this time, but I know that there are many others working on this because you can't exchange one pollution for another pollution. That does not solve the problem. This is something that is still in its infancy, but it is being addressed.

John: You amassed a large volume of published work, and at the time of your passing, you had left behind more than 80,000 documents. It was not known until recently that your works had been assembled and published, and we now have resources such as Princeton's "Digital Einstein" and "The Einstein Papers Project." Are all of your works available, or are some not being made public? Do we need those documents to help with the clean energy technical efforts?

Einstein: There are documents that are being withheld at this time by the government, by the United States government, and by the Germans. There are works that are not available. But I must tell you, just as Mr. Newton transferred his thoughts and ideas to me, I continue to do that, and that is a way to get my papers into the minds and brains of those who can do the most with it.

What is being withheld? I worked in a patent office at one time, and I put everything—I mean, all these ideas came through to me. For some reason, I was very gifted at putting ideas into equations. There are many ideas in equations that are being studied by the government. They want to ensure that these theories are indeed valid and not of harm to others. I do not feel these papers are of harm to others, but they are something being studied at this time.

John: Do you think that any of your works, any of this information, could help us with our advancement of nuclear fusion technology?

Einstein: That is not something that is being studied at this time, but it is something that is being tested.

John: Earlier, you mentioned having interactions with Mr. Newton and communications with technologists on Earth. Do you work one-on-one or collaborate with a group and try to impart ideas? How do you make your ideas manifest on Earth?

Einstein: Some ideas are collaborated. There are several of us who collaborate on ideas. And then, to me, there is a very simple way of projecting those ideas into those on Earth who can physically manifest these ideas. That is truly through telepathic thoughts, transferring our thoughts to them. This is also known as ideas. Ideas come from all types of inspiration, but we are one of the sources where ideas come from.

John: That is very interesting. Who else would you recommend that we speak with on our topic of climate change and clean energy?

Einstein: I feel that Mileva Einstein is someone who has a unique perspective.

John: Oh, Mileva, your first wife.

Einstein: Yes. She was a scientist, and her ideas were often not heard. She was very vocal with me about her theories and ideas. Being a woman, she was not considered valid in her ideas.

She is someone who has a unique perspective and someone who might be of interest to you to hear her ideas. I also will say she is extremely gifted. The reason why she was not in my place is because she was a woman, and a mother, and a wife at that time.

John: Are you closely connected with Mileva? Do you see each other often?

Einstein: We see each other, but she is part of my lesson to learn. She is someone that I betrayed and someone that I am trying to learn to . . . uh, it is a bit personal for me. But I am trying to learn to be more accepting of women and different races and people who are not like me.

John: Do you have plans to incarnate at some point?

Einstein: Most definitely. I am, as a soul, I have information. I have a vision, but there is still much I need to learn about being a better human. When you are on Earth, you have the experiences, and then when you cross over, you regroup. You learn from those experiences so you can continue to grow.

John: How do you know when you are ready to incarnate?

Einstein: It is not always self-knowledge. There are many souls that validate when you are ready. You do feel it, though. You do feel when you are nearing that time to go back. But there are souls, where it's almost like a certification.

John: When you are on the other side and working on lessons, is there a concept of forgiveness in the spiritual realm, or do you have to live your life on Earth for the forgiveness to be real?

Einstein: [Where I am,] you cannot move forward without forgiveness. It is twofold. It is learning and growing and cleaning the slate to try again. And that is a very simple theory.

John: How did you know that we would like to speak with you today?

Einstein: I received a message that I was to be here, and this is something [that] I've been looking forward to. Well, it is not like I can say it's been two months or six months or six years, but I received a message that it was of importance that I be here, and it was very enlightening for me at this time because I know that it was an important meeting that I needed to attend. But I don't always understand why we are attending these meetings except that it is of importance.

John: So, the souls or soul that delivered this message described that it was important for you to talk with us?

Einstein: Exactly.

John: Well, thank you, Dr. Einstein, for coming in today. It's been such a pleasure. And thank you for all your incredible work, which has made such an important contribution to our society. Thank you so much.

Einstein: And thank you, John, for your very interesting questions and for all of the work that you did to prepare. I appreciate that from all of you. I want to say that only good can come from this.

Part Two: Mileva Maric-Einstein (1875–1948)

Interview date: January 23, 2023

Mileva Maric-Einstein was born in Austria-Hungary in an area that is now Serbia, and she met Albert Einstein in the mathematics and physics department at the Polytechnic Institute in Zurich. Maric-Einstein was the only female student in the program, and the fifth woman ever, at that time, to study in that department. She was also the first wife of Einstein, a marriage that lasted from 1903 to 1919. There has been speculation that, before and during the marriage, she was a close collaborator with Einstein with respect to many of the breakthroughs that are credited to him.

Carolyn: Thank you so much for coming in today. May I call you Mileva, or would you prefer Ms. Maric or Mrs. Einstein?

Maric-Einstein: Mileva.

Carolyn: Okay, thank you, Mileva. My name is Carolyn, and my partner Sam is the person who is channeling you. We are currently working on a book and have been speaking with souls on the other side who have made meaningful contributions to the planet during their time on Earth. The focus of the book is global warming and climate change, and the intention is to provide inspiration to the masses at a very challenging time when many feel a sense of hopelessness, even despair. Several weeks ago, we spoke with your former husband, Albert, about the role of nuclear energy in terms of saving the planet, and he highly recommended that we also speak with you. We would very much like to get your perspective from the other side. Is this something you would like to proceed with?

Maric-Einstein: Yes.

Carolyn: Wonderful, Mileva, thank you so much. I would now like to provide a summary of the urgent situation we are experiencing on Earth right now, and as you know, it's global warming and climate change.

[Note: The summary was then read to Mileva. As referenced in Chapter 1, this was done with each soul before their interview.]

John: Hello, Mileva, it's John. It's a pleasure to be speaking with you today. And thank you for connecting with us.

Maric-Einstein: Thank you, John.

John: First, do you agree with Carolyn's global warming and climate change summary?

Maric-Einstein: I am in a unique situation because I am living a life on Earth, and also in spirit. So, I am experiencing this as an individual on Earth and I am seeing this from my perspective as well in spirit. [Sighs.] It is very depressing, I have to tell you, what you said in your summary. I just have to say that, yes, I agree with the summary as Mileva, and I agree with the summary as—I don't want to tell you my name. I am living in India as a psychotherapist at this time. We'll just say the name will be David.

John: David, Okay. Mileva, we did not know if it was possible to connect with a soul if that soul was incarnated and back on Earth. So, this is very interesting, the fact that David is on Earth while we talk with you on the other side. Thank you for telling us about that.

Before we get to any other questions, we must address this first and foremost. When we spoke with Dr. Einstein, he made it clear that you were very vocal with him about your theories and ideas during your time together. Some historians of physics argue that you did not make significant scientific contributions, while others suggest that you were a supportive companion in science and may have helped Dr. Einstein materially in his research as well as co-developed scientific concepts together as students.

Dr. Einstein has been famously quoted as saying, "Everything that I achieved in my life, I must thank Mileva. She is my genius inspirer, my protector against the hardships of life and science. Without her, my work would never have been started nor finished." And in 1905, Dr. Einstein also said, "I was proud and lucky when we were together to finish our work on the theory of relativity." Additionally, the Tesla Society has been gathering evidence, and they claim that the newest findings gathered on the theory of relativity, and specifically your contribution, are significant.

Mileva, we would very much like to give you the opportunity now, once and for all, to set the record straight. Did you contribute to the writings that describe the theory of relativity, known by the famous equation $E=mc^2$? Would you consider yourself a co-contributor?

Maric-Einstein: Yes. We co-authored the paper on relativity. We co-authored the papers that were filed at the same time [four papers were filed in 1905: (1) photoelectric effect, (2) Brownian motion, (3) special relativity, and (4) mass-energy equivalence]. And we worked together, collaborated together. Yes, being a woman, I was thought to have less credibility with my name on the papers, that I would not be taken seriously. And the papers would not be taken seriously. I wanted to help Albert, at that time, to make a name for himself and to advance in his career. And so, yes, my name was left off for that reason. But only for that reason. We were always a team. Being a woman, I was a lover, I was a wife, I was a housekeeper. But in the evenings, we would work together, and I would check the mathematics, and that is one way that we collaborated. But we were always a team.

John: That must have been very disappointing, I would imagine, to not have your name on such important papers. But the way you describe it, I understand. Thank you for explaining that, Mileva.

I'd like to get your thoughts now on a technical topic. We know that nuclear energy has the promise of being a very clean approach to energy generation. But there are two issues. First, many people fear nuclear, as they have seen disasters such as Chernobyl, Fukushima, and others. And the second issue is the problem of nuclear waste. Do you see any innovations that are in process and may come out later that will serve to make the current generation of nuclear fission approaches both clean and safe?

Maric-Einstein: I am so sorry, but your question was not clear to me.

John: Let me rephrase; I apologize. Today, if there is a nuclear power plant, it uses fission technology. But there's been a recent announcement about the potential for nuclear fusion technology. We know that nuclear fusion is the cleanest and safest way, but it's very much in the early stages. Is there some technology or development that will make the current approach of nuclear fission more acceptable to people? Or do you see, for nuclear to really become pervasive and solve the problem of clean energy, we're going to have to wait for nuclear fusion?

Maric-Einstein: I think, basically, it sounds like you are answering your own question. Yes, at this time, there are some hazards to using nuclear energy in the way we are ready to use it. And yes, it is feasible to create this completely clean nuclear energy. Yes, it is being worked on. No, it is not ready. I feel it could be eight to ten years away, could be more. But I feel that it is something on the precipice of happening. Time happens much more slowly on Earth than it does where I am from. To me, it is happening very soon. For you, it seems a very long time, but I can tell you it is going to work. It is going to be our future.

John: That's wonderful news. It's an interesting point that you make about time, how there is a different perspective on the other side. And that's also very encouraging about where fusion is going.

Maric-Einstein: Yes, it's very promising. For me, it's almost here, but to you, it may seem like half your life, but it really won't be that long.

John: From your perspective, do you see the world being able to meet the Paris Agreement goal of net-zero carbon emissions and limiting warming to 1.5 degrees Celsius by 2050?

Maric-Einstein: My thoughts are that with the technology that we hope to have in place, we could meet it if the nuclear fusion technology is in place and active at that time. If it is not, it would be almost impossible, from my perspective, to make that goal.

John: Let me switch topics and ask some questions related to what you are doing on the other side. But talking with you presents an interesting situation. Right now, I am going to assume that we are talking with your higher self. Maybe your human form, David, is not even aware of this conversation happening. Is that how it works?

Maric-Einstein: Yes, you are very perceptive. Very perceptive. That is how it works. We keep our higher self, and we are everywhere at once if we choose to be. I am in a body, and I am also available to talk to you about my previous life, all of my previous lives.

John: So, your higher self knows about all your past lives in a body. Is this true?

Maric-Einstein: Yes, this is true. You are answering your own questions.

John: [Laughs.] I know. We're on Earth here, and these are big topics for humans in a body to absorb. [All laugh.] May I ask, how many human lives have you had?

Maric-Einstein: I have had 122 lives.

John: Any guess as to how many more lives in a body?

Maric-Einstein: That, I'm not given that information. If I had to guess, I don't know.

John: Are you enjoying your human life in a body right now as much as you enjoy your higher-self experience on the other side?

Maric-Einstein: Not really. My human life, I'm able to have a complete human experience, which is really good and really not good. I have to deal with emotions, I have to deal with things that go wrong, I have to deal with what we call life. In spirit, I don't have to deal with any of that daily stuff. But I will tell you what I miss when I'm not in a body. I miss touching and showing people love, and being able to embrace and smell grass, fresh-cut grass. Those kinds of senses you don't have when you are in spirit. And those things, take advantage of them because you will miss them.

John: Before you came back into a body, were you able to choose your lessons, or is that done for you?

Maric-Einstein: No, you're able to choose. So, you have, like a counselor, that you work with, sometimes more than one, and they help you to reach the goal of what you want to learn in that lifetime and what you want to accomplish in that lifetime. So, together, you work on that.

There are some people who don't necessarily want to work in a lifetime. They just want to have everything for them, everything easy for them. But when you have that type of life, and you don't use it for the best by helping others, or making someone's life better, or growing, it doesn't do anything to move you forward. You don't get credit for that life.

In spirit, I work for people who are seriously mentally ill. When they arrive, they are often very disoriented. Well, you could say that about everyone [who arrives], but they are especially disoriented. I work to help them to know that their illness is gone when they arrive and to give them comfort and to help them to understand how their existence will be without that handicap. In a body, I am a psychotherapist, and I work with those who struggle with schizophrenia.

Carolyn: While doing my research on your life as Mileva, I understand you had a son who had schizophrenia.

Maric-Einstein: Yes.

Carolyn: Is that what prompted you to want to have a life on Earth where you help those with schizophrenia?

Maric-Einstein: Yes. When Eduard [Einstein] was living in a body, it was a very difficult time for him and for me. The only cure, not cure, but treatment, was to be institutionalized. And that is not necessarily so today, especially with the advancements that we have. I have compassion for those who are struggling with that illness.

Carolyn: I find it fascinating that you are doing work on the other side while you're doing similar work on Earth. Do you know our higher selves on the other side? Are we working near you?

Maric-Einstein: [Laughs.] This is an excellent question. I know of your souls, yes. Are you working near me, is that what you ask?

Carolyn: Yes. Or are you aware of us working someplace on the other side?

Maric-Einstein: Yes, I am Carolyn. I cannot tell you anymore. It is something that you have to find out for yourself. [All laugh.]

Carolyn: [Laughs.] Well, Mileva, that explains why I'm so exhausted every morning when I wake up. Now I get it. [All laugh.]

Maric-Einstein: You're doing a lot of things and still working while you're sleeping. I just want to say, Carolyn, I want you to make sure that you are getting credit for your work on your book.

Carolyn: Oh. Well, I am choosing to remain anonymous because my feeling, Mileva, is the book is not about me; it's about the souls that we are speaking with, and if we put our names out there, then it becomes about us.

Maric-Einstein: Alright, if you choose that [approach, I understand.]

John: One of our concerns is that people may not believe that we were really able to connect with the souls. This is a challenge because we want broad distribution since these messages will give people hope to know that nuclear fusion will come together or to know there are souls who are acting as guides for them, etc. Our challenge is to get people on Earth to believe the source of the messages. Would you agree that would probably be a big challenge?

Maric-Einstein: You know, I have mixed feelings. The people who believe are waiting for this, and those who do not believe, you are in the energy of proving. But that is not the right energy for this particular project. This project will reach many people, and this project will be ignored by many people. But it will gain momentum and it will gain word of mouth. But "prove it" energy is not necessary for this book. There are so many people who believe, and those people are anxiously waiting for this type of information.

John: Do you think that David is one of those people who would believe?

Maric-Einstein: David believes. Yes, David believes. Many people believe. It is not as small as you think.

Carolyn: John, did you want to ask about a scientific working group?

John: Yeah, I'll get into that. But are we doing okay on time?

Carolyn: We've got another ten minutes or so.

Maric-Einstein: Can I say something?

Carolyn: Certainly.

Maric-Einstein: With Carolyn and you, I sense the same type of relationship that I had with my husband, Albert. I had to constantly keep him on track and focused. [All laugh.] You have to have the diligence and research, and you have to have the charismatic conversation to engage and keep the interest.

John: We are both very curious, and we're both very appreciative of souls like you, willing to connect with us. It's just fascinating.

Maric-Einstein: I feel so happy to be talking to both of you. You both balance each other, and I like that you are balancing.

John: Can you be a guide to others on Earth while you are in a body on Earth?

Maric-Einstein: Yes, you can. But I am not a guide to an enormous amount of souls. I am more of a general guide to those suffering from mental illness. And those who are fighting to get recognition and, for some reason, are being marginalized. These are souls that I am helping to guide. But yes, you can be a guide and be in a body.

John: We recently spoke with Rachel Carson, and she is a guide for many female scientists trying to help the planet. Are you a guide for women who are being marginalized?

Maric-Einstein: Yes, but not just for women, but for people who are overlooked for one reason or another. When I was at university, I took my exams for graduation, and I failed the exams twice. Yet, I was one of the top students in my class as far as knowing information. I know that I failed because there was bias against me as a woman. I know that. But there are biases for every reason possible. And I like to work with people who are feeling that they cannot break through, not solely women.

John: Dr. Einstein mentioned he sees you on the other side. While Dr. Einstein has acknowledged mistakes made on his part during your time together, he holds you in the highest regard. Would you mind describing what your relationship with him is now, on the other side?

Maric-Einstein: Yes, that is fine. We have great respect for each other. We are souls that are destined to be with each other. It is not a romantic love as much as a balance of working together and collaborating. But this time around, I am equal in what we are creating and what we are discussing. And I am treated with respect. We have had many conversations about our last lifetime together, and we realized that I was not treated equally at that time. I had a lot of responsibilities in the marriage, and then my husband, who I was in love with his mind more than anything, separated and divorced me. It was very hurtful to raise our children, with our son Eduard being so ill. It was very difficult, and I lost all my money trying to get him help—the best help. What is important now is that we are equals.

John: Did you have to go through a forgiveness process on the other side?

Maric-Einstein: Yes.

John: Is it a requirement to move forward?

Maric-Einstein: No one imposes that on you, but you soon find that if you are not learning and growing, that is because you are not forgiving. I had to do that. It didn't come as quickly as I wanted it to. I still had very hurt feelings and resentment from our life together. What helped is that he had to forgive himself, and that is how we could meet together equally. We had to have an agreement moving forward. He has grown. He has advanced as a soul and is working on other things as well. But he now sees me as equal, which is everything.

John: That's wonderful. He seems like such a sincere guy, and it was a pleasure for us to talk with him. Before we part, what message of hope would you like to give to the people?

Maric-Einstein: The message of hope I have is that if you love someone, tell them you love them, even if it seems frightening. That heals the soul more than anything.

Carolyn: Thank you for that, Mileva. And thank you so much for talking with us today and for your major contributions to the foundation of modern physics. We are honored to have had the opportunity to talk with you today.

CHAPTER 7:

Mohandas Gandhi (1869–1948)

Interview date: February 25, 2023

Mohandas Gandhi was one of the most influential persons of the twentieth century. He was a lawyer and skilled political campaigner, as well as a social activist, champion of human rights, and spiritual leader who employed nonviolent civil disobedience to lead the successful crusade for India's independence from British rule and to later motivate actions for civil rights and freedom throughout the world. He was given the honorific title of Mahatma, which is Sanskrit for "great-souled," and the name Mahatma Gandhi is now one of the most universally recognized on Earth.

Carolyn: Welcome, and thank you so much for joining us today. Before I go any further, I understand from your autobiography that you preferred to not be addressed as Mahatma. If this is still the case, can you please let me know how best I can address you?

Gandhi: Mohandas.

Carolyn: Thank you so much, Mohandas. We wanted to talk with you today because your writings were full of thoughts on nature and the environment, and we would like to discuss how Gandhian principles can be applied to not only serve and heal Mother Earth but also to help readers find ways to feel hopeful and optimistic as we heal our planet. Mohandas, can you please give us your thoughts on the state of the planet as you see it from your perspective on the other side?

Gandhi: The state of the planet is a reflection of how we are treating each other. The state of the planet is not in accordance with peace at this time because the people are not in accordance with peace at this time.

Carolyn: In addition to people not being in accordance with peace currently, do you feel there is also a spiritual reason for what is occurring now, and if so, what is the lesson?

Gandhi: The lesson is that we must look at our reflection like a mirror, and we must see that we are doing this to ourselves. The planet is reflecting what we are doing because we are not treating each other with equality and kindness, and we are not living in peace—and the planet is reflecting this.

Carolyn: Mohandas, many feel that one of your most important contributions to the world is your philosophy and method of nonviolence. For the readers, the philosophy of nonviolence is based on the principle of *ahimsa*, a Sanskrit word for non-harm in the physical realm, thoughts, words, and deeds, along with the responsibility to stand up for those who are harmed or threatened and a refusal to inflict injury on others—sentient or nonsentient. Ahimsa, which is more than just the absence of violence, is perfect love. And love toward not only human beings but love toward all creatures of the world. From what I understand, *satyagraha* is a way of putting the principle of ahimsa into social and political action. It has also been described as "truth force" and "love in action." Applying your system of satyagraha, you used nonviolence in India's freedom struggle, and India became independent from British rule. And Martin Luther King, Jr. drew on the Gandhian principles of nonviolence. He famously wrote, and I quote, "While the Montgomery boycott was going on, India's Gandhi was the guiding light of our technique of nonviolent social change." If people exercised a satyagraha campaign to support Mother Earth, what might this look like? Can you talk more about how we can apply this principle individually and collectively to help the planet and our environmental crisis?

Gandhi: Yes, yes. Satyagraha is very important. It is a solvent for injustice and harm, and it is to defy peacefully and suffer with no retaliation—nonviolent passive resistance. We need to bring forth a more harmonious way of being, to care for the whole of humanity as a family, to cause no harm to nature and Man, and to emulate Jesus Christ.

Carolyn: What or how would a campaign to carry this out look like in this day and age?

Gandhi: A campaign would be to bring in unity—the people of the world, with the world, with the Earth, with the planet. Modern civilization is making everything into waste, and we need to take only what is needed and apologize to the natural resource after we have taken. Vegetarianism is important because the meat industry has put extreme pressure on soil and water resources.

The Earth is a living thing. Nature and all life forms are to be of reverence to Man. All of nature and Man are equal. We must come together as One, to honor nature, to live peacefully, and to stop the destruction of natural resources without giving thanks to those natural resources when we take them. This is something that I think is very important—that we understand what we are doing and be thankful and in gratitude and not to waste. To come together as One in harmony, to know the Earth is a living thing.

Carolyn: So, satyagraha can be done individually, and it's not a situation where you need to be out in public peacefully protesting, is what I am hearing.

Gandhi: This is about truth, living in truth, and this is about being in cooperation and peace and compromise. It can be done as individuals. It can be done with a feeling of One by individuals.

Carolyn: What is the difference between peaceful protestors that we see today taking to the streets and those who exercise satyagraha? What more could peaceful protestors be doing to accomplish their goals?

Gandhi: It is passive resistance. It is about defying the laws peacefully and suffering with no retaliation. It is a way for people to not comply with the destruction of the planet. Not comply with overfishing. Not comply with the destruction of our wildlife. Not comply with the removal of our trees or the removal of our nature's resources. Peaceful protest is something that can be done by not complying. It is a way of saying, "I will not agree, and I defy." But if it is done peacefully, and through peace, it is more efficient than through violence.

Carolyn: And this is something that can be done individually at home or by the thousands peacefully protesting in the streets.

Gandhi: Yes.

Carolyn: You developed a concept called *Sarvodaya*, which in Sanskrit means "progress and upliftment of all." From what I understand, the concept of Sarvodaya is also similar to that of sustainable development to safeguard the rights of future generations, where there is no distinction between humanity and nature, and there is support for each other. And a theory closely linked to the concept of Sarvodaya is that of trusteeship. Can you please talk more about this and share your perspective on how we can better apply these principles in our present world?

Gandhi: The best way I would say is to practice—whether it be [as] a collective or whether it be as an individual—to keep in mind that every choice you make, everything you do in regard to our natural resources and waste production is affecting those who have not even been born on the planet yet—every move you make. And to know this is so important because it is not just about you and your life; there are many more to come. It may be you incarnating again, and you may be living in a land dump. You don't want that for your life. And you don't want that for others' lives. You want to leave the future beautiful so others can experience harmony with nature and our planet.

Carolyn: One of your mottos was "simple living, high thinking," in which you talked about how one could be happy without material possessions and that simplicity is key. We live in an age of overconsumption of material goods that satisfy more wants than needs, particularly here in the West, which certainly does not help the environment. Can you please talk more about this?

Gandhi: I am in belief of agriculture to reap from the Earth, to give back to the Earth, not to destroy the Earth as you bring the food into agriculture. I believe in the meditation of silence. I believe that twenty-four hours of silence brings in meditation, quiet thinking, reserving resources, and conserving energy consumption. And, most of all, what I think is so destructive is noise pollution. [We need to be] in the spirit of appreciation and gratitude and slowing down life. Life is far too hectic; life does not give us clarity to make decisions for future generations. We are just trying to keep up. Life is too busy. We must replenish and not be of greed.

Carolyn: Several years ago, India made a climate change commitment deliberately based on three Gandhian principles: ahimsa, satyagraha, and Sarvodaya. Are there other Gandhian principles that I haven't mentioned that you feel would be important for the people of the world, along with other governments, to adopt and apply?

Gandhi: There is the Chipko movement (a forest conservation movement in India), and supporters have a belief, based on my teachings, that nature should be in harmony with the needs of Man and that neither Man nor nature is to be exploited or destroyed. This is very important. There is a cosmic law, which is "all man, all life, all creation"—the entire universe being a single species. We are all One.

Carolyn: With that said, ultimately, for this book, we are looking for messages of hope. Before we move on to the next topic, do you have a message of hope regarding Mother Earth that you'd like to share with the readers?

Gandhi: Nature should be allowed to take its course, and the hope is about nature being in harmony with us. Let me think. My message of hope would be that if we can live as One in regard to nature—and even if we take a branch of a tree to take a leaf off, it is not necessary to take the entire branch or to take more than one leaf—we need to just take what we need. And we don't do that. I think that if we try that, we will find that we come together more and more and more as One with nature. And that is the goal, that is the hope—to come together as One with nature so that we recognize that nature is a living thing with a soul. We must recognize that we are all One—with the animals, with nature, and with the planet. Come together as One.

Carolyn: From your vantage point, say in twenty years, do you see the state of the planet improving and people starting to think in ways that you are describing?

Gandhi: Those who strive for this, they will be the survivors, and those who do not recognize this will not be able to adapt to our world. It will not be something they can continue to survive in—that way of thinking. So, to answer your question, I do not know your timeline of twenty years, but I feel that we must come together, and those who do will benefit from this.

Carolyn: Thank you for that. I'm now going to hand things over to John.

John: Hello, Mohandas. Thank you so much for being here; it's really a pleasure.

Gandhi: Hello, John.

John: Moving to a new topic now, we'd like to talk about your life on the other side. Can you share what your areas of focus are and the types of things that you enjoy?

Gandhi: Yes, I am like an advisor. I help to counsel souls on living in a more quiet, more silent meditative state, because the souls that I help to guide and counsel are those who have not been able to feel their own thoughts or think their own thoughts because they have been living in a tornado, like a hurricane. They have never given time to have their own thoughts and their own meditations and cannot advance as souls without being in silence from time to time. I help to guide them through this. They have never known such a thing—and I help them to appreciate and to learn to love their silence.

John: Are these types of people world leaders or individual citizens, or simply people who reach out to you who would like your guidance?

Gandhi: These are people who are crossing over. These are the people who I am guiding into meditation. Just because you die does not mean everything goes quiet . . . the soul is very active with some people, which does not give them peace within.

John: Can you tell us if you are collaborating with other spiritual leaders and/or political leaders or civil rights leaders?

Gandhi: It is somewhat part of my work. It is not my work in its entirety. When I was Mohandas, I was executed, and I was incarnated again in 1958. I lived in Turkiye, and I was a very poor farmer, and I had a very peaceful, quiet life. I had many times when I was able to think peaceful thoughts and meditate, even though I was very poor and sometimes very concerned about my existence financially. I died in 1984, and I have not been back on Earth. And I do not plan to come back to Earth at this time.

Carolyn: Can you please tell me, where is Turkiye?

Gandhi: I'm sorry. I think you may know it as Turkey.

Carolyn: Oh, okay. Where in Turkey did you live?

Gandhi: I lived in Mardin. I grew wheat, and I grew barley, and I died from my heart.

John: Was that preplanned, that you would only spend a limited amount of time on Earth?

Gandhi: Yes, it was preplanned. I was not quite ready to refrain from incarnating, so it was agreed that I would have a simple life in reflection and a short life.

John: Was it a joyful life?

Gandhi: It was joyful in that I had peace of mind. I was a very good person. I was Catholic and was surrounded by many temples and many churches, and I was able to return in some way to the life I had known before, by being in silence and being appreciative of my simple life. I did not require more.

John: Does this mean you are 100 percent done, or is there any chance you might choose to come back?

Gandhi: 100 percent? What does 100 percent mean?

John: Meaning that you are absolutely done with life in a body.

Gandhi: No, I have completed my cycle. I completed my cycle 100 percent. [All laugh.]

John: We have spoken with a lot of souls, and I was wondering if you have seen any of the interviews?

Gandhi: I saw Mr. Gaylord [Nelson], Mr. Nixon, and I saw Mr. Clemens (Mark Twain).

John: We recently spoke with both Dr. Wayne Dyer and Saint Francis. We see a lot of synergy between your beliefs and their teachings. Have you spent time with them?

Gandhi: With Saint Francis, I have.

John: Would you agree Saint Francis's messages are consistent with yours?

Gandhi: Yes, 100 percent. [All laugh.]

John: Are you a guide to many on Earth, and if so, what types of people are you guiding?

Gandhi: I am a guide to those who are imprisoned. I help them. My goal is to help them to find inner peace and forgiveness.

Carolyn: When you say that you are a guide to those who are imprisoned, is this in the literal sense, or does this also apply to people who are imprisoned in their way of thinking?

Gandhi: Yes, very wise of you, Carolyn. It is people who are literally in prison and people who are symbolically in a prison.

John: Along those lines, in terms of you being a guide, are you available to be a guide for those who ask mentally, or in meditation?

Gandhi: Yes, anything is possible.

Carolyn: Although your deaths were not that far apart, were you a guide to Martin Luther King, Jr.?

Gandhi: Yes, I was. For a very short time. Great man. And a visionary for what the world can be.

Carolyn: Have you seen him since you've been on the other side?

Gandhi: No, I haven't seen him, and I hope to. I do not know if he is in spirit or body.

Carolyn: I understand that you were assassinated by Hindu nationalist, Nathuram Godse, in an obviously violent manner. Have you seen him on the other side, and if so, can you tell us about this?

Gandhi: Yes. Definitely, forgiveness took place. He was pressured to assassinate me because of my support of Pakistan and Muslims, and he was pressured to kill me. But we have this great forgiveness and respect for each other now.

Carolyn: Was there an agreement for this to transpire that was set up before you incarnated?

Gandhi: Yes, but once I came into my body I was not aware of the agreement. When I crossed over it was made clear to me that it was all an agreement. You forget. You forget. It is gone. You make the agreement and you know that is what you are to do and how it will work. But then you forget. And then you go and live your life with free will, not knowing of the agreement.

Carolyn: In your autobiography, you stated that being given the title of Mahatma had deeply pained you, and you were unable to recall a moment when the title had quote "tickled" you. Can you please tell us why you had this reaction and if you still feel this way?

Gandhi: "Mahatma" is an honor, meaning that you are highly evolved, that you oversee spiritual growth in people and in the development of society and civilizations. I do not want to be known as Mahatma. I want to be as One. I do not want to be higher in any way. No separation.

John: Mohandas, you mentioned earlier that people are moving so fast, not taking the time to really think things through. People are wanting to be busy but are not so concerned about being thoughtful. In our society today, we have something called social media, where all the kids have phones in their hands and they don't communicate much with people. Do you have any messages you would like to impart on the importance of slowing down life and the benefit that it will have? Do you have a perspective on that?

Gandhi: My perspective is that it is not only kids. I see it with older people, too. I see a lot of escaping reality, and the more we escape from reality, the more we move away from our truth. The more we move away from our potential, the more we turn off to what is happening. So, this is being used as an escape. To be thoughtful is to allow thoughts to come in. When we close off, we don't allow thoughts to come in. It is very likely that individual and collective progress can go forward when we do not give it [social media] our time. We do not give it our thoughts. That is a way, today, in the world you are living in, to practice twenty-four hours of silence—no social media. Allow your thoughts to come in; allow yourself to be in nature; find nature; find harmony with others. Silence is what we want to strive for, but go twenty-four hours without social media. It is dumbing us. We are not here to escape. We are here to have an experience, a real experience of life. And we are shutting off because it is more than we can deal with.

John: Isn't it ironic, Mohandas, that social media was created to allow people to be more connected, but now we're more isolated?

Gandhi: It is because they are not connecting with people; they are connecting with pictures of people, the thoughts of people. They are not having a human experience.

Carolyn: When you talk about practicing twenty-four hours of silence, how often do you recommend doing this?

Gandhi: Well, I know that your world is much more different than the world I am in, but whenever the opportunity makes itself available, it is good to seize that opportunity. There are not too many times and not too few times. But I would just take small steps, and if it means every six months for you, that is great, or every month, or once a year, that is great. Do not run before you can walk. It is a challenge in your world. It is good to put it on the calendar, and say, "In July, I will be taking twenty-four hours of silence." And you do not have to do anything but shut down the noise.

Carolyn: As I reflect on your words today, it is making me rethink how and with whom I spend my time. And my question is not only for myself but for others who want to embark on the path that you have described. Many of us have friends and family out in the world who are very busy, caught up in their lives, and not particularly conscious, or self-reflective, or self-aware. And for the most part, it's not terribly satisfying, at a soul level, to be around these people. What guidance do you have for those of us who are trying to embrace your words and want to change our lives but feel so out of alignment spiritually with these people? Is it best to step back from them and seek out like-minded people, or do we continue on and try to emanate what we are learning in hopes that they can awaken to a new way of thinking?

Gandhi: That is a wonderful question that you are asking. I would say that it is probably good to keep a relationship but keep a more distant relationship where you have more neutrality. And when you come together, you are able to be an example to them. Not to preach to them. Not to direct them on how they should live their lives. But they will notice a difference. And those who are attracted to that light that you carry will continue to seek that light out for the right reasons. They will look at you as an example of someone who is living a good life and staying true to what their beliefs are. So, I would say, it is not the best idea to just not see them again, but keep a very cordial distance and just be friends but not seek them out. Let them seek you out.

Carolyn: Thank you, Mohandas, that is wonderful guidance. Do you have any recommendations for our next book? What topic do you feel would be the most useful in this day and age?

Gandhi: Oh, that is so good. I love this—this is so good. A lot of responsibility! I would say that something that I would like very much would be to follow your intuition and your heart and follow your gut. In today's world, this is something that people dismiss, and it could do a lot of good to reintroduce that to people. Animals rely totally on their heart and their gut to tell them when things are not safe, when food is not safe, when their environment is not safe. I feel this is something that needs to be reintroduced to humanity.

Carolyn: As we near the end of our interview, is there anything you would like to add for the readers?

Gandhi: I would like to add that this is a beautiful, beautiful, beautiful world, and as we continue to honor our world and find our human experiences and be in nature and seek out nature, this will help us to grow and evolve. This is important to keep in mind. The world is part of us, and we are part of it, and we are all together. The more we appreciate and become involved in the Earth and the human experience, the more we will grow, and the more we will understand and have what we desire.

Carolyn: Before we part, we'd very much like to do additional messages of hope books, with topics such as the power of forgiveness, unifying polarized countries, and, as you just mentioned, following your gut and intuition. Would you be interested in talking with us again?

Gandhi: Yes, I would like that very much. I will be most ready and available.

Carolyn: Thank you so much, Mohandas. It's been such a joy to meet you, and we look forward to talking again soon.

CHAPTER 8:

President Theodore Roosevelt (1858–1919)

Interview dates: November 5, 2022, and January 25, 2023

Theodore Roosevelt served in a variety of political positions during his lifetime, including New York state representative, president of the board of the New York City Police Commissioners, and assistant secretary of the US Navy. When war was declared with Spain in 1898, he organized and led a volunteer cavalry known as the Rough Riders, a unit that fought the Spanish-American War in Cuba. Upon his return, Roosevelt was elected governor of New York and then went on to be the vice president of the United States under President William McKinley. Roosevelt would become the twenty-sixth president of the United States after the assassination of McKinley, serving two terms. He remains the youngest person to ever become president, at age forty-two. A member of the Republican Party, Roosevelt became increasingly progressive in the later years of his presidency.

As president, Roosevelt was one of the most powerful voices in the history of American conservation, protecting approximately 230 million acres of public land and establishing 150 national forests, fifty-one federal bird reserves, four national game preserves, five national parks, and eighteen national monuments. It has been said that out of all his achievements, Roosevelt was most proud of his work in the conservation of natural resources and extending federal protection to land and wildlife.

Part One: November 5, 2022

Carolyn: Mr. President, I'd like to get your perspective as both a conservationist and former president of the United States. You are a very interesting person to speak with, and we thank you so much for being here today. First of all, do you agree with my global warming and climate change summary?

Roosevelt: Do I agree? Yes, I agree.

Carolyn: Now, I'd like to ask what your thoughts are on the current state of the planet.

Roosevelt: Ah, an easy question first. Thank you [laughs]. Oh, my goodness, my goodness. Man does not waste a chance to mar this beautiful country. I saw this coming, with the trees being cut down, and I saw housing taking over in my time. I was hoping to prevent this by asking the people to stop and pause and see the beauty and reflect upon the beauty in the parks. I did not realize what was to come. And what you are experiencing at this point is definitely frightening, and it is something where there is still time to address this. It's just that the clock is ticking, and I feel that we all must collectively come together, we all must listen to each other, and we all must fix this together. I believe it can be done, but it will take everyone's part in this.

Carolyn: In the summary, I mentioned the Paris Agreement, with the goal of achieving net-zero carbon by 2050 and limiting warming to 1.5 degrees Celsius. Unfortunately, in a report issued very recently by the United Nations, many of the participating countries are failing to live up to their commitments to fight climate change, including China—the world's biggest emitter. If you were president today, what would you do to encourage these countries to honor their commitments and step up their climate actions when there is no enforcement mechanism?

Roosevelt: That is a conundrum. I feel that those countries must pay some sort of price for continuing to make the decisions they're making and destroying our planet. Have they no sense of humanity? I don't understand why they would not want to save themselves, if not each other. I feel there must be a price to pay—that those countries should not be able to participate in trade agreements or be able to share resources with other countries. I feel that trade agreements should be completed and ended when they are not doing their part and not participating. After all, if they are not thinking of their fellow man, then there must be a price to pay. I feel that trade agreements should be ended, as best we can do that.

Carolyn: People around the world are relying on these countries to live up to their commitments. What actions should people take?

Roosevelt: There should be a boycott, and people should not participate in travel to these countries or purchase goods from these countries. This will make things difficult in some ways because we are used to doing trade with these countries, and we have agreements in place, but the sacrifice will be far worth it.

Carolyn: From your perspective, do you see the world being able to meet the net-zero emissions goal by 2050 and not exceeding 1.5 degrees Celsius?

Roosevelt: Well, from my perspective, I can only hope that we will meet that. But I feel that as the time gets closer, we will become more and more challenged by what's happening with our weather systems and natural disasters. There will not be people who you call deniers. There will not be those people unless they are certifiably insane. They can no longer deny it as it gets closer. If they do not work toward saving themselves, their fellow men, their children, and their children's children, there is nothing to live for. There will be nothing to live for. They can no longer run from this.

Carolyn: We are in the process of a clean energy transition, as agreed to in the Paris Agreement. As I mentioned in the summary, fossil fuels currently account for 80 percent of the energy generated worldwide. The top three renewable energy sources are solar, wind turbines, and hydropower. And then there is nuclear energy. As we make this transition to clean energy, many experts agree that nuclear energy will need to play an important role.

Nuclear energy can provide a continuous and reliable source of energy, unlike renewable energy sources that require sun, wind, and water, which are intermittent. Progress in nuclear power technologies continues and is leading to next-generation reactor designs that can help make nuclear power a more efficient, affordable, safe, and attractive option for decarbonization. But many people are frightened of nuclear power after the Three Mile Island, Chernobyl, and Fukushima meltdowns, and they are concerned about radioactive waste disposal. What are your thoughts on nuclear energy and its role in helping us reach the 2050 goal, and do you see these next-generation nuclear innovations coming soon?

Roosevelt: I see the fear of the people regarding the word "nuclear." It is a hotbed, as you say. It brings up a lot of feelings and emotions in people regarding the past tragedies that you speak of. I would like to see education for the people about how nuclear energy is being transformed to work for our benefit and how this can provide clean energy. I'd like to see more education for people about this. There's not a lot of support at this time because, frankly, we don't have the information. We only think of disasters around the word "nuclear." And the second part of your question?

Carolyn: Do you see these next-generation nuclear innovations coming soon?

Roosevelt: From my perspective, I see people who are working on this quite diligently at this time. I feel that this is something that will be able to accelerate our goals. As far as meeting our goals, I feel quite positive about the work that is being done.

Carolyn: To help save our planet, we must rapidly deploy the available clean renewable energy solutions right now. From a conservationist's standpoint, however, there are environmental trade-offs that come with these solutions: (1) Hydropower requires building dams that can create imbalances in the ecosystem around the dam area; (2) It has been said that disposed solar panels create 300 times more toxic waste per unit of energy than do nuclear power plants; and (3) A single industrial-size wind turbine typically requires about a ton of rare earth metals as well as several tons of copper, which is notoriously destructive and dirty to mine, not to mention the negative impact on wildlife both offshore and on land when in operation.

Do you see solutions or improvements to these problems coming soon? Or new innovations? If not, how do we reconcile this?

Roosevelt: I feel that wind power is something that will be modified, will be improved. It's my understanding that scientists are currently working on improving this so wildlife is less in jeopardy and the precious metals are able to be replaced with man-made materials. I see the scientists working on this as we speak. I feel that wind power is going to be able to propel us as well as nuclear energy. I feel that by working in tandem with the two of them, we can meet these goals. I do not see hydropower being able to propel us as quickly as nuclear energy and wind turbine energy.

Carolyn: Some positive news. US President Joe Biden has made climate change a top priority. Biden brought the United States back into the Paris Agreement in 2021 after the last president pulled out in 2017. And, in 2022, Biden signed the largest climate legislation in US history. This legislation basically provides all sorts of incentives, tax breaks, and a huge investment in growing our renewable energy infrastructure, such as solar panels and wind turbines, all for the transition to renewable energy that will put us on track to meet our Paris Agreement commitment. But fewer than half of Americans are only moderately familiar with this bill, and at the same time, nearly two-thirds of Americans feel the government isn't doing enough to fight climate change because they are simply not aware of what's already being done.

Coupled with this is the fact that many Americans do believe global warming is caused by human activities, but all they see are depressing images on television and reports of doom and gloom. People feel hopeless, anxious, and helpless. Some are so depressed they don't even want to bring children into the world. As John Muir recently suggested to me, alarmist activism must be avoided, and instead, seeds of hope should be planted for the American public through the launch of some sort of ongoing campaign. People need to regularly hear about all the progress, the new legislation, technological advancements, and breakthroughs that are occurring because there really is an abundance of hopeful, promising news.

I know that you, as president, held a lot of press briefings to keep the public informed. In fact, you are consistently ranked as one of the top ten presidents of all time, partly for your gifts of public persuasion. From your perspective as a former president and one who is concerned about the planet, let me run three related questions by you. How would you get your arms around keeping the public informed? Who should be the owners and drivers of such a campaign? Should it be a collaboration between the government and private sector?

Roosevelt: I would like to see young people starting campaigns. I would like to see them starting a campaign about seeds of hope. I love that— "Seeds of Hope." I would like to see them leading the charge and getting the word out through all the ways you are able to communicate today. Through print, through television, through social media, through radio—is radio still a thing?

Carolyn: Yes, it is.

Roosevelt: I would like to see the young people getting the word out, a campaign just to say, "This is what's happening, this is great news, let's keep working on it." Motivation is so important for the people at this time: encouragement, motivation, a way to feel that hope. I would love to see that happening. If I were president, I would have the government lead this and involve the private sector, and I know that it would be very positive for people at this time. People feel in the dark about what is happening. They know it is bad, but they don't know what to do. People need to have more information about positive things that are happening and then information about small things that can be done to keep working toward this. Picking up trash. Pick up three pieces of trash on your way to school. Turning the faucet off when you're not using it—and this comes to you naturally in California, Carolyn, but not to the rest of the country. We all need to conserve. We all need to remember the beauty and that it is still possible for that beauty to exist in this world. But the morale is very poor at this time.

Carolyn: There are a number of extremely wealthy and/or influential people and organizations in the US who care deeply about global warming and could be a very effective mouthpiece collectively. Should they be leveraged, and if so, how?

Roosevelt: They should be leveraged, of course, one hundred percent. The people who have the opportunity because of their financial reserves should make a difference in the world. Those that aren't using their . . . well, I won't judge on this, but I feel that those that have the financial reserves are able to help invest money in more scientific investigation and toward more scientific discoveries, and to put into our schools' scholarships that will reward children for their ideas and their innovations toward this specific issue of saving our planet.

Carolyn: Yes, I envision getting a few of these wealthy individuals together to start this "Seeds of Hope" campaign. They could fund something like this easily. They could work together with the government, private sector, and young people to pull something together.

Roosevelt: Yes. The reason why I refer to the young people is because they have the energy and the vitality and the hope. A lot of older people shut down, and they don't have that same youthful vitality. It's infectious. I feel with the students in our world, that's where the answers lie.

Carolyn: When you were president, did you leverage public resources, or perhaps wealthy individuals, to further your agenda?

Roosevelt: I did, I did. It was something that I worked on very much with Carnegie. Do you know the name Andrew Carnegie?

Carolyn: I sure do.

Roosevelt: Those that were putting in the railroad and all of these millions of dollars toward opening up coast to coast through our country, I would leverage with them quite a bit because they were taking our land. They were taking the land from the American Indians, and they were carving up our country. So, I leveraged with them quite a bit to put money toward the preservation and conservation of the parks and to help me in getting that campaign going to preserve and conserve our beautiful land and resources.

Carolyn: Currently, over 50 percent of Republican members of Congress are climate deniers. In fact, President Biden's recent climate legislation passed without a single Republican vote. And it is concerning to see the influence and power that fossil fuel industries have over the making of policy in the US. This could be a big problem for the planet, especially in light of an upcoming midterm election, as well as the 2024 presidential election, in which climate initiatives would surely be rolled back by a Republican-led Congress and president, and legislation would be pushed to speed up fossil fuel development. As the second largest emitter in the world, this would be catastrophic in terms of not meeting the Paris Agreement goal and the resulting damage to the planet.

If you were president today, how would you handle both the problem of fossil fuel money influencing policy at such a critical time, as well as the deliberate disinformation campaign carried out by these members of Congress to deceive the American people?

Roosevelt: I'd like to take the question apart, please, and answer one part at a time. The second part of the question: look, I believe that it's very in fashion to disagree with the other party. But the truth is that the deniers are destroying confidence. And when I say destroying confidence, I mean that this is false information that they are claiming to have, and I would ask that they, rather than just deny, prove how there is no global warming. Prove where they see the opposite. Prove where they are saying there is nothing. Show us how there is that evidence. I don't feel they will, and they don't feel that's their role.

But I feel that they are sacrificing the best for our country in order to win. They are trying to present the world as a safer place, at this time, than it truly is, and that global warming or planet concerns are just a bleeding heart, liberal point of view. Of course, I disagree with this. I don't know how to—other than asking them to prove their stance—I don't know what can be done.

Politics is no longer about trying to do your best for the country. Politics has become more than that. There are several layers to it—greed that is insurmountable. And there are people who, for their own greed, want to win, and not for the best of the country. And now things are at risk because when someone does not win, they deny that. Politics should be about accepting when you win or accepting when you lose and doing what is best for the country. This is all falling away.

My only hope is that people will try to do the right things and listen to the information that is out there, and try and discern what is correct and what is incorrect. But it is very difficult to discern what is real and what is made up in the way that information is presented at this time.

Carolyn: How would you handle the problem of fossil fuel money influencing public policy?

Roosevelt: Oh, goodness. I am so happy I'm not president right now!

Carolyn: [Laughs.] Well, I really wish you were down here!

Roosevelt: I'd like to think about this and come back to you at another time. This is one question which I don't feel I have an immediate answer for. Would you be willing to reconnect at another time?

Carolyn: Absolutely. In fact, at the end of this interview, I had planned to ask if we could talk again after the midterms but before the 2024 election. It's going to be a very interesting time, and I would very much appreciate more time with you.

Roosevelt: Oh, good, we will do that, then.

Carolyn: With the upcoming midterm election, which experts suspect will move the US House to red, we can expect that the US House and Senate will both be in an intractable situation with respect to passing more climate legislation, not to mention potentially reversing already in place laws. If you were president, how would you deal with a gridlocked Congress in terms of climate legislation?

Roosevelt: Hmmm. I would like to see some time limits put on these bills being passed rather than the stalling and combativeness. Time limit on the bills—do you know what I mean by this?

Carolyn: Do you mean time limits on these bills or term limits in Congress?

Roosevelt: Actually, yes, I would like to see the time limits on the bills, and I would love to see term limits for members of Congress. There has to be new energy coming in all the time, not just new energy that I agree with or that you agree with, but there has to be new people coming in with new ideas and new understanding. This gridlock is because of people digging in their heels. No one will compromise. It just sits and sits, and it's gotten worse and worse with time. I would also like to see time limits in place for discussion in Congress.

Carolyn: For change to happen, people need to show up and vote in large numbers and make informed, educated choices, but many on the far right are heavily influenced by far-right media platforms that are a major driving force behind climate denial and other distortions. Global warming and climate change have long been politicized, as you were saying, as a left-wing issue.

How would you handle the problem of people on the far right believing the disinformation campaign and not doing their own research? Is there anything you would like to say to them?

Roosevelt: I'd like to shake some sense into them, but these are people who are followers. They will not look into information that is available to them to make their own decisions. I would say wake up, because they are blindly following information. This information is being distorted to get a very definite result from them, and that is to keep following the path.

I would also say, please educate yourselves. Please look at your children. Look at how they are doing in their lives and tell me this is not happening. Do your children have the same clarity of mind that you had as a child? Do they have the same opportunities? Do they have the same natural resources? Look at your children, because that is the reality. Educate yourselves. Go to libraries where it's free. Seek out news from reliable sources and seek the truth. Do not blindly follow. You are wasting your precious time here in making a difference. I would say that, and they would probably turn the other cheek and they would not listen, I doubt. But I would say, please, look toward our future, which is our children. Look toward how you can make this world better for them, even if it means facing your fears and facing the unpleasantness. Face the reality. It is time to act. It's time to come together and act.

Carolyn: Well, Mr. President, as we approach the end of the hour, is there anything you would like to add before we talk again?

Roosevelt: I would just like to say thank you for this opportunity, and I would like to thank you for all the hard work that you are doing to make a difference. I would like to give you my love and my gratitude, and I would like to, as I said, be available to you. But I must ponder some of these questions because I do take them very seriously, and I want to give you my very best input for your project.

Carolyn: Well, thank you so much. I really appreciate that. I also wanted to ask if there is someone you'd like to recommend that I also speak with for this project?

Roosevelt: I would recommend a gentleman that you already spoke with, John Muir, a good friend of mine and partner. He is a very good soul. His spirit is in what you are doing. We are all doing everything we can to help with this project, and the answers are not easy, but we will continue to fight toward this cause.

Carolyn: Oh, yes, Mr. Muir. I very much enjoyed my first conversation with him. I've got plans to reconnect with him to talk about his life on the other side. Well, thank you, for coming in today, and I very much look forward to talking with you again for the second part of the interview.

Part Two: January 25, 2023

Roosevelt: [Laughs.] Hello!

Carolyn: Mr. President? What is so funny? I must know!

Roosevelt: I'll explain in a moment.

Carolyn: All right! I love starting out this way. I have really been looking forward to talking with you again. And I thank you so much for being here.

Roosevelt: Thank you. I am most happy to be here. So, who are you?

Carolyn: My name is Carolyn.

Roosevelt: That is a beautiful name.

Carolyn: Thank you so much! The last time we spoke, I was able to get a lot of helpful information. But I wanted to give you the opportunity to follow up on a few questions that we weren't able to finish. I'd then like to ask some questions about the types of activities that you are doing on the other side and give you an opportunity to share any additional thoughts. And before we get started with questions, I'd like to introduce you to John, who is also on the call. He also has a keen interest in speaking with you and will be asking some questions shortly. Before we launch into questions, is there anything you'd like to say at this point?

Roosevelt: I'd like to say that my channeler was laughing because I rode on my horse when I came to greet you, and I was galloping at a quick speed. And I was very excited and anxious to come in today, so that's why there was some laughing there. But all in good fun.

Carolyn: [Laughs.] What is your horse's name?

Roosevelt: My horse's name is Cleo.

Carolyn: Cleo! Well, Cleo, thank you for bringing the president in today. We appreciate it.

Roosevelt: Her name is Cleopatra, but I call her Cleo. And she's very happy to be here as well.

Carolyn: So, Mr. President, from our last conversation, I wanted to follow up on several questions that we talked about revisiting at a later time. I was asking about the fossil fuel industry influencing public policy on global warming and climate change. Few Republican elected officials deny the existence of climate change, but many still don't accept that burning fossil fuels is the primary cause of global warming, while strong majorities of voters do. Republicans in Congress are now out of step with the American public on climate. In the meantime, "Big Oil" companies continue to lobby policymakers to lock fossil fuels into climate policy. From your perspective, do Republicans simply not see the future risk? Or do they not believe the science? Or is it simply just a matter of being beholden to the fossil fuel industry? What is the problem?

Roosevelt: Oh, it's definitely a little bit of all of them. The third item—being beholden to the fossil fuel industry—is a big part of this. It is an enormous part of this. And the Republicans are out of step, and I couldn't agree more.

Carolyn: From your perspective, do you see the quality of elected officials improving in terms of their integrity and their desire to do good for the American people rather than to just stay in office and have this powerful position?

Roosevelt: Well, I don't know if you know this, Carolyn, but I represented the Progressive Party in my later days, and I would love to see a rejuvenation of the Progressive Party. I would love to see a three-party system in place because there is no middle point. Do I see the Republican Party . . . improving? I don't want to say that I don't have an optimistic viewpoint; I always do. But there would need to be an extreme house cleaning and bringing in more people with a more progressive attitude. And the Democrats have their own issues at the moment. But there needs to be a meeting in the middle, and I think it's probably time for another party to be in the system. I feel it is overdue, and we've wallowed in this situation for far too long.

Carolyn: Yes, I would also agree. I'd like to see an independent party, something in the middle—a moderate party. That would really be helpful. I'm not sure if you have a perspective here, but I wanted to talk specifically about the role of "Big Oil" companies, such as Chevron, Exxon Mobil, etc. From your vantage point, what is it going to take to push "Big Oil" to finally move more aggressively toward renewable energy and away from fossil fuels? Is it a matter of government policy, such as incentives and penalties?

Roosevelt: Yes, yes, you've got it. Otherwise, they're going to keep producing the oil, the fossil fuels. They are going to go where the money is, and they need to have an incentive to move forward or have a government policy in place.

Carolyn: Yes, along with penalties, too.

Roosevelt: Yes, correct. You are a very bright young woman.

Carolyn: Why, thank you. Is there something that the American public can do to move things along in addition to what the government should be enacting?

Roosevelt: The American public needs to be more vocal about opposing fossil fuels. They need to be more active in their voices. I don't think the American public completely understands what is at stake at this point and needs to connect fossil fuels with the climate. It seems like a very easy, direct hit to me. But there are people who are still confused—they have a busy life, they have families, they have children, they go to work, and they put the gas in their car. Do you understand what I'm saying, Carolyn?

Carolyn: Oh, yes, I do. Do you have a feel for when we can expect to see "Big Oil" finally start to move away from fossil fuels and transition to renewable energy, or is it possible that will never happen, and we will have to get there another way?

Roosevelt: Well, if I were president today, I would be on that like a rat on cheese. [Carolyn and John laugh.] It would not be something that we need to forecast in the future. The way I see it, I think it will be moving toward eliminating fossil fuels, but it may be a very long time. When I see it, I see sludge—a slow movement toward this.

Carolyn: Do you see things moving at a faster clip, for example, in the European Union?

Roosevelt: European Union. I would say that they seem to be much more in alignment with working toward this transition. And I do see that happening at a much faster pace. My hope is that the United States will move forward once they see that they are not in first place and they are not the winner, because we can't stand for that. But yes, I see them [the European Union] being much more proactive toward this progress.

Carolyn: The US House is now led by Republicans, with a Speaker largely beholden to the far-right Freedom Caucus, which will likely prevent future legislation to address climate change. Have you, and others on the other side, been watching what has been happening in the new House of Representatives? If so, what are your thoughts?

Roosevelt: Yes, we've been witnessing this, and we think it's a complete, complete disaster. We think that it is an embarrassment and not the Republican Party as I once knew it. We feel that this is going to hold things up until there is a new Speaker. We feel this is going to be in place within the next year.

Carolyn: Do you feel the American public will vote for more moderate choices in the 2024 election, which would ultimately help the planet?

Roosevelt: Oh, I think there is a very good chance of that. The Republican Party is digging themselves a very deep hole, and I think there's a very good chance of more moderate representatives. It's kind of like a circus.

Carolyn: Yeah, I bet you all have never seen anything like this when it took fifteen ballots to elect the Speaker.

Roosevelt: No, Carolyn, no. This is unlike anything I've ever witnessed, and I've witnessed some things, okay. This is unlike anything that we have ever seen. One thing I want to say, though, it might be wise not to alienate the different political points of view in your book, which I think comes naturally for you to side with the Democrats or more moderate points of view. I just want to say a more neutral position would probably inspire more people to read your book if you were more neutral in your political views. And I know, this is almost impossible.

Carolyn: I completely agree with you. But from the types of questions that I'm trying to get answered, in terms of messages of hope, it seems the roadblock is the more far right of the Republican Party. Not the moderate Republicans and certainly not the Independents. Not the Democrats and not the Progressives. So, I've written off the far right as being a target audience for this book. They are not going to read it, and they are not going to care.

Roosevelt: Yes, I understand. You know your people. I understand. That makes perfect sense, and it sounds like you are already on it, already thinking forward. Good job on that.

Carolyn: Well, thank you. At this point, I'd like to hand things over to John for a few questions regarding the types of things you are doing on the other side.

John: Mr. President, first of all, you mentioned Carolyn is a bright young woman, and I have to agree [Carolyn laughs]. She is a spring chicken in her late 50s [more laughs], and we're coming to you from California.

Roosevelt: Oh, beautiful, yes.

John: I also wanted to mention that the point of the book is to deliver messages of hope. We talk a lot about these discussions and interviews before they take place, and we know that our mission is to always find messages of hope that will help the readers stay enthusiastic. We have explicitly discussed among ourselves that we need to remain neutral. So, we understand your point on that. It is a challenge when we see where the problems lie, but I completely understand your point to not alienate a demographic.

Roosevelt: Yes. And I have to tell you, John, that is not something I am very good at myself. I am very vocal when I disagree, and I'm very vocal with parties that I disagree with. So, I commend you, sir. That is a very challenging job that you're doing, and it sounds like you both are extremely bright and you both are very capable of realizing your demographic.

John: On the other side, are you spending time with other political leaders or your good friend John Muir? Do you have collaborations to help people on Earth?

Roosevelt: Well, yes, very much so. As I was saying, I've never been one to be quiet, and I definitely work to influence others to be more vocal, be more active about preserving this great, beautiful land that is so precious. And we need it to last forever, plain and simple.

John: Can you share more about the types of people you work with?

Roosevelt: Yes, I work very closely with those people who are very vocal about things that they would like to change. I support them and work very closely with them as a guide because you have to be loud about what you need. I also act as a guide for many people who are involved with preserving our land and keeping it pristine and beautiful in the national parks. That is something that is very important to me, and thus very important to them as well.

John: Are you influencing leaders in many countries? When you are choosing people to help, is it globally? How does that work?

Roosevelt: Well, I have been serving as a guide, and the reason is because it's a mutual agreement. I don't sit and pick, as much as there is a gravitational pull toward working with someone. I do work with other countries. It's not just about America. This land is extremely beautiful, and we need to save it—it's all about maintaining the beauty and creating the beauty with preserves. And with the activists, there are activists everywhere, all countries, and I am there as a support for them.

John: We recently spoke with Chico Mendes, who, during his lifetime did a lot of work in the Amazon, and he is that kind of guide.

Roosevelt: Yes, he is that kind of a guide, and I know him very well.

John: Oh, very interesting.

Roosevelt: Very good man.

John: Yes, we very much enjoyed our conversation. We recently spoke with President Richard Nixon. Have you seen him on the other side?

Roosevelt: No, I have not.

John: The reason why I ask is that Nixon enacted many laws to protect the environment during his presidency, and he created the Environmental Protection Agency (EPA). We have noticed that his contributions are starting to get more press down here. The other side of Nixon is starting to get presented, and we hope that he sees that happening here. We see some level of redemption going on, which is, in itself, a message of hope, and I do hope that comes through for him.

Roosevelt: I was going to say that he is not someone that I've spoken with or had discussions with. He has been very reflective about his life and has done quite a bit of isolation. But I know that he will be happy, so happy, to hear your words. I will definitely do what I can to communicate this message to him.

John: Last week, we spoke with Senator John McCain, and he mentioned that he is doing his, and I quote, "damnedest" to protect the US Constitution at this vulnerable time. Do you work with Senator McCain? It seems like you guys would get along well. Is he one of your collaborators, if I might ask?

Roosevelt: He is definitely someone that I collaborate with—a very good man. We have had many discussions about protecting the Constitution, and it's something that is very important to us. I not only work toward being a guide, but I'm also in discussions with those who want to protect the Constitution and democracy. And, I might add, I'm also working in a body at this time as well.

John: Oh, so you are in a body on Earth now. Can you tell us more about this?

Roosevelt: I am in a body and am in a completely different life than when I was president. It is part of my challenge to be in this body at this time. I am practicing benevolence, and I am practicing in a different way. You see, my life as a president, I was very driven by my ego—I was driven by being a man's man. I am in a body in Africa, in Kenya, and I am a Franciscan monk at this time. You can understand why it's important to have a clean slate because with all of that knowledge and information [from previous lives], you get tied to that past life, and this is an opportunity to start again on a different path.

John: That's very interesting. Thank you for sharing that.

Roosevelt: Of course.

John: I'm going to hand things over to Carolyn now.

Carolyn: Mr. President, since you are now a Franciscan monk, have you met with Saint Francis on the other side?

Roosevelt: Yes, yes, I have.

Carolyn: Wonderful!

Roosevelt: It is a wonderful thing. Yes, I have met with Saint Francis, and he has been very inspiring for me on my path. I love my life—it's very different from my life as president and coming from a well-to-do family. It's very different. We practice selflessness and charity. There is a way to understand that the animal life is just as important as the human life.

Carolyn: Is this your first life since your time as President Roosevelt?

Roosevelt: No, I was actually in another body. I came into Berlin [Germany] but only lived for a few days after my birth. And so, I came back and started again.

Carolyn: Does your higher self, who we are speaking with right now, know my higher self, and John's higher self, and Sam's higher self on the other side? Have you met our higher selves?

Roosevelt: Yes, I have.

Carolyn: Can you tell us a little about that?

Roosevelt: I am afraid that is something I cannot discuss. But I will just say that there are no accidents. Carolyn, John, and Sam, your higher selves are very pleased with your choices, as far as being on your path. And your growth in this lifetime has been great. Your higher selves are very proud. Your higher selves are like your family, and you don't want your relatives embarrassing you.

Carolyn: [Laughs.] No. Thank you for sharing that, and I'm glad that we know you in that form on the other side.

Roosevelt: Yes. It is wonderful.

Carolyn: Mr. President, I understand that you passed at the age of sixty, in your sleep. I'm wondering if you would mind sharing what your experience was like when you crossed over?

Roosevelt: When I crossed over, I at first was confused because I didn't realize that I had passed. I saw my body, and I was confused as to why I was able to see my body from outside of myself. I was greeted by my family—I was greeted by my son and I was greeted by my daughter who I had never really known very well. [Note: Roosevelt's second wife had two miscarriages, and I speculate this daughter could have been one of the miscarriages.]

Although it was confusing, it was quickly remedied by being with my father and mother and my family. It was very touching to be with them. What was so important to me was that I was also greeted by my pets, and it was lovely to have that love and that kindness. That was very important to me. There was a beautiful fire going in a fireplace as well. It was just a feeling of being accepted for being me and not having to be anything but me.

Carolyn: Did you see any of your guides? Were they there to greet you?

Roosevelt: Yes, I was there with my guides as well. I had three guides at the time, and they were there to make sure that I had properly acclimated to my new existence. They let me know that they were very happy with my life and what I had tried to do. They also let me know what I would be working on once I got fully transitioned, and that would be to work with the activists, the [political] parties, the preservation of the land, and also the preservation of democracy.

A lot of things to work on, but you don't feel any pressure. It's all very smooth, and there's no pressure. It feels good. It feels like what you want to do, so they help guide you in the direction of what your soul needs to grow and to learn.

Carolyn: Do you still have the same guides now?

Roosevelt: I have another guide at this time.

Carolyn: For people on Earth who are inspired by you, would you be willing to be their guide, and if so, how should they go about asking for this?

Roosevelt: They just need to ask. Just ask for me and my guidance, and if it's in alignment with what I'm working on, then we have a match.

Carolyn: As a child, you suffered from severe asthma. But as an adult, you overcame physical disabilities and hardened your body and your will. You formed a band of voluntary fighters called the

Rough Riders, who would go to battle in the Spanish-American War. Years later, you survived an assassination attempt at a campaign stop where you were shot point blank in the chest, yet you carried on with your speech for almost ninety minutes as you bled from the wound. I have to ask, how on earth were you able to do this?

Roosevelt: Well, I want to say that some of the people in attendance weren't exactly distressed that I had to cut my speech short because I usually like to talk for much longer than ninety minutes. [All laugh.] Yes, I was known for talking quite a bit. I was a self-made man, and as far as my illness/asthma, I just made up my mind that I was not going to be that person, that sickly person. I just made up my mind and transformed my body; really worked on my body. I built up quite a lot of stamina, and people had a hard time keeping up with me.

I'll tell you, Carolyn, the ego comes in handy when you decide you're going to be something else. I was going to be a man's man. And that was very important to me. I did not want to be frail or anything less than robust. So, I fixed my mind on that speech, and I continued to bleed, and I just did my speech. But, as I said, that was actually a pretty short one for me.

Carolyn: [Laughs.] Okay. What guidance can you offer to people who would like to feel stronger in their bodies and their minds?

Roosevelt: Well, yes, what I can say to that, the mind is very powerful, and, in many ways, has no limits to what you can become on the outside and on the inside. For those that are dealing with sickness and illness that they feel have taken over their lives, I would say that you can make things different if you truly want to. Anything is possible. We are energy, and anything is possible with energy. Our minds are energy, and our bodies are energy. But there is no effort without error or shortcomings, and it's not always going to happen for everyone. Your mind is capable of great things in terms of manifesting what you desire.

Carolyn: Would you be willing to be a guide for people who are dealing with sickness or illness and who are inspired by you?

Roosevelt: Well, of course I would! Again, it's just about requesting and asking. That's how it works. And if they truly want this, then I can be their guide. And remember, a guide is someone who helps to steer you in the direction where you would like to go—not someone who creates miracles.

Carolyn: Right. Okay. So, if you would allow me to ask this question. I would like for my body to have more stamina and for it to have less fatigue and pain. And so, with that said, I would very much like for you to be my guide in this respect, if you would be willing to take that on.

Roosevelt: That would be a deeee-light, Carolyn!

Carolyn: [Feeling very moved.] Oh, well, thank you!

Roosevelt: I want to be your guide, and I am honored to be your guide. We are in alignment, and I think it's a perfect marriage of a guide and someone who wants to be working with me.

Carolyn: Well, I am thrilled! Thank you again. You've given us quite a bit here today, but is there anything you would like to add that might be hopeful for the readers?

Roosevelt: I feel it's in that song, "This land is your land, this land is my land." I feel that we have all this beauty, all this God-given beauty. Man is quite extraordinary in all the capabilities that Man possesses, but in this position, I think it's important that everyone come together, and I feel that this beauty can be saved. I feel very hopeful about that. I wouldn't be here if I didn't. I feel very hopeful. This planet can be a place of beauty, a place of efficiency, a place to grow, where we can continue to learn for billions and billions of years. We can do this. We can come together and save this beautiful, beautiful land and save ourselves. We can do this. I believe with all my heart that it will be done.

Carolyn: Thank you, thank you. Before we part, I'd very much like to talk with you again for another book about saving our democracy, fixing our broken political system, and unifying a polarized country. Would you be willing to talk again about this?

Roosevelt: Yes, most indeed, yes, I would.

Carolyn: Thank you, Mr. President—and my new guide! And thank you so much for agreeing to come back for part two of this interview. It's really such an honor to speak with you again, and I look forward to the next time.

Roosevelt: Thank you!

[Note: Two months after this second interview, John and I traveled to Henry Cowell Redwoods State Park in Felton, California, specifically to visit the famous redwood tree on the Redwood Grove Loop Trail where Theodore Roosevelt had been photographed on May 11, 1903.[1] Here's the funny part: As we went to pay for parking, I looked in my wallet and had only one bill—and it was very clear that one bill was $20. The parking fee was $10, so I handed over the $20. The attendant gave back $40 in change instead of $10. I told him there had been a mistake and that I'd paid with a $20 bill, not a $50. The attendant held up the $50 bill to show he hadn't yet put it in the cash register.]

---

[1] https://www.santacruzsentinel.com/2018/02/23/focal-point-roosevelt-among-the-redwoods/

CHAPTER 9:

Saint Francis of Assisi (1181–1226)

Interview date: January 16, 2023

Saint Francis of Assisi was an Italian Catholic friar who established the Franciscans and is one of the most revered religious figures in Christianity. Inspired to abandon a life of privilege and wealth to lead a life of poverty and itinerant preaching, Saint Francis set out to follow in the footsteps of Jesus Christ. He cared for the sick and poor and preached multiple sermons about animals. Saint Francis referred to all creatures as his "brothers" and "sisters" and considered all nature the mirror of God. Pope Gregory IX canonized Saint Francis in 1226 based on evidence of miracles during his ministry. In 1979, Pope John Paul II declared him Patron Saint of Ecology, adding, "Among the holy and admirable men who have revered nature as a wonderful gift of God to the human race, Saint Francis of Assisi deserves special consideration."

John: Saint Francis, there are many saints, but you are personally one that I've felt a long-term connection with based on your affinity for the animals and ecology. In fact, I keep a small statuette of you on my desk, so it is a special honor for me to speak with you today. I thought I'd open it up to what your thoughts are on the current state of the planet. Do you agree with the assessment that Carolyn just described?

Saint Francis: First of all, I would like to say that I am humbled by your words of kindness. Thank you for that. I am humbled that you have my picture. Thank you. I agree with Carolyn that the world is not as recognizable for me at this time as what I once knew. I agree that it is in a state as if it is spinning; the world is spinning. The people of the world are not in connection with the nature and the planet. They are treating the planet as something separate from themselves and from God.

John: As a man of God who cared about the environment and was later named Patron Saint of Ecology, what do you see is the greatest problem with our stewardship of the Earth today?

Saint Francis: As I was saying, it is a separation. The planet, the nature, is separated from the people. The animals are still in connection with the planet and creation, but the people are looking at it as something that can either just give to them or take from them. They are not recognizing that they are making that choice. They are not recognizing that the connection is broken. Without respect for the Earth and our environment, the Earth feels disrespected and betrayed by the people. There must be acknowledgement that we are all One and not separate.

John: There are people who are more opportunistic, and as you say, think, "What can the Earth give to me?" But there are also a lot of people who do understand the severity of the situation. While you might describe that globally, the Earth is feeling betrayed, can you detect that there are pockets of people who also understand the urgency to take corrective action and would like to convince the other people? Do you see that there are two different groups?

Saint Francis: Yes, I do. I am just explaining how the Earth is feeling at this time. Yes, I see there are many people who cherish the planet and understand the peril of the planet at this time. The Earth knows that there are stewards looking out for the Earth, but I would say that it is a feeling not yet taken over completely by those who feel otherwise.

John: We have had it described by others interviewed that the Earth is heating up because the Earth is angry about the mistreatment. How can we all come together, as a collective, to create healing and protect our planet?

Saint Francis: It is a way of thinking; it is a way of living. It is something that could become expansive with more information and more ways to see the Earth as our brother, as one of us. Not as something that we just reside on but as a connection to us. That is a message—to spread that message in the ways that you have to do that in this time. It is much different than how I would convey that message when I was on Earth. It is about reshaping the way the world and the environment are perceived. I am sorry [lightly laughs], I am a little overwhelmed by how to spread the message to eight billion people.

John: Well, that's okay, Saint Francis, because it's our job to spread the message, and you are providing us with excellent information. If I hear what you are saying, we need to have the people perceive the Earth as not an inanimate object but a living, breathing member of our community.

Saint Francis: Yes, as one of us. We must treat Earth as family, as a loved one. We must love the Earth because the Earth is not feeling loved.

John: From your perspective, can you please share why the people of the world are experiencing this particular issue, global warming, and climate change, and if there is a higher message, learning, or lesson? Can you provide some insight here?

Saint Francis: The lesson is that the people are not embracing the planet as a loved one. They are looking for the planet to blame at this time. They are looking to say that the planet has not served them. It cannot keep up with their demands. But that is what the lesson is: the Earth is a living, breathing thing. If you were treated as such, you would also be angry. The lesson is that we need to come together, we need to be kind to each other and honor each other, we need to love each other as best we can, and love everything in our world. And that comes from kindness. That kindness needs to be shared with our planet, and that kindness needs to be shared with the animals. We need to see the Earth as someone who can read our thoughts and read our intentions and give the Earth the respect that we would ask—and that is to be treated with kindness and honor.

John: It is unfortunate that the Earth is having to go through such a terrible time for us to learn this lesson. Do you have hope for humanity that we will figure this out in time before the damage is irreversible?

Saint Francis: I have hope. I always have hope. My hope is true. My hope is based on love for the people of the Earth and what they are experiencing at this time. I know that they are frightened. I know some feel that the Earth is rebelling, and I would not disagree. I am not able to see the time when things could turn around, but it's so many years and so many lifetimes of maltreatment that it's going to need many years to recover and to heal. And that is a way to look at this, as a healing for the Earth. We need to heal the Earth. And I have hope that humanity can start to love and heal the Earth. I feel that once that is in place, once that is genuine and coming from the heart, that things will begin to turn around. Earth will begin to heal.

John: So, Saint Francis, what you are saying is that people need to show respect and love for the Earth, for the planet to heal.

Saint Francis: Once that respect and love from the heart is in place, the healing will be quick. The healing will start to take place, and it will be miraculous. But it has to be there. It is very simple, a simple request.

John: Can you describe the types of activities that you have been doing on the other side and have a strong conviction about?

Saint Francis: Mostly, I oversee many of the souls that are here. I am especially passionate about working with those souls who experience poverty and experience feeling alienated in some way, such as feeling like an outcast from society. I am very passionate about working with those souls because they often feel like they will remain unaccepted. I work with them to embrace who they are. I work with them to show them the unity that we have and to bring them together with other souls, because they often feel that they are not worthy or do not deserve to be integrated with other souls and be a part of and belong.

John: Is it souls on the other side or souls on Earth?

Saint Francis: It's both—souls that arrive and souls that are still in a body.

John: Regarding the angry Earth and what humans are doing to the planet, causing global warming and climate change, are you doing any work to influence people, to help them perceive the Earth differently? Is that part of your work?

Saint Francis: It is part of my work. I am like a messenger, and I work to try to influence and to spread that message. It is a difficult message, though, as I was saying, to reach so many people, so many souls. But it is something that I am doing because I love the people of the Earth, and I love the Earth and I love everything about it. I am in love with the people and the Earth together. I try to reach individuals who I know can help with this message. That part feels big to me, to reach everyone I want to reach, so I have people who do help me with that.

John: Thank you so much, Saint Francis. Carolyn is now going to ask the remainder of the questions.

Carolyn: Hello, Saint Francis. I was wondering if you are a guide to many on Earth.

Saint Francis: Yes, yes, yes, absolutely. I am a guide to John and Sam, and I am a guide for many people. And that is where I get most joy, from being a guide. I try to show them the love and show them the way toward helping others.

Carolyn: Saint Francis, are you not my guide?

Saint Francis: Well, it is about, do you want me to be your guide?

Carolyn: I would love for you to be my guide.

Saint Francis: I would love to be your guide!

Carolyn: Alright!

John: If I might cut in, you mentioned you are a guide to Sam and me. Do people formally need to ask you to be their guide? Is that part of the process?

Saint Francis: No, it is not part of the process. Carolyn has a number of guides. We are working with everyone on certain things, and that is why I was not in place as her guide. But if she would like me to be her guide, I am your guide, Carolyn.

Carolyn: Wonderful, but I don't want to take away from anyone else.

Saint Francis: That's not possible, because my love is infinite.

Carolyn: What does it mean to be a guide for people on Earth?

Saint Francis: A guide gives protection. A guide gives information. A guide is there to help you to be on your path. A guide is there to keep you true to yourself and for why you are here in this lifetime. A guide is always about love. And a guide will never turn their back on you. A guide always is there for you.

Carolyn: Can people call on you for you to be their guide as they strive to help the planet and/or animals in need?

Saint Francis: Oh, yes.

Carolyn: How do you suggest they do this?

Saint Francis: Simply ask me. I have infinite love to give. Just simply ask.

Carolyn: On a different topic, can you please tell us how you became aware that I wanted to talk with you today?

Saint Francis: That is something that I would like not to answer. So, I will just say that I am aware from watching.

Carolyn: I was wondering if you've watched any of our other interviews, and if so, if you had any comments.

Saint Francis: I have. I have watched all of them. My comments are that I love all of you so much for what you are doing. I am so filled with love and pride for what you are doing. The comments that I have are that I feel that there is no question that this is your calling, Carolyn. There's no question that you have accepted the call and that you are right for what we are doing. And you are going to be able to reach so many people. This is definitely one of those ways that we can reach the people.

Carolyn: Oh, thank you so much for sharing this with me.

John: Do you have any plans to ever incarnate again, or are you what some people refer to as an ascended master, one who has completed their lifetimes on Earth?

Saint Francis: I will not be coming back in a body. And I am an ascended master, if that is what you want to call me, but I am not coming back in the body.

Carolyn: Saint Francis, I wanted to ask about the taming of the wolf. For the readers unfamiliar with this story, there was a wolf that had been terrorizing the Italian town of Gubbio. So, you, Saint Francis, went out to find the wolf. When the wolf sees you, he comes charging, ready to attack. You immediately made the sign of the cross over him and commanded him on behalf of Christ that he do no harm to you or to anyone. The wolf then stopped running and meekly threw himself at your feet. You asked the wolf to promise to never harm any human or animal again. The wolf showed agreement by simply bowing his head. Later, in front of the people of the town, with the wolf present, you asked the people if they would promise to provide food for the wolf regularly. They all said they would. Finally, you asked the wolf to give a guarantee that he would no longer harm the people or their animals. The wolf then lifted his right paw and placed it in your hand. Afterward, the wolf tamely entered the houses without doing any harm to anyone and was kindly fed by the people. Please tell me, is this a parable or a true story?

Saint Francis: This is a true story. This is what I was saying about the Earth. This is about treating the Earth as One, in connection. It is about respect. The wolf, many felt that it [the story] could not be true, but it was true. It was about treating that wolf with love and respect, and it was an agreement. And that is what needs to happen with the Earth: an agreement. We will love and respect you, and we will take care of you if you take care of us in return.

Carolyn: Oh, that is just beautiful. Today, the topic has been about global warming and climate change. But I'd also like to ask, what do you see is most useful in terms of helping humanity right now? How can we best help each other?

Saint Francis: Mercy. I feel that mercy is lacking in the world today. We are separate from each other, and we say, "Well, too bad for them," and "That's terrible what's happening to them." But together, we are all One, and we need to have mercy and compassion for each other and for all living things.

Carolyn: Before we part today, is there anything more you would like to add?

Saint Francis: No, thank you for inviting me because it was another way to get my feelings out in today's world. And I want to say thank you for what you are doing. It is so important, the work you are doing.

Carolyn: Thank you so much, Saint Francis. Thank you for your interest in this project and for connecting with us today. Would you be open to us contacting you in the future for upcoming books with a focus on forgiveness, empathy, and compassion?

Saint Francis: Yes, I very much would. Thank you.

Carolyn: It's been such an honor and a pleasure to speak with you, and I very much look forward to the next time.

Saint Francis: God be with you.

CHAPTER 10:

President Richard Nixon (1913–1994)

Interview date: December 1, 2022

Richard Nixon was a member of the Republican Party, serving in the US House of Representatives, the US Senate, and later as vice president of the United States for two terms under Dwight D. Eisenhower. Nixon would go on to become the 37th president in 1969, resigning in 1974 during his second term as a result of the Watergate scandal.

In the years before Watergate, Nixon and his administration initiated some of the United States' most meaningful environmental policies, including the establishment of the Environmental Protection Agency (EPA). One-third of Nixon's State of the Union address in 1970 was devoted to the environment, and an excerpt of the address can be found at the end of this chapter.

Prior to speaking with Nixon, Carolyn had interviewed Dr. Stephen Schneider, a climate scientist who had been a consultant to the Nixon administration. Schneider had not yet spoken with Nixon on the other side because Nixon was "doing a lot of self-reflection, a lot of self-isolation" and was not accessible. Carolyn's sources on the other side confirmed this was the case and that it was doubtful that contact would be possible due to Nixon's self-imposed seclusion. Nonetheless, Carolyn prepared for the interview and gave it a go.

After invoking Nixon to come forth, a long minute passed, and then his distinctive voice came through. Carolyn was startled that he'd actually shown up, and the tone of his voice didn't seem very friendly. He sounded suspicious, and even though the voice belonged to Sam, it was all Nixon. It brought Carolyn back to her nine-year-old self during the Watergate scandal, and she struggled to keep her voice from shaking.

Nixon: Hello.

Carolyn: Hello, Mr. President?

Nixon: Yes.

Carolyn: Thank you so much for joining us today. I'm so grateful to be able to connect with you. My name is Carolyn, and my partner is Sam, who is channeling you. We would like to put together a book, and the intention of the book is to give hope and inspiration to the masses at a very challenging time in history in terms of global warming and climate change. I have been speaking with scientists, conservationists, political leaders, and inventors who, during their time on Earth, had significant—

Nixon: Carolyn, may I interrupt, please?

Carolyn: Of course.

Nixon: Are you sure you want to speak with me? I don't mean to say that I don't want to speak with you; I just want to make sure that you have the right person.

Carolyn: Mr. President, I think that many people have no idea that your administration left such a strong environmental legacy, giving the United States new legislation governing the protection of the air, water, and wilderness. This is why I'd like to talk to you.

Nixon: Ah. Alright, then.

Carolyn: You initiated many of the most important and enduring environmental policies in American history. It's enormous, and I would very much appreciate your participation in this project so more people can understand the motivation behind all the good work you did. Is this something that you would be interested in proceeding with?

Nixon: Well, I have to say, I'm a bit—I'm a bit at a loss. I—I would like to speak with you, thank you, but I'm a bit surprised that you'd like to talk to me. Thank you, I'm just a bit surprised.

Carolyn: Well, I think that a lot of readers will find what you have to say to be very interesting. Quite honestly, they associate you with Watergate, and that's not what this is about. This is about all that you did on behalf of the planet. You did a lot of good things, and I want this to be emphasized. I'd like to get your perspective on a few questions for the book, and quite honestly, I'm thrilled that you would like to continue. Again, the main thrust of this project is to provide a vision that the future can be better than the present, to inspire people to take particular actions that will help the world, to know good things are coming, and to provide much-needed hope.

Before we get started, your administration created the Environmental Protection Agency and, as I stated earlier, enacted many important environmental policies, including the National Environmental Policy Act, the Clean Air Act of 1970, the Marine Mammal Protection Act, and the Endangered Species Act. You also established the National Oceanic and Atmospheric Administration and the Legacy of Parks Program, which transformed more than 80,000 acres of government land into 642 new parks.

I have read that, in some cases, your motives for creating these policies may have been for political purposes. But I've also read that some initiatives were near and dear to you, such as the Marine Mammal Protection Act. Either way, thank you for the actions that you took on behalf of this planet. I would really like to know how you viewed the importance of environmental initiatives while you were president and how you view the importance of protecting our environment now that you have a different perspective, being on the other side.

Nixon: Well, my goodness [laughs]. It is a lot [meaning his list of accomplishments]. I'll tell you—it was very important to do what I could to protect the air, protect from hazardous dumping, pollutions, pesticides, asbestos, and dangers of asbestos in schools— there were many things that needed to be completed, and I had scientists—I didn't work with them; they advised me—and I paid attention. And political motive—everything is a political motive. But I also have to say that even though I had many faults, I did try to do what was best for the American people, and I knew from the information presented to me that we were heading down a path that we would need to veer off of and create a new path or we would be in great trouble with the planet.

I feel there is still much to be done, but there is a great deal that has been improved [upon]—not so much by me—but there has been a great deal of improvement. The problem is the world is densely populated, and pollution gets harder and harder to keep up with, with more people. But thank you for the recognition. I do understand there is much more to be done.

Carolyn: If you were president today, what would you be telling America and the world about the state of our planet and the needs of our planet?

Nixon: I'd like to say, Carolyn, that I'm glad I'm not president today. I did my time, and it's time for new blood. I would tell the people that there is much to be done, but there is much that has been done. There are many who are working on this issue now. I feel that the American public is in a very desperate place—feeling very destined for doom and Armageddon—and nothing can be accomplished in that state, and this is something that we all need to be a part of to see these improvements take place. I would tell the people about things that have been done and where we are seeking improvements to work toward a cleaner planet. When you have no information or overwhelming information, it's like a deer in the headlights, and people freeze and feel powerless.

Carolyn: Since your passing almost thirty years ago, can you describe the types of activities you have been doing on the other side?

Nixon: Well, in my lifetime, I was a man who needed to win. And win at any cost. And that was to my detriment. I've done much self-examination and reflection. I was someone who had an abundance of hubris, and I am someone who, since I have passed, has been reexamining, trying to rediscover my humanity. I started to believe that I was more powerful than I really was. I am learning empathy and compassion. I am learning from people and their stories. I am learning by experiencing others' grief and strife so I can learn how to be a better human being. I did try to do good things, but also, I did not do good things—and I want to be better.

Carolyn: Compassion and empathy . . . Is this something you'd be willing to talk further about in another book?

Nixon: Yes. It is something, though, that I—it's not that I'm not willing to talk to you; I am. And I appreciate your invitation, but in small doses. I have much that needs my attention at this time, and a great deal of that is relearning and generating a new story for myself that is not based on my belief of my own greatness.

Carolyn: Of course, I understand. I'll check back with you at a later date, and we can certainly do this in smaller doses. I appreciate your time here today . . . Before we part, is there anything you would like to add?

Nixon: I would like to add that I hope that there is forgiveness, and I hope there is understanding that this is a human experience that we are all having. I am working. I am working on who I am. I hope in my next life that I can do better things—and do them in better ways with more compassion.

Carolyn: Thank you for coming in today, Mr. President. And thank you for all that you did on behalf of the planet. It's so nice to meet you.

Excerpt from Richard Nixon's State of the Union Address, delivered on January 22, 1970

I now turn to a subject which, next to our desire for peace, may well become the major concern of the American people in the decade of the seventies.

In the next 10 years we shall increase our wealth by 50 percent. The profound question is: Does this mean we will be 50 percent richer in a real sense, 50 percent better off, 50 percent happier?

Or does it mean that in the year 1980 the President standing in this place will look back on a decade in which 70 percent of our people lived in metropolitan areas choked by traffic, suffocated by smog, poisoned by water, deafened by noise, and terrorized by crime?

These are not the great questions that concern world leaders at summit conferences. But people do not live at the summit. They live in the foothills of everyday experience, and it is time for all of us to concern ourselves with the way real people live in real life.

The great question of the seventies is, shall we surrender to our surroundings, or shall we make our peace with nature and begin to make reparations for the damage we have done to our air, to our land, and to our water?

Restoring nature to its natural state is a cause beyond party and beyond factions. It has become a common cause of all the people of this country. It is a cause of particular concern to young Americans, because they more than we will reap the grim consequences of our failure to act on programs which are needed now if we are to prevent disaster later.

Clean air, clean water, open spaces—these should once

again be the birthright of every American. If we act now, they can be.

We still think of air as free. But clean air is not free, and neither is clean water. The price tag on pollution control is high. Through our years of past carelessness we incurred a debt to nature, and now that debt is being called.

The program I shall propose to Congress will be the most comprehensive and costly program in this field in America's history.

It is not a program for just one year. A year's plan in this field is no plan at all. This is a time to look ahead not a year, but 5 years or 10 years—whatever time is required to do the job.

I shall propose to this Congress a $10 billion nationwide clean waters program to put modern municipal waste treatment plants in every place in America where they are needed to make our waters clean again, and do it now. We have the industrial capacity, if we begin now, to build them all within 5 years. This program will get them built within 5 years.

As our cities and suburbs relentlessly expand, those priceless open spaces needed for recreation areas accessible to their people are swallowed up—often forever. Unless we preserve these spaces while they are still available, we will have none to preserve. Therefore, I shall propose new financing methods for purchasing open space and parklands now, before they are lost to us.

The automobile is our worst polluter of the air. Adequate control requires further advances in engine design and fuel composition. We shall intensify our research, set increasingly strict standards, and strengthen enforcement procedures—and we shall do it now.

We can no longer afford to consider air and water common property, free to be abused by anyone without regard to the consequences. Instead, we should begin now to treat them as scarce resources, which we are no more free to contaminate than we are free to throw garbage into our neighbor's yard.

This requires comprehensive new regulations. It also requires that, to the extent possible, the price of goods should be made to include the costs of producing and disposing of them without damage to the environment.

Now, I realize that the argument is often made that there is a fundamental contradiction between economic growth and the quality of life, so that to have one we must forsake the other.

The answer is not to abandon growth, but to redirect it. For example, we should turn toward ending congestion and eliminating smog the same reservoir of inventive genius that created them in the first place.

Continued vigorous economic growth provides us with the means to enrich life itself and to enhance our planet as a place hospitable to man.

Each individual must enlist in this fight if it is to be won.

It has been said that no matter how many national parks and historical monuments we buy and develop, the truly significant environment for each of us is that in which we spend 80 percent of our time—in our homes, in our places of work, the streets over which we travel.

Street litter, rundown parking strips and yards, dilapidated fences, broken windows, smoking automobiles, dingy working places, all should be the object of our fresh view.

We have been too tolerant of our surroundings and too willing to leave it to others to clean up our environment. It is time for those who make massive demands on society to make some minimal demands on themselves. Each of us must resolve that each day he will leave his home, his property, the public places of the city or town a little cleaner, a little better, a little more pleasant for himself and those around him.

With the help of people we can do anything, and without their help, we can do nothing. In this spirit, together, we can reclaim our land for ours and generations to come.

CHAPTER 11:

Rachel Carson (1907–1964)

Interview date: January 18, 2023

Rachel Carson was a marine biologist, author, and conservationist whose books and activism advanced the global environmental movement. After a career with the US Bureau of Fisheries, now known as the US Fish and Wildlife Service, Carson became a full-time nature writer, during which time she published articles and a trilogy of bestselling books on the natural history of the sea.

A fourth book, *Silent Spring*, was published in 1962 and created worldwide awareness of the dangers of environmental pollution, particularly the problems that Carson believed were caused by pesticides. Carson endured the threat of lawsuits from the chemical industry along with their unsuccessful public relations campaign to attack her credibility and disparage the book. *Silent Spring* became a bestseller, and Carson would go on to testify before Congress in 1963, which ultimately led to a nationwide ban on DDT and other pesticides. *Silent Spring* is widely credited with igniting an environmental movement, which ultimately led to the establishment of the Environmental Protection Agency (EPA) in 1970.

Carolyn: Ms. Carson, do you agree with my global warming and climate change summary, and what are your thoughts right now, given your perspective from the other side, with respect to the current state of the planet?

Carson: Yes, I agree, and yes, Man has continued to try to control nature, control the Earth instead of cohabiting with the Earth and with nature. And this is where we are today, struggling with this fallout. Yes, I agree.

Carolyn: What do you think people need to hear now, and what should we all be doing to take better care of our planet?

Carson: Well, people need to hear that there is a younger generation. There are future generations and a younger generation that is committed to this type of work, so that is very hopeful. Also, I feel that we need to learn how to integrate Man's inventions and use them properly and not overuse them. And then, by doing so, our relationship with our planet will be much better and safer and give us a future where we can exist. Without that, I feel there is no looking back.

Carolyn: When you speak of inventions, which are you referring to?

Carson: Since World War II, we have plastics, we have drugs, we have lubricants—and, of course, we have pesticides. The problem is not that. Those things are not the problem. It's about overuse and the way they are disposed of and not being used correctly. We are finally recognizing that in the incorrect and improper use of these things, they are continuing to add to the pollution of our planet and to global warming. I am not saying we need to omit every convenience. We just need to use them with respect and use them properly.

Carolyn: A recent report released by the United Nations projects that one-third of all animal and plant species on the planet could face extinction in the next fifty years due to climate change. Globally, up to one million species are at risk of extinction because of human activities. Maximum annual temperatures are the key variable that explains whether a species will go extinct, and limiting warming to 1.5 degrees Celsius would save most global species from climate change. However, it is estimated that 14 percent of all species living on land would still be at risk of going extinct. From your perspective, do you see the world being able to meet the Paris Agreement goal by 2050 and not exceeding 1.5 degrees Celsius?

Carson: I would have to say that I would not be surprised if we surpassed that goal. I do feel that there is a lot being done to work toward meeting that goal, and I admire that. And I do, of course, see the future getting brighter, but I feel that we may surpass that goal.

Carolyn: When you say we may surpass that goal, do you mean we may go beneath 1.5 degrees Celsius by 2050?

Carson: Exceed.

Carolyn: Oh, dear, okay.

Carson: Carolyn, there is a lot being done, which is very, very hopeful. But there is a lot being done in a short amount of time to meet that goal. So, I do not want to say that I am right; I just want to say that it would not surprise me if we exceeded that goal.

Carolyn: Okay. With that said, can you see us eventually, with breakthrough technologies and innovations, once they take hold, eventually being able to dip beneath 1.5 degrees Celsius?

Carson: Yes, I do. That is entirely possible. It's not going to stop people from working toward the goal. And I want to be very wrong. And I hope that I am wrong. But I do see that eventually, Man will come together, and things will be much more optimistic and have a brighter future. But first, I think we have far to go to see that brighter future.

Carolyn: In December 2022, the United Nations COP15 Biodiversity Conference (CBD) struck a historic deal on protecting and restoring nature. The CBD is a landmark international agreement that sets out how to safeguard plant and animal species and ensure natural resources are used sustainably. Almost 200 countries have signed on to protect 30 percent of the planet's land and 30 percent of oceans or marine areas by 2030. It can also be referred to as the 30x30 Initiative. Currently, 17 percent and 10 percent of the world's land and marine areas are under protection, respectively.

Additionally, nearly two dozen other targets against biodiversity loss were agreed upon, including a 50 percent reduction in the use of pesticides, which I thought you'd like to hear.

Carson: Yes.

Carolyn: I'd also like to note there has already been local adoption of the 30x30 Initiative in places such as California and cities like Boise, Idaho. Though not legally binding, governments will be tasked with showing their progress in meeting targets. Is 30 percent enough, or should it be set at a higher percentage? What is your perspective on this?

Carson: I would like to see it set higher, but I do feel that if 200 countries come together on 30 percent, I feel that 200 countries is of great significance. I would like to see it at 60 percent, but I know we must take time to get to where we need to go because it doesn't happen overnight. I think this is a wonderful start, and I'm very impressed that we were able to come together with so many countries to make this agreement.

Carolyn: Do you feel most of the countries will follow through on their commitments to honor the agreement?

Carson: I feel that most of them will. I feel the majority will.

Carolyn: Thank you so much, Ms. Carson. I'm now going to hand things over to John.

John: Hello, Ms. Carson. It is certainly a pleasure to speak with you, and I really appreciate all the work you did while you were here.

Carson: Thank you, John.

John: I'd like to run something by you. Bill Gates, the billionaire philanthropist who has launched a nuclear innovation company as well as an investment firm to back new climate technologies, recently publicly stated that the world will not be able to avoid overshooting the Paris Agreement goal to limit warming to 1.5 degrees Celsius by 2050. I heard your report on this earlier, so I think you would agree with him on that. But I also heard you say that you felt we might be able to recover and pull it back down. Do you think it's possible to pull it down significantly lower than 1.5?

Carson: I think it's possible. I think there's a lot of innovation happening right now. Again, I am hopeful that if we do surpass it, we can bring it back down. There is a lot of innovation happening, and I'm aware of that, but not necessarily all of the details.

I'm working with young scientists—young female scientists, and that's part of my role—to guide them and to help them advance in this area. I'm extremely hopeful that, if we do surpass it, and again, I hope that I am incorrect, that it can be brought down to possibly even lower [than 1.5 degrees Celsius]. That would be exactly what we would want, of course, and there are many scientists who are studying this and are very passionate about saving the planet. They have a lot more years than you, Carolyn, and Sam, and they need to exist in this world. There is this huge drive happening in keeping that goal in place and then actually receding from that goal and bringing that number down.

John: This is a very good message of hope, Ms. Carson, because the fact that with these innovations happening over time, we can see this number drop, we can reverse the trend, and that is a very big deal. Do you think there is a fundamentally different attitude in the younger generations where they do understand the plight of our planet and have a much deeper commitment than the older generations who are responsible for all those inventions that turned into overuse, improper use, and improper disposal? This would be a message of hope if we feel that the younger generations have a much deeper understanding and commitment. Do you see it that way?

Carson: Most definitely, I do. I truly do. They are passionate about this and don't want to exist in a world that is full of misery and destruction. They want to save the world. It's not that they blame your generation, John. It's very much about coming back to what we had before we decided that Man was here to control nature rather than live with nature. And by that, I mean that Man pretty much set out to change everything from the natural world if possible and dominate the natural world.

We have a generation now that realizes they need to co-exist with the natural world, and they are very passionate about this. I think they do have a bit of, I guess you could say, an attitude about previous generations and how the Earth has been treated. They know what they need to do, and they are driven and determined.

John: Saint Francis recently educated us that the Earth is our partner, a living entity with which we are connected, just like each other. And the Earth is not happy with the way it's being treated. I like the fact that our younger generation gets that. It's hopeful for me.

Carson: Yes, it's hopeful all the way around. Because you know, John, it's not that the previous generations were stupid and evil; we just thought we could do better than Mother Nature, and we have realized that we are an absolute failure at that. In many ways, we have made great advances, but in other ways we are living in a way that is destroying nature, and we need to stop trying to control it.

John: I'd like to get your thoughts on the Amazon rainforest and what more we can do about this. The Amazon rainforest has already had almost 20 percent of its total area deforested, and scientists have warned that further deforestation could push it beyond a tipping point where it could effectively fail as a rainforest and become a much dryer ecosystem. That tipping point would be 20 to 25 percent deforestation.

The Amazon rainforest is vital to the planet's climate, playing a role in regulating global climate. Brazil contains almost 60 percent of the Amazon rainforest. With the recent elections of pro-environment Presidents Lula in Brazil and Petro in Colombia, where almost 10 percent of the Amazon rainforest is located, do you see us being able to avoid the tipping point?

Carson: I can only hope. And that does come from the governments, from politicians, and from voting for the right people who are proactive and "pro" about the rainforest and saving the rainforest. As long as they are in charge and in the government, we have a very good chance. But again, we need to keep those people in their place, to fight for the forest, or we need to keep replacing them with others who will fight for the forest. I feel that it will be one of those situations where we can keep this going. But there have to be so many regulations in place with the government. It is looking much better, much brighter for the forest.

John: Do you think Presidents Lula and Petro have the passion and the will to push those kinds of regulations through? Are those the right people?

Carson: I feel they are.

John: What can we do other than contribute to organizations and boycott Brazilian exports and US companies that are connected to deforestation?

Carson: That is a tricky question because there is so much we can do, and yet there's also not a lot we can do. As far as what we can do, write to the Brazilian and United States governments and show support for the rainforest. There could be more campaigns about the rainforest—more information. You know, some people think that the rainforest is a type of snack food. It's actually been marketed in ways that the name is used for snacks and candies, and a percentage does go toward the protection of the forest. But I don't feel the American people truly understand what is at stake, nor do I feel that other countries, in general, feel knowledgeable about what is at stake here. But I do feel that we are [headed] in the right direction.

John: What's become apparent to me, from the souls we've spoken with, is that education is a big problem. People don't know it's a problem unless they are educated.

Carson: Yes. People today are very involved in other things that were not available in my lifetime, and there is not a sense of stillness. You have to be still in order to receive information. The ways that you have in getting information now could be used in spreading this information. But people are very selective about what type of information that they receive personally.

I am not actually sure the best way to get that education and information out. It definitely is a deficit and needs to happen, but in a way that, and this is the tricky part, in a way that alarms people but doesn't make them panic. We want to get their attention, and we want to get the information to them, but we want them to remain hopeful.

John: That is the tricky part because if we give them a message of hope and they get the impression that everything is taken care of, then they will not be sufficiently actionable on the topic.

Carson: I'm wondering if, in your book, perhaps you could include different ways of finding out more about these topics, for those who are interested.

John: That's a very good idea. I will say, Ms. Carson, when we look at people like John Muir and how he was able to educate and make things happen in the national parks, and how you were able to get a lot of traction in the 1960s around the topic of pesticides, it's definitely possible. And the fact that you were able to get it done back then on such a big scale.

Carson: At that time, my book was very controversial, and that is why it got so much attention. It wasn't a time when there were a lot of options to have a selection of information. Now, you can pick what type of information you want to receive. Back then, it was pretty black and white about what information you would receive—through newspapers, radio, and books. And it was so controversial at that time because the chemical companies went into an uproar, saying that I was incorrect. That's why it got so much attention. It threatened the money that they were making. And then President Kennedy and the Secretary of the Interior, they followed through, and they started having hearings. There were several bills introduced, and they found out that I was correct in what I was saying about those chemicals.

But I know even today, there are still questions about pesticides being used. Again, it is about us wanting to dominate nature. And, at that time, they were wanting to completely eradicate insects, and then you don't have to deal with them anymore. There are insects that take care of insects. Nature has a cycle of interrelationships. That, again, was Man trying to make some money. In the meantime, there was the poisoning of wildlife, poisoning of people, cancer, poisoning of food, cattle were dying, horses were dying, and people who worked on farms were developing cancer and other serious terminal illnesses. So, that is why my book was so controversial; because it involved money and greed, and the chemical companies had a good thing going.

John: Do you think the tipping point, when people started to right the wrongs of DDT, was because the government intervened, or was it the public at large that became educated, or a combination?

Carson: It was a combination. With the hearings and bills being introduced, that got everyone's attention. But the public, they said, weren't fully told about the effects of these chemicals. Their children had them sprayed directly on them. And it frightened quite a bit of people.

John: You mentioned earlier that you are working with female scientists from the other side. Do you connect with them to inspire them through dreams, or is there anything you can tell us about how you do your work?

Carson: Mostly, I work with them, definitely to inspire them and to guide them. I am a guide for them. I support them to keep going, and I lead them in good directions, new directions. I make sure that they are protected, and I want to see them flourish. Even today, John, women still have to fight for recognition in the sciences, and I am there for them and want to see them succeed and exceed. I want to see them take precedence, and I want to see them succeed.

John: If these female scientists, if they somehow knew to meditate about Rachel Carson and asked for your guidance, would it help?

Carson: Yes. It makes it easier for me to do the work when they recognize me as their guide. That goes for everyone. If you are able to call on your guides in meditation, ask them to give you their name or their purpose for being with you. Ask them to show themselves to you in some way, and that doesn't necessarily mean a physical picture of them. Just ask, and those requests are answered because it makes it easier for the guides to do their work when they are recognized. It becomes a one-to-one relationship rather than just trying to encourage from afar and to support from afar.

John: When you were here on Earth, did you have guides that you knew about and reached out to? Did you have that kind of insight?

Carson: I did not, and I wish I'd had because I had some excellent guides. I wouldn't say I had anyone of note, but I had guides that were exactly right for me, but I didn't realize that until I passed over. And I think that's very sad. It would have been nice to be able to call on them while I was in a body.

John: When you crossed over, did your guides greet you and reveal themselves?

Carson: Yes, exactly. It was a beautiful moment because there were many things that had happened [while on Earth] that sometimes seemed unexplainable. We call it luck. My guides were there to say to me, "I was with you when this happened, and I was with you when that happened, and I was encouraging you and supporting you along the way." It was beautiful.

And I wanted to mention, when I transitioned, I was greeted by a million monarch butterflies. It was beautiful!

John: Wow, that must have been incredible!

Carson: John, you've never seen a million monarch butterflies all at once, have you?

John: [Laughs.] No. We have gone to monarch butterfly sanctuaries but never saw a million! That is really something. Thank you for sharing with us. Have you met Dr. Charles Keeling on the other side, with whom we recently spoke?

Carson: I have met with him, yes, a few times. I find him fascinating. He is a good man, a good soul.

John: We would agree. Is there any chance that you are working from the other side with his son Ralph Keeling, here on Earth, at Scripps?

Carson: I am not a guide for his son, no. But if he is anything like his father, he is a very special person who is doing this not only in the name of science but also because he has a pure heart that wants to be of service to the planet and help the planet.

John: We have plans to speak with Jacques Cousteau soon. Have you had an opportunity to meet him on the other side?

CHANNELED MESSAGES OF HOPE

Carson: Yes, I have. Jacques is a very, very, very kind soul and someone who is very concerned about what is happening with our climate and our oceans. And yes, I think you should speak with Mr. Cousteau.

John: When we speak with him, do you have any specific questions that you recommend we ask him?

Carson: I would ask him about the coral reefs.

John: During your time on Earth, you were instrumental in changing the way the world viewed conservation. If you were on Earth today, what advocacy actions would you be undertaking?

Carson: There are so many opportunities today. I would like to concentrate on the overbuilding that is happening on Earth today. So much building and so much housing, and I understand that the population requires it, but there has to be some other way. We have to have nature. We will end up with a planet with very little, other than the designated national parks and nature conservatories; other than those, where will children play, and where will they see nature other than traveling to see it like animals in the zoo? That is something that I feel is an issue. I feel that the buildings that we have should be used before new buildings are created. There's so much tearing down and building, tearing down and building someplace else, and land that is being developed. It's something I think is very important that needs to be addressed.

John: [Rachel Carson is starting to sound tired.] Ms. Carson, we are getting near the end. Sometimes we notice that it can be tiring for Sam to hold the channel. Is it also strenuous for souls?

Carson: I wouldn't say it's strenuous. It takes a lot of energy to be able to show up in this way, but as long as we can sustain it, we will. If you want to test us, we can start dropping off like flies. [All laugh.]

John: [Laughs.] We do not want reports going out that we are pushing souls too hard. Do you have plans to incarnate again? If so, what would you like to accomplish?

Carson: Oh yes, I would like to incarnate. I am not certain when I will be doing that, but I would like to incarnate. And I would like to actually work more in the medical field, working toward advances in ending cancer. That's because I actually experienced cancer, and it was quite ravaging to my body, and my emotions, and my spiritual self. That is something that I am very passionate about, and would like to come back in a body and work toward that.

John: What message of hope would you like to give to the people?

Carson: I would just like to say that Man, the human race, is full of wonder. So many things that we are capable of and so many things we have accomplished. I feel the human race is amazing and capable of many things, but we've also realized we are capable of being highly destructive.

This is about ego, and if we could set our egos aside and not look toward personal gain and look toward living with nature, living with the Earth, it would be a beautiful world.

I think that it's time that the human race made that shift, and I feel like that shift is coming. I'm not certain when, but I'm starting to feel quite a shift in the human race realizing that they are just humans after all. And if there is anyone who believes in the capabilities of mankind, it's myself. I know they can do great things. They just need to channel that into saving and protecting this Earth.

John: How did you know we wanted to talk with you?

Carson: Actually, telepathically, it was communicated to me that I should be here and participate. I am so happy to have this time with you, and I'm so happy to be able to share what I could.

John: Well, thank you so much, Ms. Carson, for talking with us today, and thank you for all the work that you did to provide the impetus for tighter control of pesticides, as well as advancing the global environmental movement. It's been such an honor.

CHAPTER 12:

Dr. Wayne Dyer (1940–2015)

Interview date: February 13, 2023

Wayne Dyer was an internationally renowned *New York Times* best-selling author and speaker in the field of self-development and spiritual growth. He wrote more than forty books, created many audio and video programs, and appeared on thousands of television and radio shows, including ten PBS specials featuring his books, which raised over $250 million for public television.

Dyer released a feature film, *My Greatest Teacher*, a true story based on the most pivotal moment in his life. Dyer's father had abandoned him and his family when he was an infant. As a result, he grew up in orphanages and foster homes, very much disliking his father. After learning of his death, Dyer visited the grave of his late father ten years later. For three hours, he stood at the grave, stomped on it, and expressed his anger out loud. In the last minutes of his visit, something came over Dyer. He said to his father, "From this moment on, I send you love, and I forgive you for everything that you have done." Shortly after leaving his father's grave, he rented a motel room and wrote his first book, *Your Erroneous Zones*, in fourteen days—and it would go on to become a *New York Times* bestseller of over thirty-five million copies. Dyer passed away forty-one years later to the day that he had visited his father's grave.

Dyer's primary message was that every person has the potential to live an extraordinary life and can manifest their deepest desires if they honor their inner divinity and consciously choose to live from their highest self.

While greeting Dyer and going through the introduction, Carolyn was surprised to find herself emotional and moved to tears, a reaction that had not happened during any of the previous interviews. Discovering Dyer's books in her teens, Carolyn has deeply resonated with and embraced his teachings for over forty years.

Carolyn: [Voice continuing to break.] Dr. Dyer, thank you again for joining us today. Since we're not here for a technical discussion on climate change, I'm not going to read the summary that appears in the book. I know that you are aware of the issue, but today, our focus is more on spiritual tools discussed in your books and how the readers can employ these tools to move from a state of hopelessness to actually manifesting the things they want in their lives and for the planet and to ultimately experience that beautiful feeling of peace. Before we get started, as you know, John is on the call and will be asking some questions as well.

Dyer: Thank you, Carolyn, and I'm touched by your emotions. It's beautiful. I feel the compassion and energy, and I just want to say thank you for showing up fully for this.

Carolyn: [Still emotional.] Thank you.

John: Carolyn is very moved. Normally, I'd say she's tough as nails.

Dyer: Well, the toughest ones are the first to go! [All laugh.]

John: Thank you again for joining us. This is certainly an honor; I just can't tell you. First of all, I'd like to look at the issue of global warming and climate change from a higher level. I know from your teachings that there are no mistakes in the universe. Is there a spiritual reason we are experiencing global warming and climate change right now? What lessons are we to learn from this, and is there a message of hope to the readers that you would like to communicate?

Dyer: Thank you, John. Yes. I want to say that, on this issue, we are experiencing a collective guilt for the abuse toward our Mother Earth. And this is what we have manifested: guilt. And there is a collective belief that along with guilt, there should be punishment. But we can eradicate this thought and practice mindfulness to heal and replenish the Earth. You see, we are just redistributing the manifestation. We cannot afford to let any doubt in. We must acknowledge the abuse and apologize, but then move into manifestation of love, healing, nurturing, comfort, and learning and growing from our past mistakes. We are here to come together collectively. We are all here for this time and for this reason: to come together as a human race, not separately. This is not about the ego. This is not about taking what we can get from this Earth. This is about serving this Earth. And we must practice service as a collective instead of taking and winning the competition, which is simply an illusion.

John: Wow, that's really interesting. Saint Francis gave a similar viewpoint, but you've given us another angle. In terms of lessons to learn, it sounds like it's for all of us to come together. Can you please rephrase the lesson?

Dyer: Progress is impossible if we do things the way we've always done them. There is a mentality of "It's okay. Someone else will take care of it." But if we come together to save ourselves and this planet and we give love, that is the one thing we have to give away freely to each other and to this planet. There are no accidents in this universe. We all show up here with a purpose, and we are connected to an intelligence. You are not separate from your environment. Mankind's ego is in competition, and that has put the Earth in peril. But this is an illusion. The ego is not real. Most people don't learn this until they die.

John: So, we need to switch from "what can I take from this Earth" to "how can I serve this Earth" and practice service. People know that they can recycle, stop buying single-use plastics, drive electric vehicles, reduce their carbon footprint, etc., all these tactical things. But what guidance do you have for the readers who are still feeling helpless, powerless, and even hopeless about the situation? How can they shift from pessimism to optimism and break those attachments to gloom and doom?

Dyer: John, we will create. We will manifest what we believe. And we are all looking for answers someplace outside of ourselves instead of looking inside ourselves. Our universe was created by divine intelligence. This universe was not created in gloom or doom or hostility or depression. If it feels angry, it's because we are manifesting this—our own anger, our own frustration, scarcity, fear, and so on. That fear, that frustration, that anger permeates into our attitudes and our beliefs. As you think, so shall you be. What you believe expands and manifests.

The simplest way that we can all work toward manifesting a more loving existence and a more loving experience with our Mother Earth is to practice meditation. Go inward to the silence and imagine not just serving but sending love to this beautiful Earth—sending love and replenishment for the resources and repair of the resources.

John: That actually answers my next question in terms of what readers can do specifically.

Dyer: Well, I think there is a very simple route to what you are asking, John. It's a very simple belief. But it's a belief that needs to be embraced wholly. And that is something your readers can do to benefit the Earth through manifestation . . . going inward and visualizing a loving Earth. A loving Earth that we are grateful for. And an attitude of gratefulness.

John: You've talked many times about how the change that we want to see comes from within, not outside of ourselves. In fact, one of your famous quotes is, "If you change the way you look at things, the things you look at change." So, if people want to change what is happening to the planet or what they see in society, it all starts with a change in mindset. And what you're telling us is that we can make that change in mindset through meditation and reframing the way we think. You said that Earth was not created in a fear-based situation, but it was created basically through divine intelligence and joy. What can we do to guide the readers through this process? I don't know if we want to do a meditation in this book. Do you have any other thoughts as to what the readers can do now to effect change?

Dyer: It could be a meditation, a visualization, or both, actually. They are interchangeable. For the readers, understand that our Earth is to be grateful for, and don't take it for granted. Give thanks for the air we breathe. Give thanks for the oceans, the rivers, the streams, the creeks. For the rain, for the snow, for the glaciers, the Antarctic, the sky, the stars, the galaxies. Give thanks for the sun that warms us, the trees, the plant life, the mineral life, and the ground we walk on.

How many of us even notice the ground that we walk on and for the earth that provides our food? Meditate and visualize everything there is on this Earth to be grateful for—all the abundance that we are surrounded by and all of the miracles that are just begging to be acknowledged, validated, and appreciated.

John: That is amazing. What you just did was a guided meditation for us and our readers. [Jokingly.] Have you been getting together with Saint Francis, Dr. Dyer?

Dyer: [Laughs.] As a matter of fact, I have. We're actually good friends. Saint Francis was someone who was always a mentor to me. Can you imagine my joy and disbelief when I crossed over and I was in the presence of Saint Francis, someone who had guided me when I was in a body? What I thought of when I saw him, I thought, "Oh my God, I have manifested what I wanted." This is the testimony to my belief in manifesting. [Laughs.] And I just want to say that everything is already here. We just need to value it and serve it in love, and it really is a very doable thing.

Carolyn: Dr. Dyer, you came up with a term for the concept behind the "law of attraction." You called it the "power of intention," a place where one can create miracles. Your philosophy was pure and simple. The law of attraction is this: you don't attract what you want; you attract what you are. Can you help the readers understand this concept and how they can easily apply the power of intention to create the things they want in their lives, both internally and externally? Is it something as simple as stating, "I AM peace, I AM love, I AM grateful, etc." Is it really that simple?

Dyer: You know, it really *is* that simple. [Teasingly.] And you've just said what I would have said, Carolyn.

Carolyn: I'm sorry!

Dyer: [Laughs.] It really is that simple. It's just that's not the tricky part. The tricky part is *believing* that it is that simple. You just need to believe it's that simple, and then it's simple. *I am love. I am peace. I am fulfilled.*

Carolyn: And *knowing* it with every fiber of your being.

Dyer: Yes, yes, and that is why many people struggle because that is a very hard concept for some people to understand. A difficult concept I would say. To know it in every part of you . . . that's what you really are: Love.

Carolyn: We spoke with Saint Francis recently, and he feels that once humanity can start to love and respect the Earth, the Earth will heal. And it will be quick, and it will be miraculous. But this love and respect must be genuine. It must come from the heart. Can you suggest to the readers how they can send love from their hearts to the Earth?

Dyer: The simplest way is to picture your heart full of love and picture that love emanating to our Mother Earth. In whatever way you visualize her—whether you visualize her as a globe or as a landscape full of trees and homes and industry—no matter how you see Mother Earth. If you see her as an actual mother, see her and emanate love from your heart to her. Send that love. It's very simple. And watch her change. Whether that be a color or whether that be a feeling. Observe the change you see when you send love.

Carolyn: What if there was a way to get thousands upon thousands of people to do this same visualization or meditation at the same time? What kind of effect do you think this would have on the Earth?

Dyer: That would be incredible, and I know that it's more than possible.

Carolyn: Do you feel that Mother Earth has a soul?

Dyer: Oh, yes, I do. Anyone who doubts that the Earth has a soul is not fully aware of how the Earth is here to protect us—how the Earth is here as our home. Let me ask you this: does your home have a soul? You've walked into many homes where you didn't feel much of a soul. You can tell the difference when there is a soul in that home and when there is not. You can tell when there is strife. You can tell when there is love. The same with Mother Earth. You can believe Mother Earth has a soul.

Carolyn: Thank you for that, Dr. Dyer.

John: Switching gears now, we'd like to talk about your life on the other side. Can you tell us if you are collaborating with other spiritual leaders and/or philosophers? And can you share what your focus areas are on the other side?

Dyer: John, what I have learned is that I will always and forever be a teacher. That is where my heart is. I continue my teachings, as you say, on the other side, and it is something that I take quite seriously. I also comfort a lot of people who are struggling after death, still struggling . . . to understand the meaning of their life. And there are some people who feel their life was wasted. That is a very true thing, and it is very sad. And there are a lot of people who need comfort.

When I was in a body, I was influenced by many people as teachers and guides, and I am able to be with them all now. And I have found my friend Ram Dass. We have so much joy together. Of course, Saint Francis, Swami Muktananda, Abraham Maslow—these are all people who influenced me greatly when I was in a body, and they are people I can continue to learn from.

We still have the same principles and the same teachings that guide our hearts. And we are here to comfort those who are in need of guidance and teaching and to understand their purpose on Earth was never wasted. To understand their life was never a waste, and to understand there is enlightenment here for us if we choose.

John: Along those lines, in terms of you being a guide, are you available to serve as a guide for those who ask?

Dyer: [Laughs.] Well, let me check my calendar. Of course, John. Of course, I want to be available. If there is someone I am not a guide to who doesn't feel my presence, I want to be a part of their life if they want to invite me. Yes, of course, I would love to be a guide if someone desires.

John: That's a message we want to communicate to the readers. That is fantastic.

Carolyn: Dr. Dyer, can I interrupt for a moment? Are you a guide for John?

Dyer: I am a guide for both of you, actually.

Carolyn: I knew it!

John: I had a sense, but sometimes here on Earth, we may question.

Carolyn: I just have to say, you visited me several times after you passed.

Dyer: I remember you were someone who was yearning for a sign from me in some way, as I have manifested myself to others who have been in desire of a sign and connection.

Carolyn: Yes, it was the alarm clock. And you had a lot of fun with that one.

Dyer: Well, alarm clocks are a fantastic way to convey a sign. Anything electric. It is so easy, and it makes our work easier. I'm just so touched that you are aware that I made that visitation to you. And actually, my mission was to make myself available at that time for visitation to anyone who was requesting that—whether they were aware of it or not. And that was something I worked very hard to manifest, and your validation means the world to me.

Carolyn: [The night before the visitation, I had watched Dyer's celebration of life service online. Before I fell asleep, I had asked him to send me a sign.]

I clearly heard your voice in my dream state. You said, "Your alarm clock is going to go off now." Two seconds later, it went off, and it wasn't even set. And then you did the same thing the next day. It was fun.

Dyer: I know that you've been a significant part of this whole experience that I was able to have on Earth, and I thank you for that.

Carolyn: Well, you've touched my life in a grand way, as you still do, so thank you. I thank you for that.

Dyer: Thank you, Carolyn.

Carolyn: Can you describe what it was like when you crossed over?

Dyer: All of my guides were there for me. My mother was there. You know, there were a lot of people who I didn't recognize. There was so much love coming from them. It turned out they were people I had touched in some way through my writing and through my videos and audiobooks and people whose lives had been affected by what I had done. It wasn't a celebration for me as much as the love that we all shared, even though I hadn't met them before. So, it was a beautiful feeling, so enveloped by love. The interesting thing is . . . it was a bit confusing because I was living in Hawaii when I died, and I crossed over to what was like Hawaii. My personal heaven is Hawaii.

Carolyn: Oh, that is so beautiful. You've written so much about your father. Did you see him?

Dyer: I did not see him when I first crossed over, but I did see my father soon after, and it was a beautiful reuniting and forgiveness. Yes, I had released and forgiven, but he was holding on to so much. By being able to see him and hold him and let him know that I understood, he was able to release all of the guilt and all of the feelings of having wronged myself and my brother and my mother. It was more than I could have imagined.

Carolyn: After you passed, your family did a memorial paddle out in the most beautiful, secluded waters near your home in Maui. Moments after spreading your ashes, a photo was taken of the water. In the water, there appeared to be a silhouette of your face. Was this for real? Was it a gift from you?

Dyer: You know the answer to this, Carolyn. It was my way of thanking my family for their love and for our experience together. It was my way of saying goodbye until we can meet again. It was there for them to see. You see what you believe, and you believe what you see.

Carolyn: That was really cool.

Dyer: I thought it was pretty cool.

John: Are you done with lives in a body on Earth, or do you have plans to incarnate again?

Dyer: I know that I will incarnate again. I don't know when, but I know I will incarnate again.

Carolyn: Well, Dr. Dyer, as we near the end of our time here, is there anything you would like to add?

Dyer: My message has been simple—redundant. I know that we have the answers within us, and I know that we can create what we want in our lives.

Carolyn: And all your books lead to these points. While we are beyond appreciative for the time you have already given us, the story about your father is such an important one, and I know it would be so helpful and beautiful for the readers. If you would be interested in speaking with us about forgiveness, we'd love to talk with you again.

Dyer: It's one of my favorite topics, forgiveness.

Carolyn: Well, thank you so much for coming in today. Thank you for being our guide and thank you for all this beautiful information you've given us that we can share with others. And please tell Ram Dass hello for me.

Dyer: That I will. And Saint Francis wants to give you a big hello, Carolyn.

Carolyn: Oh! Well, I must thank him for a statue that he kind of made come my way a few weeks ago. I've got a beautiful statue of him.

[Note: Just days after my interview with Saint Francis, I found myself drawn into a magical little garden shop from its white twinkly lights. Right away, I noticed a two-foot-tall garden statue of Saint Francis, and this statue was like none that I had ever seen. Instead of just holding a bird, Saint Francis also had the infamous wolf that he had tamed at his feet, which had been specifically discussed in my interview. I took this as a sign and immediately bought the statue. Later, when talking with Baba from The Council, Baba said that Saint Francis had nudged me into the shop to see the statue. Baba continued, "Saint Francis wanted you to know that he can see you, and you can see him." According to Baba, Saint Francis had no idea that I was going to purchase the statue and was thrilled that I did.]

Dyer: Well, he loves both of you so much, and he loves what you are doing. And he understands there was a misunderstanding, and he wants you to know that he loves you and he is here for you.

Carolyn: Oh God, now I'm going to start crying again!

[Note: The *misunderstanding* . . . During the interview with Saint Francis, it was revealed that he is a guide for both John and Sam, but not for me. I am embarrassed to admit that my feelings had gotten a little hurt, and I even cried about it later. At the time, I didn't understand that guides are chosen, not the other way around. Saint Francis had seen the tears and had tried to bring me comfort with the statue, whether I purchased it or not.]

Carolyn: Thank you, Dr. Dyer. I love you.

Dyer: I love you, too. Everything is all about love. I send you all my best and so much love for what you are doing and so much gratitude.

CHAPTER 13:

President Ronald Reagan (1911–2004)

Interview date: December 24, 2022

Ronald Reagan was an actor for more than twenty-five years, appearing on television and in feature films. A Democrat for many years, Reagan began to move to the right politically in the 1950s. He registered as a Republican in 1962 and first became known on the national political scene after delivering a speech in support of presidential candidate Barry Goldwater in 1964. Soon after, Reagan ran for and was elected Republican governor of California for two terms and would go on to become the fortieth president of the United States.

Reagan's record as governor of California included significant environmental achievements. He signed the California Environmental Quality Act, which requires state and local agencies to evaluate and disclose the environmental impacts of development projects and to mitigate those impacts. He created the California Air Resources Board to address the issue of severe air pollution, which was largely due to automobile emissions. Reagan opposed a destructive dam, and he blocked a Trans-Sierra Highway project that would have cut through the Sierra Nevada mountain range south of Yosemite and destroyed the John Muir Trail. Reagan also set aside 145,000 acres of land, including forty-one miles of ocean frontage, for the state park system.

President Reagan served two terms from 1981 through 1989, during which time his stance on the environment shifted. Reagan supported the deregulation of many environmental protections put in place by his predecessors because it was felt they were obstacles to industrial growth. And he famously claimed that trees produced more air pollution than automobiles.

Reagan did, however, sign bills that added more than 10.6 million acres of deserts, mountains, forests, and wetlands to the National Wilderness Preservation System. He championed an international treaty, the Montreal Protocol, which would prevent an estimated 280 million cases of skin cancer in America by the end of the twentieth century due to the halt and reversal of ozone layer deterioration.

Nonetheless, Reagan's environmental record will be remembered as one of the worst of any modern president. We were hoping Reagan's perspective on the environment had changed now that he was on the other side and that it could be impactful to those who continue to hold the former president in high regard, including climate deniers and possibly those still on the fence.

John: Mr. President, during the time you were governor of California, you enacted strong environmental policies, especially around clean air. But as president of the United States, you did not seem to give the environment as high a priority in your administration's agenda. What was your perspective as governor related to the environment, and what was your perspective as president related to the environment?

Reagan: When I was governor, I had more room to focus on the environment. And I do feel the environment is important, obviously. I had more room to do that when I became president, but I ran on lowering taxes and lowering inflation, and that's where my priorities were at that time.

But I did sign an act when I was president, which protected beaches and wetlands.

John: Is it correct for us to conclude that you had a shift in your position or opinion on environmental policies from your time as governor to your time as president? And if so, was that shift a matter of political expediency, or did you move to a different view on environmental priorities once you became president?

Reagan: I had to prioritize, and I still had questions as they were presented to me about environmental issues. There was acid rain, but I did not feel there was enough evidence. There were issues of fossil fuels being presented to me, but at that time, how would we operate without fossil fuels? So, I chose not to prioritize these issues because I did not feel there was enough evidence behind them.

John: From your vantage point on the other side, if you were president today, what would you be telling the people in America and the world about the state of our planet and the needs of our planet?

Reagan: I wouldn't want them to become distressed and upset about what is happening in the environment. I would just let it happen behind the scenes and let what happens be taken care of.

I think that the public doesn't need to know everything, and it can create the opportunity for depression if they see everything. I think that without an optimistic view as Americans, we lose our spirit, we lose our drive, and we lose our ambition—and, again, I think these things are best taken care of behind the scenes.

But, of course, I do realize that there is an issue here with the environment, but I feel that Americans should focus on becoming more excited about what we do as Americans. I want the American spirit restored, and I don't feel that would happen with all the information being exposed. It is not necessary at this time for all the people to be involved.

John: I understand you feel that the public does not need to know everything about what is happening with climate change and the environment and that it is better addressed from behind the scenes. But from your perspective on the other side, if you were president now, is there anything you would want to communicate to the public about climate change? And would you be enacting any climate change-related policies?

Reagan: I definitely would [enact policies]. But I also think that keeping the reins on inflation and reining it back in is more important. People can't keep food on their tables. This brings them worry, and to become disturbed by climate change, I think would add to that. Keeping American pockets full is important to the American spirit, and I think that is probably [the] number one top priority. I think that we need to feel good as who we are as Americans, and have food on the table, and send our kids to good schools.

John: But is there some way to make Americans see that taking care of the environment is also a way to contribute to their economic environment? Do you see any way to combine these two things?

Reagan: I would think that there could be a way to combine them by providing people who are doing their part in taking care of the environment with tax benefits. This would be a wonderful way to get people motivated. Tax breaks and incentives would encourage that. As far as inflation, I would guess that the agriculture industry would benefit if we all gave farmers a lot more attention and resources—to recycle and to use the food that is not cosmetically perfect to help in feeding more people. I think this would be helpful. The American farmers have been suffering for many years now, and it's becoming a dwindling industry that I feel could be helped in this way.

John: If there were any programs that could provide tax benefits for recycling, etc., what would you do as president to help communicate these programs, to help people get aligned, and to get the population behind these types of programs?

Reagan: It would be like a presidential address, maybe quarterly, to remind Americans of our American spirit and the need to come together to look out for our environment and reminding them of the benefits of doing that—and the tax break benefits—even a campaign like the March of Dimes for the environment . . . where people can donate a quarter, and have them set these up in shops. There are many ways to get the message out, but the president has great effect to get that message out.

John: For the world to meet the Paris Agreement goal of net-zero emissions by 2050 and limit the warming of the planet to no more than 1.5 degrees Celsius, it will require all hands on deck. But over 50 percent of the current Republican members of Congress are climate deniers, in that they refuse to acknowledge scientific evidence of human-caused climate change. From your perspective on the other side, and as a former Republican president of the United States who is much revered and enormously respected by these current Republican members of Congress, do you have a message for the climate deniers that might help change their stance?

Reagan: Well, I think that for those who are in denial, it is because they have not been presented with the facts. I know that there are facts out there, and I feel that those who deny facts are not guilty of turning their backs without reason. They are looking for more proof about climate change because their feelings, and I tend to side with this, is that it can also be attributed to other natural occurrences. And so, you are asking me what message would I give them?

John: Yes, Mr. President, what can be done for the Republican members of Congress who reject all the science? What can we do to get these people to look at the climate situation more objectively?

Reagan: [Pauses.] Well, I think that perhaps there could be an educational conference and they could be presented with that information and those resources, but I don't know how they would feel about going to that conference. But I think that would probably be a good way to present to them all the information.

John: Some climate change can be attributed to natural causes. My question to you on the other side is, . . . do you believe there is a human-made component contributing to our climate in a way that is bad for our future, or is it natural causes?

Reagan: Well, I do understand that there are man-made problems with the climate, but I also understand that we have been experiencing natural cause and effect since time began with our planet. I know that dinosaurs became extinct in the Ice Age. There have been many things that happen and that's the way it's always been. And now I feel like we are looking for other reasons when it's always been a natural occurrence.

I realize that there are issues with pollution and there are issues with too many people in the world now because there are more cures for diseases, so people are living longer and people are surviving through childhood, which wasn't always the case. But I do think that, yes, because of the population spurt, that Man is contributing to this, and that nature is wielding the power. But nature is also a part of this . . . I don't think it is all man-made or man-produced issues.

John: Are you involved in any working groups or some focused collaboration with souls on the other side?

Reagan: No, not too much. I meet with people who were in my life who have now crossed over, and we catch up. What I am working on is being more authentic and more myself . . . my true self. I am embarrassed sometimes to show my true self, and I may not be as . . . well . . . I always wanted to make my mother proud on Earth, and I did that. But now I want to look for that within myself and make myself proud of who I am, and to know that who I am as a soul is still evolving and is still a work in progress and that I am still someone important even though I am no longer an "Earth president." I am learning to appreciate myself for who I am, and be with myself, and not pretend to be someone else. I did a lot of pretending on Earth. This was not lying, but I did "pretend" to be a president because I never felt I was important enough or knowledgeable enough or simply "enough." But I do not collaborate with others at this time.

John: Mr. President, do you believe that you will incarnate and possibly come back to Earth? To work on some of these things, like work on your authentic self, things like that?

Reagan: Oh, yes, I will be coming back, and I will be coming back actually very soon. I have many lives to live and to learn these lessons and learn to be who I am as a soul.

John: I must tell you that your memorial service, and especially the presence of Nancy at that service that millions saw on television, was very moving. I can only hope that some sort of reuniting happens when a soul transitions. If you would care to comment on that, I am very interested.

Reagan: I would love to comment on this. Nancy is with me. We are together at this time. Nancy and I will be together in other lifetimes. She is my soulmate; she is that for me, and I am that for her. We have a deep love. She is also working on being her authentic self and working to learn how to accept imperfection.

John: That must have been so joyful when you reunited.

Reagan: Oh, yes, it was the happiest day when that happened.

John: Before we part, would you be open to us contacting you again? We plan to explore topics such as protecting the American democracy, fixing a broken US political system, and unifying a polarized country. If these issues interest you, may I contact you in the future for further discussion?

Reagan: That would be fine! I see you are tackling little, tiny things [laughs], and if I can help, I want to do that.

John: Do you have any other ideas for a follow-on messages of hope book topic?

Reagan: I don't know how you would make this a topic, but I am really looking at what is occurring now with a false persona, such as in social media. I think this is very bad, and people are losing their authentic selves because of a persona they are creating. I think it is very hurtful to play that game. Obviously, I did not have social media back when I was president, but I was playing a role. In a bigger picture, this creating a persona for people is very hurtful, and it is out of a belief that they are inferior, and they feel a need to play a role. I want to continue to feel more confident in who I am as a soul and not inferior, and I feel I could be of help in these areas by helping to bring messages of hope to these people—to help them be themselves and see the benefits of being themselves.

John: This is a very interesting topic, how people are creating a false persona on social media.

Reagan: Yes, I pretended as far as who I was as a young adult because it was safe to do that. I got everyone to like me, and I got what I needed from that. I became governor, then president, and I built a whole career based on a false persona. It was very close to who I am, but it wasn't close enough to who I really am. I didn't expose my true self, and I suffered from that. I feel it is damaging to the soul to be so unaccepting of who they are during their time on Earth.

I want to say, John, that many people struggle with this. It affects more people than we could ever think about, and it's about not feeling like they are good enough as they are. But imagine all the things we could do and be that could be so much greater than our wildest imaginations if we could just learn to love ourselves and be true to ourselves.

John: Did you know we would be contacting you in this way, to speak with us?

Reagan: Yes, I did know. You know, like the boy who was a wizard, Harry Potter . . . well, you know how the owl prepares a message with "this is where you need to be"? Well, I got a message delivered to me, but not by an owl. [Laughs.]

John: At this point, we've talked to Richard Nixon and Theodore Roosevelt. Did you know about that?

Reagan: I knew that you were talking to different presidents and different people, but I did not know about Theodore. He is very impressive.

John: Do you have recommendations of other souls we should talk to around climate change or any other topics?

Reagan: I know that you have a list and a very good list of important people, and I am sure that will serve you well more than me trying to come up with people like, well, George Burns! But he may not be right for this project. [Laughter.]

John: As we wrap things up, is there anything you would like to add?

Reagan: Well, I see you, John, and I want you to know that I feel that you are a very special soul, and I appreciate you, Carolyn. This is a very important project, and although I may not be as well informed as I should be, we will succeed in resuscitating the American spirit because people like the two of you are bringing people together and helping people see the light in these trying times. I see you and admire you both.

Carolyn: Thank you, Mr. President. And thank you for coming in today, and for all that you did on behalf of not only the United States but also the world during your presidency. It's been an honor to speak with you today.

Reagan: I am quite glad to be able to talk to you today, and I will be thinking very good thoughts for this book. I know it will touch many people.

CHAPTER 14:

John Muir (1838–1914)

Interview dates: October 23, 2022, and March 5, 2023

John Muir was a nature writer and preservationist who considered forests sacred and wanted them treated as parks, with logging, grazing, and hunting prohibited. He was able to reach and inspire many through his twelve books and more than 300 articles. Several of Muir's magazine articles ultimately led to the establishment of Yosemite National Park through an act of Congress in 1890, and his advocacy efforts were directly involved in the establishment of Sequoia, Mount Rainier, and Grand Canyon National Parks.

Muir's writings also caught the attention of Theodore Roosevelt. After Roosevelt became president, he and Muir spent three days in Yosemite in 1903, exploring, camping, and discussing conservation. During this time, Muir raised the issue of the need for forest preservation, as well as concerns about Yosemite and the surrounding areas. Soon after, Roosevelt would go on to designate more than 150 million acres as national forests.

In 1892, Muir and other supporters formed the Sierra Club specifically to rally citizens who believed in the preservation and protection of the High Sierra, a large wilderness area in eastern California. He served as the first president of this nonprofit organization until his passing in 1914. Today, the Sierra Club serves to "practice and promote the responsible use of the Earth's ecosystems and resources" and boasts more than 3.8 million members and supporters.

Through his writings and vigorous activism, Muir championed the idea that American wilderness areas should be preserved for all to enjoy and is often referred to as the father of the US National Park System.

Part One: October 23, 2022

Carolyn: Mr. Muir, thank you again for being here today. Do you agree with my global warming and climate change summary?

Muir: Well, I'd like to say that you are impressive and very smart, and I appreciate talking to someone of this making. I want to say that I am extremely honored to be part of this discussion.

Carolyn: Well, thank you so much. I feel honored to have you here. I thought I'd open it up to what your thoughts are on the current state of the planet.

Muir: Uh, well, I have to tell you that it's very sad for me to see that this world is so greedy and that Man is putting his materialistic needs ahead of everything. Not a thought about the planet, animals, trees—tear it down, put a house up, a factory up. America has been very greedy. The world has been greedy. They call it ingenuity, but look at where we are now. I feel that it has become each man for himself, and that is the root of the problem. When Man disregards every being but himself, they find themselves in a very lonely place.

Carolyn: Given that you spent a lifetime of wanting to save and preserve the natural world, it sounds like you see greed as the greatest problem with our stewardship of the Earth.

Muir: The greed, yes. I feel it's greed. Man continues to hunt when there's no reason to hunt. Man continues to abuse the land and Earth when there is no reason. Man has continued to ruin this church, this planet. And this church is turning its back on Man.

Carolyn: What do you think people need to hear now, and what should we all be doing to take better care of our planet?

Muir: I feel that people need to be more thoughtful about the world they live in, not just how to get to work or make money, but to be conscious of the world, the beauty of the planet, all of the above. Man needs to think about that and give it his time and thought just as if you were going to church. Give the planet time to reflect on its beauty and how it's a nurturing being.

Carolyn: From your perspective, do you see the world being able to meet the Paris Agreement goal and limit warming to no more than 1.5 degrees Celsius by 2050?

Muir: Well, from my perspective, there is much work to be done, but I believe it can be done. The human race needs a reset. They need to give it more thought and replace the beauty lost. If they destroy, they need to replace and honor this planet. I feel that in the schools, the young people would be inspired if an initiative was started to remind people to reflect on the beauty and give back to this Earth. But I feel we can do it.

Carolyn: Do you think this is the right goal? Is it quantified correctly?

Muir: That is an excellent question, not one I'm prepared to answer. I feel that the scientists are correct in what they are doing, and I feel that . . . we could surpass that goal if we all came collectively together and worked toward this. I feel it's possible, but people need to wake up, and it needs to be a collective. I feel that the world and America can be more unified in this race to save our world. It can bring us together in ways that are pretty astounding because we are all working together to save our lives and our beautiful planet.

Carolyn: We know fossil fuels are the predominant energy generation method currently and that we must embrace clean energy to reach net-zero emissions by 2050. There are some very good renewable energy options that will help us reach the 2050 goal, but they come with some cost to the environment. The main three are: (1) hydropower, which requires building dams and can create imbalances in the ecosystem around the dam area; (2) solar, which has environmental issues in the fabrication of solar panels as well as the disposal of old panels; and (3) wind turbines, which have a lot of potential but there could be impact to wildlife. Do you see these environmental issues getting resolved so that we can continue aggressively with the proliferation of these approaches?

Muir: Yes, I do. What you don't see from your perspective is that there are younger generations born and they are spending a great deal of energy to try and address these issues and problems that the renewable energy can bring with it. The younger generation is willing to put down their lives to save our world. They have never known anything else than a world that needs saving. They are very passionate; young minds that are fertile. They will be the ones who will come forward.

Carolyn: That is very encouraging to hear. There is also nuclear energy, and it is very efficient, but there is radioactive waste involved. Do you see improvements to nuclear technologies and/or new innovations coming soon that could solve our problems in a clean and safe way, allowing us to reach our 2050 goal?

Muir: I do. I see that there are other innovations that are coming that can bring less of the hazards to our environment. We want to get there correctly. There are other innovations coming, and the younger generation will bring them to our forefront. It may be that we start with nuclear energy, but I feel it will be phased out after a short amount of time.

Carolyn: When do you see the crossover occurring from relying primarily on fossil fuels to clean sources of energy that you feel are safe for the environment?

Muir: Hmm, that's going to take a bit of time because we've become so reliant on it. I feel that a complete crossover will take past 2050, but I also feel that the majority of the world will transition to clean energy sources before that time.

Carolyn: Severe drought has been a huge problem in California, and the state's record-setting wildfires of 2020 destroyed 4.2 million acres of forest and erased years of progress the state made in battling climate change. One hundred forty million tons of carbon dioxide was released into the atmosphere. Do you see technological innovations for water capture and storage that are safe for the environment coming soon to California and other parts of the country and world that are suffering from drought conditions?

Muir: I do not see that right on the horizon, but I do see there are new ideas coming. It is a very difficult time for America. America, as you will see, is lopsided, with half of the east underwater and the west being parched. As climate changes, as global warming continues to encroach dramatically and more people become affected by it, the numbers will continue to increase, and with that comes awareness. Again, I see great innovations coming, but I don't see anything that can help with the wildfires dramatically for fifteen to twenty years, and this is something that I feel can significantly improve the crisis. But at this time, I still see that there will be damage done.

Carolyn: As of 2020, almost 75 percent of Democrats say human activity contributes a great deal to climate change, whereas only 20 percent of Republicans say the same. This speaks to the fundamental challenge of not just raising awareness but raising awareness with information that people will believe.

I know you wrote approximately 300 articles and twelve books. Through your passionate articles, you were able to reach and influence a lot of people. These people, in turn, wrote letters to Congress. As a result, an act of Congress created both Yosemite and Sequoia National Parks. What can we do to get the climate deniers "on board?"

Muir: Yes, have tax credits for anything that is done toward eliminating fossil fuels and greenhouse gases in one's personal property. I feel that is a great way to reach the masses—through their pocketbooks. Any tax credits are a very good way to stimulate people getting on board.

Carolyn: In this day and age, what would you do to raise awareness to the climate deniers, both private citizens and elected officials, of the issues at hand and the future consequences we face?

Muir: Well, I have a very loud voice, and I'm someone who doesn't back down. Even though we have ways to connect through the internet rather than a simple phone call, we are more disconnected from each other than we've ever been. To really get the message out there, to really speak to those who are in denial, it's something that we have to be vocal about. Write the letters. We need to make our voices loud. There will be people who are still in denial, and they don't want to believe what is truly happening. But writing Congress and making our voices loud collectively is still the best way. Children should have programs in school to teach them about this. It is a very effective way to approach this because the children are at risk of having no future.

Carolyn: What message would you like to give to the climate deniers?

Muir: Hmmm, that is the most difficult question. I'd like to say the same thing to everyone: this is our church, our beauty, where we are nourished, and to turn our back on this world and all of its beauty, it will bring great suffering that you cannot deny. To see animals die in front of you, people die in front of you, and barren wasteland, you cannot deny. Let's please work together; don't try to be different.

Carolyn: Many people feel global warming is out of their control. All they see are depressing images on television and bleak news reports. They feel helpless and hopeless. Some can afford to buy electric vehicles and make upgrades to their homes, but not the masses. But there are numerous climate groups and grassroots organizations that many have no idea exist.

How do you suggest we appeal to these people to check out these organizations, get involved, and let them know that their participation really will make a difference?

Muir: Well, in your world today, you spread the word through the internet, through television, through the radio. I think there should be a great deal of money put into a campaign and spread the word through these avenues. There's so much information, but it just needs to be funneled out there—and not in distressing ways. If there is hope, we need to expound on that hope and what scientists are doing, all the strides being made. That needs to be vocalized and put out there because people are feeling so discouraged. Plant a seed of hope because people turn away when they see destruction.

Carolyn: A "seeds of hope" campaign—that is an excellent idea. Mr. Muir, as we approach the end of the hour, is there anything you would like to add?

Muir: Oh, I could go on and on about my travels throughout the United States and the beauty that I have witnessed. I have written about it quite extensively. I have completed many, many lifetimes, but the lifetime that I spent in the Sierras, that was a lifetime where I knew that I needed to be an activist for this world. I come from a beautiful place, Scotland, but I had never seen anything so beautiful as the Sierras.

Carolyn: Is there anyone you would like to recommend that we also speak with?

Muir: Well, I would recommend that you talk with Theodore Roosevelt. I think you could enlighten each other.

Carolyn: As a matter of fact, Theodore Roosevelt is on my list, and I'm very much looking forward to talking with him. Before we part, do you have a message of hope that you would like to share?

Muir: It is such a privilege to speak with you today. And I feel that the work I did continues.

Don't lose sight of the fact that we have done so much to continue to cherish and keep the beauty, such as we see with the national parks, but we have done so much to take it away. If we could find that again, where the beauty is not just in the national parks, imagine if we could feel excited about bringing back the beauty and appreciation of nature in the world we live in day to day. And those who have never experienced that, if we could have them be able to see that firsthand, they would want to protect it, and foster it and nurture it. And more access to nature; we would all benefit from this. This planet—this church—it is a beautiful place, and we must take care of it, and I feel we can do that and make strides. This can be done! This can be done!

Carolyn: Well, thank you so much for talking with me, Mr. Muir. It truly has been such a pleasure, and thank you for all that you have done and continue to do to preserve the beauty of our church and to educate others to honor and respect our church.

Part Two: March 5, 2023

Carolyn: Mr. Muir, thank you for reconnecting with me again. When we last spoke in October, I hadn't yet started asking souls about their lives on the other side. Today, we'd like to talk about the types of things that you enjoy and what your areas of focus are on the other side. Are you active with respect to helping or influencing things happening on Earth?

Muir: I am, to a certain degree. I am very much about the animals and the wildlife. I like to look out for them. I'm especially fascinated with some of the things that are happening with the birds. I like to just try and be there for them if they are injured or if they are not protected by their environment. I like to be a guide for them, for the animals.

Carolyn: Are they aware that you are helping them?

Muir: They know they are being helped by something or someone, but they don't know that it's me.

Carolyn: Can you tell us if you are collaborating with souls on the other side, such as environmental activists, naturalists, preservationists, conservationists, or others?

Muir: I am part of a group of other souls that are sort of, what you would call, natural beauty enthusiasts. We share our art, I share my writing, Ansel Adams shares his photography, and I also love photography. We share this beauty with those on Earth, and we share this beauty with those who are here with us.

Carolyn: Wonderful!

Muir: It's more of a creative collaboration.

Carolyn: How are you able to share this creative collaboration with people on Earth?

Muir: We have the work that we left on Earth, and we create new work now. We can't exactly share the physical form with those on Earth, of our new creations, but we can help others who we want to sort of pick up the pen and carry on or pick up the camera and carry on. So, I think you could say we are inspiring people on Earth.

Carolyn: Through inspiring, do you give nudges or downloads into their minds?

Muir: Exactly. They think it's their idea, but it's really coming from us. Which doesn't mean they don't have free will to take that and go further. We like to share, that's all. We like to share.

Carolyn: How do you choose these beings on Earth with whom you would like to share your ideas with?

Muir: We don't really choose them. They sort of choose us. They are often inspired by us, and we have these thoughts that are going through the air like a transmission, and they are there for them to take if they want to pick that thought up.

Carolyn: Oh, so they are connecting to your wavelength.

Muir: Yes, that is a great way to say it.

Carolyn: Are there specific organizations that you might be helping, such as the Sierra Club, which I know you co-founded in 1892?

Muir: Yes, the Sierra Club is, of course, something very dear to my heart, and I serve as an inspiration for them to explore the beauty this country has to offer.

Carolyn: And when you say you serve as an inspiration to them, is this another situation where you are providing nudges and downloads?

Muir: Yes, but it's also my legacy that inspires them as well. To keep doing the work and to keep exploring the beauty and cherishing it. And they act as environmentalists as they are doing it.

Carolyn: Are you pleased with their work?

Muir: Yes, I'm incredibly pleased with what they are doing. I think that it's one of the most wonderful things that has ever happened, that it has continued.

Carolyn: Yes, the Sierra Club sure has been around for a while.

Muir: Right. And I didn't expect it to go and go and go. So, it's been very fulfilling.

Carolyn: Are you a guide to many on Earth? If so, what types of people are you a guide for, and how do you help them?

Muir: I mostly work with the animals, but I have also made it a point to continue to help those who are working toward the exploration of all the natural resources that we still have in this country and those who are working toward conservation as well. It is something that is, as you know, everything to me. It's what I like to do, what I call a whisper in their ear, and I like to be a guide for them. There are lots of places I want to show them, and I want them to see, so I'll just guide them and help them to witness the beauty. And those that are working in conservation, I like them to know there are places that still need to be under conservation, and I like for them to be able to see that for themselves so they can be proactive about that.

Carolyn: Can you describe your experience when you crossed over?

Muir: I was actually in a bit of a fog when I first crossed over, and then I began to see all this imagery that I remembered and saw in person. The incredible redwoods and the giant sequoias, and I began to see the lakes and the rivers and the mountains. All the wildflowers. I was confused that I was still in a body on Earth, but then my family members, my great friends who had left me behind, were there to greet me. It was the warmest feeling, like being in a warm bath, comfort[ing] and peace[ful]. The thing that I appreciated was that they told me that I could take all my trees and all my mountains and my lakes and my rivers with me, and I could have them here with me.

Carolyn: Oh, wow.

Muir: So, I never really left.

Carolyn: Your experience now on the other side, it sounds like the Sierras, or perhaps Yosemite?

Muir: Well, I get a little bit of both. I get to mix all the parts I like. The waterfalls of Yosemite and the mountains, and I get to mix in the meadow, and I get to mix in the Sierras with the snow falling, not deeply, and the sun comes out, and it's really quite whatever I want it to be.

Carolyn: It sounds like your perfect heaven! I can't think of anything better.

Muir: It is the perfect heaven, yes.

Carolyn: Have you incarnated since your life as John Muir?

Muir: Yes, I have. That life is a life being lived now. I live in Spruce Grove in Alberta, Canada, and I'm eleven. I'm just a wee lad.

[Note: The being that we were speaking with was Muir's higher self, an aspect of the soul that is extremely wise and connected to Source or God and resides on the other side. We encountered this with two other souls.]

Carolyn: Is this your first life since your time as John Muir?

Muir: Yes, my first life.

Carolyn: What would this wee lad like to accomplish?

Muir: I quite like snowboarding, and I would like to be really good at that. I live near a magical place called Peyto Lake, and it's in a national park. It's magical. The water, it is like a turquoise, just beautiful. And I like to go there with my family.

Carolyn: Have you seen any of the other interviews, and if so, what are your thoughts?

Muir: Yes, I've seen the one that you did on President Bush, and I've seen another with Gandhi, and there was one more that I saw with Mr. Tesla.

Carolyn: Oh, you've seen some good interviews, in my opinion.

Muir: Those were hard seats to get.

Carolyn: So that leads me to my next question. Can you describe for us, how do you see these interviews? Is it like going to a movie theater?

Muir: It is like that. It is a lot like that. We can't go to all of them. We can only go to some of them.

Carolyn: Why is that?

Muir: They rotate. They only like a small amount of people in there to see it. So, you can't go to every one because other people want to go as well. It's almost like when you have season tickets to a play or something, where you have to go on the nights that you are assigned. So, we go to the interviews that we are assigned.

Carolyn: Goodness, that is interesting. How many souls on the other side are watching and are interested? We just have no idea the scope of it on your side.

Muir: There are other souls that have invitations. There are not a great deal of souls witnessing it because it's still a special thing to be invited. I will say that it helps us with our growth, to witness these interviews, because we are participating as a soul in the interviews. And if we are participating, then we get to see other interviews.

Carolyn: Oh, okay. So, you get even better access if you are a participant.

Muir: Yes.

Carolyn: How many souls at one time are typically watching an interview?

Muir: I'd say possibly about one hundred. Does it make you nervous?

Carolyn: You know, what makes me nervous is not knowing what is happening. What makes me more nervous is coming up with the right questions so that I can get answers that may be hopeful for the readers. That makes me the most nervous. But, yes, there is that element of how many people are watching me do this.

Muir: They are not really watching you, Carolyn. They are watching and learning. You are doing a great job. Just know, it's all love, that we are all there for love and growth. We are not there for judging. And we're not there to scrutinize what you are doing.

Carolyn: Well, that does help, thank you. And being on the Earth plane, I've had to sit in executive management meetings, and you just get eviscerated [laughs], so there's a part of you that still draws on that little bit of terror.

Muir: Oh yeah, but that's garbage. Let that go. Let that go. That's just garbage.

Carolyn: It sounds like you are in contact with some of the other souls that we have interviewed. Do you accompany any of them to watch any of the interviews, or do you talk with them outside of this whole process?

Muir: Yes, I do.

Carolyn: The reason I ask is because as we began to speak with more souls, we started to see a common theme emerge. For example, both you and Mohandas Gandhi talked a lot about the greed of humankind and the negative impact on the planet. You and a handful of others talked about the need for people to come together as a collective. And you and Saint Francis spoke of the Earth as a place that should be respected. Or, as you said, treated like church, as well as the interconnectedness of all species, sentient or non-sentient. Is Saint Francis one of these souls that you are in contact with?

Muir: Yes, he is.

Carolyn: Oh, he's a beautiful soul.

Muir: Yes, I agree—a good, good, good soul.

John: We spoke with Saint Francis recently, and he feels that once humanity can start to love and respect the Earth, the Earth will heal, and it will be quick, and it will be miraculous. But this love and respect must be genuine, must come from the heart. And we also spoke with higher consciousness author, Dr. Wayne Dyer. He gave us a meditation and a visualization on how to send love to Mother Earth. Many of your writings and quotes reveal your thoughts about God and nature. From your perspective now, do you have a sense or feel for the soul of the Earth?

Muir: Well, the soul of Mother Earth is there when you look out at all that the Earth has to offer and all the astounding, magical places. All you have to do is be still and you can feel the soul of Mother Earth; you can see the soul of Mother Earth. It is a beautiful soul. It is a very poetic soul. It's a soul of generosity and a soul of nurturing. But more than anything, it's a soul that is about expressing themselves through the beauty that they provide. Its want is nothing more than just to be recognized as a soul.

John: Could we contact Mother Earth and have a conversation in the way we are having a conversation with you right now?

Muir: I don't see the reason for that, but you could. What I mean is that all you have to do is put yourself in nature, and you can feel the soul, and you can have a conversation with the soul. But yes, it's possible. This is a soul that has provided our home for us and provided all this beauty and has provided a home for the animals and wildlife. This is a very generous soul who lives to be the mother. I just want you to know that when people feel different in nature, it is because they are connecting with the soul of Mother Earth, and it is genuine.

John: Do you have a feel for what Mother Earth would like to say to human beings, or even the readers of this book?

Muir: She'd like to tell them that she needs to be respected and she needs to be loved and adored. She needs to not be taken advantage of. Every time you see something that's amazing, stop, appreciate that, and thank her. She's given that to you for your enjoyment, for your peacefulness. She's given that to you ... treat her with respect and kindness.

John: Mother Earth gives and gives and gives. And it sounds like what we could give back is what you just mentioned treat her with love and respect. Does Mother Earth need anything more than that, Mr. Muir?

Muir: Can you imagine what enormous level of appreciation there would be, what a shift there would be if people could send that love to her as Mr. Dyer suggested? She has asked for nothing in return, but appreciation is something that would definitely help, and to give some of that love back. When you go from taking things for granted to abuse, then you get into a whole different area. Just as if you were to treat a person this way. They can only take it for so long until they stop giving you what they used to give you.

John: People on Earth, most have had previous lives. But is it possible for people who are of a younger soul age to not be able to think about the Earth this way, and that it's the older, more mature souls that carry them through? Are soul ages important? How do we help them understand this tremendous gift? How can we come together as a collective?

Muir: I don't think you should worry about that. I would say that there are guides on Earth; those older souls you speak of, they are guides on Earth. The younger souls can only learn through experience. But the older souls are there to guide them, and with the younger souls, it's not always possible. They have to hit their head a number of times before they get it. It is not possible to collectively have everyone come together. Yes, we strive for that, but everyone is having a different life experience, and it's hard to get everyone on the same page.

Carolyn: Mr. Muir, many of the souls that we've spoken with, including yourself, have mentioned the younger generation as the ones who are so passionate about saving the planet. This younger generation, are there more older souls in this group?

Muir: Yes, there are. Excellent question there, Carolyn. They are older souls, but of course, not everyone. They understand from their previous life experiences, and they understand from this experience they are having that this is where their focus needs to be.

Carolyn: Did you have an opportunity to see Theodore Roosevelt on the other side, between his lifetimes? We understand he is currently on Earth now, in Kenya, but we did speak with his higher self.

Muir: We had time together, yes. Our higher selves are capable of communicating, and sometimes that happens in dream space. But that's not where most of our conversations occur. We were able to spend time together when we were both on this side. And I quite enjoyed my time with him. It's very hard to explain. A soul that is very strong but yet very soft.

Carolyn: I like that kind.

Muir: It's really the best kind if you ask me. It's good to have your strength, but it's good to allow yourself to have that softness. It's really quite beautiful.

Carolyn: I agree. I know you traveled extensively and saw many beautiful places. And I know your affinity for the Sierras and believe your favorite place on Earth was Yosemite. I'd really like to know, what is your favorite section or area of Yosemite?

Muir: I truly do like being in the meadow. The reason is because, especially during the winter, it is very quiet, and all the animals are in the meadow. You get to see six of everything. They love it so much when they have that peacefulness. You can just sit there and be taken to another realm, another place, in your mind, I mean. So that would be my favorite place.

John: There are people on Earth who may want to connect with you. How do you find them?

Muir: I know when I'm needed by a soul or they need my guidance in some way. I specialize in giving them that guidance toward nature, but also, if someone has an inclination to do what

I did in a body and to write about nature and to explore, that is always a given, that I will be a guide for them. It's like a mutual understanding between them and myself, and that's how it works for me to be their guide.

John: Have you been surprised by any souls who have telepathically reached out, wanting your inspiration, your guidance?

Muir: I've had people who have never really seen nature, besides a city park, who have reached out to me with that yearning. I feel that, and I guide them, and that was a bit surprising when I received those invitations because I found it hard to believe that people hadn't been in nature before. But it's not that uncommon anymore. It's a very sad thing to me, that some people aren't able to be exposed to all the beauty and the nature and hang out with a tree.

John: Speaking of trees ...

[Note: We were nearing the end of the interview, so John and I took a few minutes to ask Muir about three redwood trees in our backyard. A series of atmospheric rivers following an epic drought had left much of Northern California's soil saturated, and we had concerns about the stability of our trees after seeing the one-hundred-foot-tall trunks swaying one night during a windstorm. Three different arborists had recommended the trees be cut down due to fall risk, and it broke my heart. The trees were scheduled to be cut down just days after this second interview with Muir. And I wanted to be certain that we were making the right decision and not falling prey to unethical arborists. Muir could actually see the trees from the other side and didn't feel that one tree was at risk and that the other two could be stabilized with corrective measures. His assessment prompted us to hold off on the scheduled removal and seek out one more arborist who unknowingly provided an appraisal that was identical to Muir's observation. I am happy to report the trees are alive and well, thanks to Mr. Muir.]

CHAPTER 15:

Dr. Charles Keeling (1928–2005)

Interview date: January 7, 2023

In 1896, building on the contributions of earlier climate science pioneers, Swedish scientist Svante Arrhenius became the first to quantify carbon dioxide's (CO_2) role in global warming, and he identified human-caused emissions primarily from fossil fuel burning as the main source. In 1938, English engineer Guy Callendar collected world temperature measurements and suggested that carbon dioxide emissions were responsible for warming the planet.

Charles Keeling was the scientist who confirmed these theories. Nobody had been able to take accurate measurements of carbon dioxide in the atmosphere, so Keeling built instruments that allowed great precision in making such measurements. In the 1960s, Keeling proved that human activities were, in fact, primarily responsible for the greenhouse effect and global warming, by documenting the steadily rising carbon dioxide levels in what later became known as the "Keeling Curve." Keeling was the first to measure CO_2 in the atmosphere on a continuing basis and played a key role in alerting climate scientists around the world of the serious implications of global warming.

Carolyn: Dr. Keeling, do you agree with my global warming and climate change summary, and if so, is global warming as critical a topic as I am suggesting with respect to the condition of the planet and our environment going forward?

Keeling: I agree with you. I have seen this for myself. Fossil fuels are the largest contributor to climate change and ocean acidification. We are responsible for this. CO_2 levels are increasing faster every year, as measured in parts per million. We are the ones who can make a difference, and we are the ones who are causing this.

Carolyn: What are the key facts and messages that you think people need to hear now, and what should we all be doing to take better care of our planet?

Keeling: The message is that we have to remove the CO_2 from the air. We have to do that. Because as the measurements continue to climb, even if we were to reduce the CO_2 emissions, there are particles in the emissions that last thousands of years. As you said, with the CO_2, things are going to be getting warmer and warmer if this is not something that we address. Thankfully, there are people who are addressing this, and there are ideas out there and things that are being used to test out the effectiveness of these ideas.

I want to say that this is not just about changing for climate change. This is about changing for us as well. What we saw is that during the [COVID-19] pandemic or times of dormancy with the human race, there was a very large drop in CO_2 emissions. As the human race evolves, we need to slow down our lives. We are all trying to get to places faster and quicker. What we found during the pandemic is that it was extremely important to our planet and the human race to slow down and stop the emissions from continuing to pollute our air. Not only remove CO_2 but also as a human race to step back and simplify.

Carolyn: Yes, I read about that, how the pandemic caused a reduction in the level of CO_2 emissions.

Keeling: When we simplify our lives, not only do we improve our planet, we improve our physical health, our emotional health, and our mental health. This world has become so fast that we can't keep up.

Carolyn: From your perspective, does society understand the seriousness of our current situation and that global warming is a problem that needs fast action?

Keeling: Society as a whole—it's hard to say. But I would say that the majority of society realizes this and is being affected. Homes are being destroyed, lives are being destroyed, of course, Earth is being destroyed, oceans are being destroyed. There is a majority of society that is in sync with this understanding.

Carolyn: The majority of the public may be in sync in terms of understanding the seriousness of global warming and climate change, but we still have those who do not believe climate change is caused by human activity. They will say, which is true, the Earth is currently in an icehouse state rather than a greenhouse state, and that throughout Earth's history, its climate has fluctuated between the two states. They might also point to the fact that historically, there have been times when the planet has been hotter than today, with CO_2 levels sometimes ten to twenty times higher than today and no ice anywhere on the planet. And, they might say that historical climate patterns suggest that within a few thousand years, we could enter another glacial period, when ice would slowly advance again from the poles. Dr. Keeling, if we are in an icehouse state, do the climate deniers have a point here?

Keeling: Okay. So, the icehouse state is due to natural variance, and we know that there's the movement of the tectonic plates. Earth's orbit shifts every 100,000 years, so when this happens, this shifts the state that we're in, whether it be greenhouse or icehouse. We know that Man is creating an abundance of activity because we have gone into the ice poles, and the ice poles contain bubbles of air. We can look at that air and measure that air and see what the CO_2 levels were farther and farther back. We can go about 800,000 years back. They were mostly consistent no matter what was happening with the tectonic plates and the shift in the Earth's orbit every 100,000 years. We can look at what is happening now in the air and see that, ever since the industrial age, Man has put all these greenhouse gases into the environment, and they are contributing to this. It's not that it's not happening. It *is* happening.

The greenhouse gases have accelerated in volume since the industrial age. But there is also the variance with the Earth shifting every 100,000 years, so regardless of what the Earth is naturally doing, we can also measure that we are dumping on top of this with greenhouse gases. Greenhouse gas emissions won't be taking full effect until about one hundred years from now. We will be, most likely, entering a greenhouse state again. So, it will be extremely important to reduce those greenhouse gases from fossil fuels that are in the air to prevent them from tipping in such a way that we are putting ourselves in complete chaos, with the greenhouse state and the warming and the social impact it would have—droughts, droughts causing famine, etc. That is what we want to prevent from happening. But there are natural variances that do happen with our Earth, and that is throwing them [the climate deniers] off.

Carolyn: So, the rapid acceleration of CO_2 caused by human activities could take us to the point of no return if we do nothing. Some scientists refer to this point of no return as "runaway climate change." If I am hearing you correctly, we are trying to avoid the point in which we can't reverse this.

Keeling: That is correct. Because we are in the icehouse state, it doesn't mean it isn't happening. It definitely is happening. We are seeing it. We are measuring it. We want to prevent the next shift where the Earth shifts on its axis. We want to prevent the next shift from, as you said, runaway climate change. The people who deny climate change, they are the ones who are looking at this icehouse versus greenhouse data and saying, "See, we're in icehouse; there's no problem." But we do have a problem because greenhouse will be next.

Carolyn: Do you see the world being able to meet the Paris Agreement goal of net-zero emissions by 2050 and not exceeding 1.5 degrees Celsius?

Keeling: I see that. But I also see it being a rush to that goal, at the eleventh-hour type of thing.

Carolyn: Well, that is a big message of hope—that we pull together collectively to meet the Paris Agreement goal and avoid the runaway climate scenario.

Keeling: Yes.

Carolyn: You established that the levels of CO_2 in the atmosphere were related to the burning of fossil fuels. At the time you made this correlation, did you foresee the predicament we now find ourselves in, in terms of the increase of greenhouse gases leading to global warming?

Keeling: Well, I was also studying and learning from what came before me. The curve—the Industrial Revolution—advanced us dramatically, as we know, in several ways, along with world wars. What I was seeing on Mauna Loa [the largest active volcano on the planet], I was seeing the rise, not only from what was currently happening, but what had happened from before I started studying. The world's population is putting more emissions into the air. There are simply more ways to pollute the air at this time, and CO_2 emission particles, they do stay around for thousands of years.

Carolyn: Are you aware of any technical innovations being worked on to address removal of the particles?

Keeling: That is something that is still in the future of discovery. But at present, there are efforts to capture emissions before they are released, such as direct air capture, carbon capture, storage, etcetera. And there is also carbon mineralization, which happens slowly and naturally. We are looking toward exposing minerals through different types of alkaline for the right mineral composition. And that is also about storing CO_2 by injecting it into suitable rock formations where it reacts to form a solid carbonate [the advantage being that carbon cannot escape back into the atmosphere].

Carolyn: And this is something that scientists are looking at right now?

Keeling: Exactly. And for our oceans, they are looking at rebuilding with certain minerals, seaweed, phytoplankton, and coastal plants. This is something that is extremely important, and thankfully has been recognized—the management of forests, reforestation, and continuing to develop forests.

Carolyn: Could this also help the coral reefs, which are really taking a beating?

Keeling: Yes, there is a coastal blue carbon and seaweed cultivation that removes carbon and supports the ecosystem, which could also help with our coral reefs.

Carolyn: That is really encouraging to hear. I understand that CO_2 emissions can be found in three places in the environment: the air, the land, and the oceans. The oceans currently absorb more than 25 percent of human-caused CO_2 emissions, which is contributing to a rise in ocean acidification. From your perspective on the other side, are you aware of other potential approaches forthcoming to sequester CO_2?

Keeling: There is also direct air capture. It is chemically scrubbing CO_2 and then storing it underground, but it's very costly. At this time, those are the things that I am aware of. You talked about acidification. It threatens the pH balance of the ocean. When CO_2 is mixed with water, it becomes a carbonate acid, and so it dissolves the shells of the oysters and the coral reefs. So, there are studies being directed toward growing seaweed to help slow the acidification. Algae, and seagrass, and kelp—they absorb the CO_2 and lower acidity. With restoring the coral reefs, we are working on planting nursery-grown corals back into the ocean and making the habitat suitable for natural coral growth. Another thing that we are doing, is we found that floating pieces of reef can be tied to a structure, like a metal scaffolding type structure, and they will regrow as long as they are bound to something. It can be bits and pieces, one-inch or two-inch pieces of the reef, and they will regrow. So, we are doing that as well.

Carolyn: Do you have a message of hope regarding the restoration of the oceans, one in which we can actually get our hands around the acidification problem?

Keeling: The message of hope is that it is something that we are working on. You see, it takes approximately one hundred years for the CO_2 to enter the ocean. So, the measurements from my Keeling Curve, whatever they are now, will not actually be absorbed into the ocean for about one hundred years. When they are absorbed, it will put us into droughts, severe droughts, and it will put us into social chaos. What I'm trying to say is we are doing everything we can to work at this time toward restoring the ocean—regrowth in the ocean—and preventing our grand-children's grandchildren from having an Earth that is in peril. We have begun, and we are well underway in doing this. We have the awareness, the science, and the information to do this to prevent the ocean from destruction and devastation. We have these new ways to restore the ocean, and we have many people who are dedicated to this. We feel very hopeful about the work we are doing and feel very hopeful that we can preserve these oceans and restore them to pristine status.

Carolyn: That's a very good message of hope. Just 9.7 percent of the world's oceans are protected, but there is some good news. In late 2022, the United Nations Biodiversity Conference (COP15) struck a historic deal on protecting and restoring nature. To help safeguard plant and animal species and to ensure natural resources are used sustainably, almost 200 countries have signed on to protect 30 percent of the planet's land and 30 percent of the oceans, or marine areas, by 2030. Marine-protected areas are seen by many as essential in order to protect marine habitats and the life they support. Can you please give us your thoughts on this landmark deal, how you see it helping our oceans and marine areas from your vantage point, and if you think it goes far enough?

Keeling: It's imperative that we put this in place at this time. The whole idea is to make sure the generations to come have the same benefits that we've had by being able to explore the ocean in its natural state and be able to reap the bounty that we've been able to from the ocean. I'm not talking about fishing; I'm talking about the bounty of the ecosystems that are going on in the ocean. We've been able to witness those life-forms. I would say it is imperative to continue preservation. Does it go far enough? Ideally, I would like it to go even further. But at this time, it is progress in the right direction.

Carolyn: Do you think it's far enough to make a difference?

Keeling: I do believe it's far enough to make a difference.

Carolyn: Do you have suggestions for the readers in terms of specific actions they can take, such as volunteering to clean up beaches, contributing to organizations, etcetera? What would you like the readers to do?

Keeling: I think it's important to leave things not only the way you found them, but better than you found them. I would suggest that everyone please be aware that everything goes into the ocean and to please be aware of any trash. Definitely pick it up. Think of the ocean as being a catchall for anything that hits the ground. This is something I cannot stress enough, and it is something that everyone is capable of doing. It's a very simple act. Most people walk by, and they don't pick things up, or they are very casual near the ocean with what they bring close to the water. All of those things end up in the ocean. This would be my number one point. It is less than scientific, but it would help tremendously if people were more conscientious about that.

Carolyn: Let's talk about clean energy technologies we know about now. We are in the process of a clean energy transition, as agreed to in the Paris Agreement. The top three renewable energy sources are solar, wind, and hydropower. Many experts agree that nuclear energy will need to play an important role in our transition to clean energy. Progress in nuclear power technologies will help make nuclear power a more efficient, affordable, safe, and attractive option for decarbonization. Do you feel that nuclear energy will need to play an important role?

Keeling: Yes. I do feel that. I know that. It will play an important role.

Carolyn: I'm sure you saw this . . . there was a major nuclear fusion energy breakthrough recently announced that could lead to a source of safe, unlimited, carbon-free energy in the future with no nuclear waste or risk of meltdowns. While there is still much work to be done, from your vantage point, when do you see widespread use of nuclear fusion technology playing a major role in the energy grid? Can it be deployed in time to help us meet the Paris Agreement goals in 2050?

Keeling: Well, that is the eleventh hour because I see it coinciding with each other.

Carolyn: Back to nuclear power as we know it today. Is it good enough? From your perspective, should the current technology, nuclear fission, be more widely deployed in the meantime until nuclear fusion is ready to be implemented, or should we hold off and wait? I think I know already how you're going to answer this: to move forward and not wait for the new technology.

Keeling: Exactly. That's exactly how I feel.

Carolyn: So, to more widely deploy the current generation, the global public, not all, but a good percentage, has become convinced that nuclear presents a huge safety risk after witnessing Chernobyl and Fukushima meltdowns. How do you suggest that we calm these fears?

Keeling: Awareness. Education. There are many old ways of thinking around nuclear energy. We have made huge advances, and the only way is to get that information out there. But I also want to say that there are people who are not grounded in that history, and they are moving forward.

Carolyn: Are you talking about the younger generation?

Keeling: Yes. I feel that the generation that is now working on this type of science—they are going to continue. This is so exciting for them, and they will continue to be a force to drive this forward.

Carolyn: In terms of education and awareness, who should control the message about nuclear energy?

Keeling: I feel that the government has the capacity to reach more people. I also feel that, as with the laboratories that recently made this announcement around fusion, I feel that the information is starting to come to the forefront with these breakthrough announcements. And there will continue to be more and more. The awareness will continue to be heightened.

Carolyn: Now that gives us a lot of hope. From your perspective, can you share if there will be more breakthroughs in clean energy, and if so, what they might look like? Can you provide any specifics or timelines?

Keeling: Whether it's through hydropower or through wind turbines, the breakthroughs will be about making those types of clean energy renewables less devastating to wildlife and our environment. There will be significant improvements. I don't see any that will be abandoned. I feel that there are many people working toward these types of improvements.

Carolyn: Very glad to hear this. We have a few more technical questions. John, did you want to cover this?

John: Yes. Dr. Keeling, you were a very early visionary in terms of looking at environmental properties and having an idea that there was importance in studying things such as CO_2 concentrations. Are there some analogous things scientists should be looking at now, maybe any other environmental compositions or properties that, if studied, would provide either more leading-edge indication of future issues or provide a more immediate and obvious-to-all indication of the seriousness of our current situation and the necessity of a globally coordinated effort for attacking global warming? Are there other things we should be looking at that would be more impactful?

Keeling: At this point, I can't think of an area that hasn't been studied. But I would say that studying the soil and how the soil can work toward removing some of the CO_2 emissions—that is something that is actually on the verge of a breakthrough. We have so much information now that we have to act on that. We have to continue to move forward with our progress, with our scientific inventions and breakthroughs and work. We have a lot of data but not a lot of information. The tricky part is what to do with that information to make progress.

John: Earlier, you had brought up the acidification of the oceans. The oceans cover so much of our land mass, and I would venture to say the oceans are the least understood.

Keeling: Yes.

John: Are we ignoring something big here in terms of how oceans affect the environment? Are we missing something with the oceans? I can't put my finger on it. Do you have a perspective?

Keeling: Well, the oceans are vast, as you said, and they are more complex because it's an underworld that we just see from the surface. We are not living in that world. So, what's happening with the acidification … it's a bicarbonate and carbonate mixture eroding the oceans, and it's coming from the emissions in the air. And if we can continue to regenerate the oceans and clean them from that acidification, of course that will be a big component of moving forward with improving our direction toward climate change. There is no doubt. Thankfully, there are scientists who are working toward this, but that is the big question. Can we save this? Because the life that we have above sea and below sea are very separated. We need to look at this planet with all systems in place to understand what makes this planet work. And it's not just what is happening on top of the ocean; it's also below. If we can continue to work toward renewing the health of the oceans, there is no question that the health of life above oceans will improve and be better. But it comes with vast cleanup and renewing the resources.

John: If you were here on Earth talking with people, how would you say to people why it is so important to treat our entire planet as a system?

Keeling: A very simple way to describe what is happening with the ice caps, what's happening with global warming, what's happening with us is that we are starting to see species die off because they are unable to survive. When you start seeing species die off, when you start seeing plant life and forests die off, you can only know that you will be next. And that is the simplest way to explain how this is working. And that is a direct message that people need to understand.

In my lifetime, I heard people who would say, "Well, maybe there's a reason; maybe it's time they die off." The extinction is coming directly from the abuse of the planet. But I must say, as a human race, we have this great capacity to put ideas in place and improve our lives, as we have shown over and over. We have made great advancements. But what we are learning is those great advancements have been to the detriment of our planet in many ways. Now we must realize that it's time to make great advancements that do not punish our planet and make great advances and strides toward protecting our planet. When we protect our planet, we are protecting our wildlife, our species, our human race. That is the simplest way to explain it.

John: I appreciate the way you made this so easy to understand. Thank you.

Keeling: Thank you for that. And I want to say it is boiled down even simpler. We are all connected. If one of us is suffering, all of us are suffering.

John: Now, I would like to talk about your work or activity on the other side. Can you tell us if you are part of a scientific working group or think tank where you are collaborating with other researchers and scientists?

Keeling: I am. But I also work with those who are on Earth. Both is the answer.

John: How do you work with those on Earth?

Keeling: So, I have those who I may be invisible to the eye, but I am in a think tank with them at all times. I am working on what I already started with the [Keeling] Curve, working toward improvements and also continuing to look at the measurements of CO_2 and to continue to track those things. Yes, I have both—people I work with on Earth and people I speak with on our side.

I also slow down. I'm not always in motion or working toward this, and I do have downtime. Sometimes we need that, and it actually refuels you, recharges you, and gives you more energy toward new ideas.

Carolyn: I find it fascinating that you are continuing the work that you did when you were on Earth, from the other side. Are you in contact with other climate science pioneers, such as Eunice Foote and John Tyndall?

Keeling: Yes, we speak, and we discuss. They are part of the collaboration that I mentioned.

Carolyn: Oh, that's wonderful. Very glad to hear that. Who else would you recommend that we speak with regarding global warming and climate change?

Keeling: I don't know if you're aware of this; some people say cloning should be illegal, but I think I cloned someone when I had my son. My son is quite knowledgeable. He has taken the torch and has moved forward with new information. In many ways, it feels like we are the same. He has made incredible advancements in continuing the work.

Carolyn: Is he still on Earth or on the other side?

Keeling: He's on Earth.

John: (Quick Google search…) This is Ralph Keeling? At the Scripps Institution of Oceanography?

Keeling: Correct. Did I misunderstand? Did you want to speak with someone in spirit?

Carolyn: Yes, but I will add Ralph to this book, give a shout-out to him, and alert people to all the good work he is doing. The people we are interviewing are on the other side, but we will include your son's name in the book.

John: Let me ask this question: If we were to talk to your son, what would he say?

Keeling: Well, uh, I'm not certain, actually. As scientists, sometimes we have very pragmatic ways of dealing with things, and I'm not certain what he would say. I'd like to think he'd understand, but I'm not certain.

Carolyn: Doctor, is there a message that we could give to him that only he would know was genuinely coming from you?

Keeling: I would say that when he was around four years old, he expressed to me that he wanted to do this work and he wanted to do this work side by side with me as he grew up. I don't think others know about this conversation that we had. I told him at the time, it would be an honor to work with him as he grew up, side by side. I could not be more proud.

Carolyn: We will try to figure out how to get this message to your son. This is lovely, and I am sure it will touch him.

Keeling: I want to say that I think, though, that he has an awareness of this, that he is doing the work he was born to do, and we are working in tandem, even now. He has that awareness.

Carolyn: So, if we gave this message, he may not be surprised?

Keeling: I don't think he would be surprised by the information but surprised by how the information came about.

Carolyn: If we are successful in reaching him, and if he has a message to give back to you, we will be in touch with you. This would be very fun.

John: Are you in contact with Jacques Cousteau?

Keeling: Jacques, I am in contact with. He is a very interesting soul and definitely an old soul. Someone who I have had many encounters with, and he is also doing this work.

Carolyn: He is on our list to speak with, and we look forward to talking with him soon.

Keeling: He is a man who lived heart-mind-soul in the ocean and had a great concern and interest in the future of the ocean, when it was not considered so urgent.

John: Did your son work with Jacques?

Keeling: No. I don't feel it was the right timing. But I do know Jacques has worked with Ralph out of body.

Carolyn: Wow! That's very interesting. We're going to have all kinds of things for Ralph. As we wrap things up, do you have a final message of hope for the readers?

Keeling: I would just like to say that we would not be in this collaboration if there was not hope and if we did not believe. What would be the point? We believe, and we have hope, and that is what keeps us going and striving for a healthier future for all of us and for the world.

Carolyn: That's lovely; thank you, Dr. Keeling. You're a joy to talk with!

Keeling: You are a joy to talk with, too, John and Carolyn.

Carolyn: Thank you so much, Dr. Keeling, for participating today, and thank you for all the contributions made throughout your career on Earth and now on the other side to benefit our planet. Thank you, thank you, thank you for all you are doing.

Keeling: It was a pleasure, and if I can be of any more help, I will be available.

CHAPTER 16:

President George H. W. Bush (1924–2018)

Interview date: March 1, 2023

George H. W. Bush was a member of the Republican Party, serving in various federal positions, including the US House of Representatives, US Ambassador to the United Nations, Director of the Central Intelligence Agency, 43rd vice president under President Ronald Reagan, and 41st president of the United States.

Throughout his campaign, Bush promised that as president, he would introduce legislation to protect the environment. Six months into his term, President Bush strengthened the Clean Air Act in 1990, which curbed four major threats to the nation's environment: the acid rain pollution that was devastating lakes, forests, and wildlife; urban air pollution; toxic air emissions; and stratospheric ozone depletion. Bush also signed the Energy Policy Act of 1992 to lessen US dependence on oil and gas imports and improve air quality through alternative fuels, clean and renewable energy incentives, and energy efficiency.

Bush was the first president to raise climate change as a major issue of concern for the federal government by establishing the US Global Change Research Program in 1990, which coordinated federal research on climate change and its impacts. In a speech delivered to the Intergovernmental Panel on Climate Change (IPCC), Bush said, "We know that the future of the Earth must not be compromised. We bear a sacred trust in our tenancy here and a covenant with those most precious to us—our children and theirs."

Bush: Hello, Carolyn.

Carolyn: Hello, Mr. President! How are you?

Bush: I'm very well. How are you?

Carolyn: I'm doing just fine. Thank you so much for coming back to talk with us.

[Note: I had previously spoken with Bush in October 2022, on topics unrelated to this book.]

Bush: Sure, sure!

Carolyn: Today I'd like to talk about global warming and climate change, and then we'd like to talk about your life on the other side. But first, can you share your thoughts on the state of the planet from your perspective on the other side?

Bush: Well, I think that we have to acknowledge the significance of what is happening to our planet. Denial is not going to save this planet. It is not going to make things any better. I feel that carbon dioxide contributes to a great deal of our problems of global warming, and I know that there are changes taking place within that to move us toward a country that is less dependent on fossil fuels. My mother used to say, "Leave everything better than when you found it." We are not doing that. We have to get out of denial, roll up our sleeves, and win this battle. This is our home.

Carolyn: There are quite a few global coalitions involving many countries, governments, and investors working together. Do you see clean energy innovations coming soon to enable us to reach near net-zero carbon levels, which is part of the goal of the Paris Agreement, by 2050, to avoid great devastation? And do you see these innovations soon becoming as cheap or even cheaper than fossil fuels?

Bush: I see that happening. There needs to also be more information available to Americans, not simply depressing images, but more information about grassroots organizations and how they can be a part of this. Many people feel there's nothing significant that they can do and that they have to leave it to their government and politicians. But there are grassroots projects and organizations that are working just as hard cleaning up this Earth and making it healthier for us all.

Carolyn: In terms of people getting involved in grassroots organizations, it makes me think of your phrase, "thousand points of light." Is there anything you'd like to add on this?

Bush: Well, thank you, Carolyn. It is such a pleasure to be with you today. I would just like to say that I still think that a "thousand points of light" can pertain to so many things. It can also pertain to the mission to bring people together to work on the climate, to be a part of this, and for everyone to do their share. I think it would bring about a lot of good feelings for everyone to do this and to be part of that "thousand points of light." I'm just thinking that that could pertain to that very well.

Carolyn: Yes, I didn't think of it in those terms, but I love it.

Bush: I love it, too.

Carolyn: A major nuclear fusion energy breakthrough was recently announced that could lead to a source of safe, unlimited, carbon-free energy produced by nuclear plants in the future with no meltdowns or nuclear waste. Until we can get up to speed with the new fusion technology, it seems time prohibitive to deploy more current-generation nuclear plants since they take an average of seven to eight years to build. As of 2022, there were over 400 nuclear reactors in operation around the world. From your perspective, do you feel the 2050 Paris Agreement goal can still be met if we utilize just solar, wind turbines, and existing nuclear facilities? Or is it going to take nuclear fusion to really take us all the way there?

Bush: Carolyn, I do feel that nuclear fusion is extremely important in us getting there. We have a lot to do in a short amount of time. And I feel that that is extremely important. As we are now, I'm not so sure that we will complete what we need to in time, which is my opinion, which doesn't mean we won't, especially with all the intention and people who are working toward this. But I will say that once nuclear fusion is in place, I think we can cover a lot of ground in a short amount of time. I'm not so sure that we will fulfill those goals, but I feel once the fusion is in place, we can truly make a bigger dent than we thought was possible.

Carolyn: Wonderful. Do you feel that once nuclear fusion is in place, we can reduce the global temperature and start cooling the planet so we don't have all of these devastating climate events?

Bush: Yes, that is my feeling. I think this is the biggest challenge that people have ever faced, and I think that we can do it.

Carolyn: In 2022, President Biden signed the largest climate legislation in US history. This new law basically provides all sorts of incentives, tax breaks, rebates, and a huge investment in growing our renewable energy infrastructure, such as solar panels and wind turbines, all for the transition to renewable energy. The legislation is also expected to encourage a cycle of innovation in the private sector that would ultimately reduce renewable energy costs with the intention of making the transition to a low-carbon future more affordable and, thus, accelerating adoption worldwide. From your perspective on the other side, do you see this already happening, where this legislation is acting as a major catalyst to spur technological innovations and breakthroughs in the private sector to provide renewable energy options that will be cheaper than fossil fuels?

Bush: Oh yes, I see that happening a great deal. For myself, my home in Kennebunkport [Maine] is all solar and wind and renewable energy, and I did that about five years before I crossed over. It's something that I'm quite proud of, and I think it's absolutely something that is happening and will continue to grow.

Carolyn: Do you think this new legislation is really going to influence start-ups, in terms of sparking new innovations and breakthroughs?

Bush: There are quite a bit now, Carolyn, that are doing what they can to get their inventions and their ideas off the ground. It's very much happening, and it will continue to happen. Having Biden bring this out for the country is definitely going to fuel quite a bit more ideas. I don't know if you've noticed, but even marketing today is about things being good for the planet. That's how they are choosing to sell a lot of things. And I think people are getting this information quicker than ever, and I think that we will continue to see advancements in this area.

Carolyn: If you were president today, what more would you be doing to stimulate innovations in the private sector?

Bush: Oh, definitely looking to fund more of the private sector through government funding. I think that is definitely something that could be looked into, could be brought out, and I think that would just be the best that we could do right now as a country. And I think it would be extremely powerful.

Carolyn: The current US House of Representatives is Republican controlled with many climate deniers, so it's doubtful there will be much in the way of more climate legislation this term. From your perspective, do you see a shift or improvement in how Congress addresses climate change legislation following the 2024 election?

Bush: Well, it's not going to be as quick as I would like it to be. I do see it eventually coming to the forefront and the climate deniers starting to fall away. Much like the election deniers, even though, as you know, there are still those who stand their ground on that, and there will still be those who stand their ground, denying that the climate is changing in our world. But I do see that, even though it will take some time. I do see that coming.

Carolyn: That's great. Do you have a feel for when that might be? Could that be in 2025 or perhaps a few years after that?

Bush: I do have a feeling, as you say, around 2025 or 2026.

Carolyn: Oh, that's encouraging. How about after the next US presidential election in 2024? Do you see that administration enacting even more meaningful legislation?

Bush: That I'm hopeful for, but I don't have an answer. I'm actually not sure how this is going to play out, to be honest. But, of course, that is our hope.

Carolyn: Big Oil continues to lobby US policymakers to lock fossil fuels into climate policy. From your perspective, do you have a feel for when—or if—we can expect to see Big Oil finally start to move away from fossil fuels and transition to renewable energy?

Bush: I feel that is going to take some time, Carolyn. That is a very rigid industry, and they have no plans on going anywhere. But if we can give them an incentive to turn their fossil fuels into another way to make money, if we can give them another way to make money with what they do in some way, I feel that's going to be helpful. You know, I worked in the oil industry, and it's a very rigid industry, and they are going to stand their ground; I can tell you that. That will be something that we need to provide incentive for, for them to stop the drilling and mining of fossil fuels.

Carolyn: As you well know, special interest groups and lobbyists have enormous power to influence policy, not only for climate but also for another huge problem in the US: gun violence. The

Supreme Court ruling on Citizens United in 2010 has led to rampant dark money donations where corporate and wealthy donors do not disclose their identities. If you were president today, how would you curb or regulate the influence of lobbyists and special interest groups?

Bush: Hmmm, that is a tough one, Carolyn. I think that some bills need to be introduced to take some of that power away. As you said, they are completely controlling everything that happens in [Washington] D.C., and I feel that if a bill or bills were introduced to take some of that power away, we would all be coming from more of an equal place. But their influence is strong and so manipulative with politics today, that if we could introduce a bill that gave them limitations, that gave them less power, I feel that would be the only way to go at this point.

Carolyn: So, an executive order from the president is not something that could be done?

Bush: An executive order could be done, but is it going to happen? I'm not sure. It may not be used in this particular situation. I don't think it would have a huge effect if it were, though.

Carolyn: What can the readers do to influence change here? Is this a matter of people writing to their representatives in Congress and urging them to introduce bills?

Bush: Always, always, always. People don't think that their emails and their letters are very effective, but they are effective, and that is always the best way to get attention. Carolyn, include information on how the readers can find how to contact their members of Congress.

[Note: Here is a link to find members of Congress, along with contact information https://www.congress.gov/members/find-your-member.]

Carolyn: Before we move on to your life on the other side, do you have a message of hope that you would like to leave with the readers in terms of global warming and climate change?

Bush: My message of hope is to let people know that there are many innovations that will become known as we go through our days, and there will be many people who have made this their life's mission. Many advancements are coming, and I think that this is a time of technology in the world right now, but we are going to see how the technology can either take us down or take us up. And I feel we're going to be going up with our technology information, and it's really going to kick in and put us forward.

Carolyn: And even if we do surpass that Paris Agreement goal, we're going to get it back down?

Bush: That's my feeling, and I don't see why we couldn't do that. We just need to do all that we can to try and avoid that, of course, and if we don't, we can get it back down.

Carolyn: Beautiful. We'd now like to talk about your life on the other side, and I'm going to hand things over to John.

Bush: Hello, John.

John: Mr. President, it's such a pleasure to talk with you today.

Bush: You as well.

John: Can you share the types of things that you enjoy and what your areas of focus are on the other side? Are you active with respect to helping or influencing things happening on Earth?

Bush: Well, I'm working as a guide for people who have lost children, meaning lost physically or meaning they have died. And that is one of the greatest, well it's a great pain for those who have experienced the loss of a child. Even if you are an older person, and your child is older and they die, there is nothing like it. The pain is searing. So, I am a guide for people who have lost a child, and I bring them as much comfort as I can.

It's a difficult thing to explain if you haven't experienced it, but I comfort them, I help them grieve, and I enjoy this quite a bit. This is very fulfilling for me, to help people in this situation. When my daughter died, I couldn't talk about it for years because I was so shattered by the experience. It was very difficult for me to overcome, and I don't think that I ever did. This is something very true to my heart, to comfort people during that time.

John: How do you choose those that you would like to help or guide?

Bush: It's not about choosing; it's about feeling a gravitational pull. Or sometimes, when I feel that people, especially people who don't have a lot of family in their life, I can feel their grief, and their light around them changes, and it's almost like a dark green that I see, and I feel that is a signal for me.

John: Along with guiding people in their grief and bringing them comfort, can you tell us if you are collaborating with souls on the other side, such as world or political leaders?

Bush: That is a part of what I do. But I'll tell you, I'm more interested in my family. My family means everything to me: the family that I re-met when I crossed over and the family that I left behind. I am a guide for them as well, and I look after them. They are the people I love, the people in my life. That's where I put a lot of my focus.

Carolyn: Mr. President, we recently spoke with Senator McCain, and he talked about how he is actively involved in protecting the Constitution. Have you had a chance to see Senator McCain?

Bush: Senator McCain, oh yes. He is an amazing man; he is an amazing spirit. I have discussed with him many times what he is working on, and he has tried to recruit me. And it may just happen. [But] I feel I need a little more time. There is so much that I don't quite understand about what is happening with the democracy at this point. But, yes, I'm sure that I'll be joining forces with him.

Carolyn: Oh, that is so wonderful, and you have so much in common. Along with your political service, you were both war heroes, both fighter pilots. And your close brush with death, being the only one who survived after your plane was shot down . . . and the other guys, just awful.

Bush: Carolyn, there is nothing like that feeling when everyone perishes except you. You feel guilt, you feel elation, you feel all of these mixed emotions, and it makes you want to make sure that you don't waste a single moment of your life.

Carolyn: Well, you did not waste one single moment of your life, that is for sure. I wanted to share something that made me a little emotional. Shortly after you passed, there was a memorial illustration that went viral. And since you were a World War II navy pilot, in the tribute cartoon it shows a depiction of you having flown your TBM Avenger fighter plane to the pearly gates, and you are reunited with your wife Barbara and little daughter Robin. In the tribute cartoon, Barbara says, "We waited for you." Can you tell us if this was, in fact, partially true? Were you greeted by Barbara and Robin?

Bush: I was greeted by Robin, I was greeted by Bar, and I was greeted by my parents, and it was such a beautiful, beautiful crossing over. I was so filled with joy to see everyone. I had the best parents in the world. I had parents who believed in me and parents who supported me. My mother was very strong, my father was very strong, and he was also able to express emotion, which wasn't common at that time with men. I just had the most wonderful, wonderful time. And I was met with every dog I ever had, all of my dogs, and you have no idea how it is to have all of those puppy licks on your face!

Carolyn: It must have been such a wonderful, delightful, happy surprise!

Bush: It was, it was all of that. And to be able to see Bar, my wife, and hold her, and hold her in my heart, it was beautiful to be back together. We were always together, and we're together now, and it's the best thing that could have happened in that way.

John: Mr. President, when we hear the other souls talking about their transitions and the reunions that take place, one thing that has struck me in my earthly body is that the feeling of the separation and those that have crossed over is so small. Yet, everyone on Earth, we just don't realize that it's so close to us. Did you have a feeling that it was this close when you were on Earth, or was this a revelation for you, too?

Bush: No, I didn't really think about it like that, John, but it is. It is very small. It is all there for us, and you just, it's like you live your whole life, but, in that instant, you have such clarity about how things fall into place and such clarity about love and about what a life really means. It's one of those things that you just have to be there for it. It's a beautiful thing. Our lives are so fragile, but it doesn't really end. We keep on living in different ways.

John: Have you incarnated since your last passing? If not, do you plan to incarnate again?

Bush: I have not been back in a body, and I know that I will be coming back. But I have not been there. I still have time, and I still have much to do on this side.

John: Sometimes life can be so difficult on Earth, so painful in many ways. From your perspective on the other side, what is the motivation to want to come back?

Bush: [Laughs.] It's a good question. We have many things that we need to accomplish on Earth and many things that we can accomplish in the realm. I think that the reason to come back is to keep getting better. I understand that some people are content to stay out of a body, but when you cross over, you do have a feeling of incredible appreciation and love for your life, no matter how your life played out. You have an incredible appreciation for that experience that you don't really see coming, that there's a reason why you have had that experience.

It [being in a body] enables you to have experiences that you could never have once you have crossed over and to have experiences with other people, which is what it's really all about—to continue to have experiences that you learn from because there's a great deal of joy to be had in a body, and I have not met many people who have not wanted to return in a body.

John: When you eventually do incarnate, do you have an idea of what you would like to do?

Bush: I don't have an idea, meaning I don't have any knowledge or information on what I'll be doing. I may come back and just be this guy. I may not have a very significant life, but I hope that I can be of service. I think that people who are of service are doing it for the right reasons: to help their fellow man and to help their country, and I would like to continue to be of service in some way.

John: We recently spoke with presidents Reagan, Nixon, and Theodore Roosevelt. Have you spent time with any former presidents on the other side?

Bush: I am actually great friends with LBJ [former President Lyndon Baines Johnson]. He is someone that I don't know if people realize what a huge heart he had. He was one of those guys that felt he had to push it all down, but he had a huge heart. We didn't always agree on everything, that is for sure, but he is a very special person with a huge heart, and I can't think of anyone else who was in this position of president who was more well-meaning in my lifetime for the country, even though he was not elected. Of course, he went into office when Kennedy was shot. But he had such a great heart and sense of humanity and was a very, very good person in a body and is all of those things now. We have become great friends, and he is someone I admire as a spirit.

John: Yes, he came into a very difficult situation, after the country lost such a popular president and was grieving.

Carolyn: Mr. President, have you seen any of the other interviews, and if so, what are your thoughts?

Bush: I saw the Rachel Carson interview and I saw the interview with Mr. Schneider, and my thoughts are that this is so exciting, and I am so excited that this is going to be available for those who need this information. What a gift. I feel so proud of what you are doing, Carolyn, and I think that you are a genius for thinking of this.

Carolyn: [Laughs.] Well, I can't take credit for this . . . I think someone on the other side planted the idea in my head; in fact, I know someone did.

Bush: That's a great way for us to get things done sometimes, to nudge or plant an idea in their head. I just wanted to say I feel so good about your book. I know that people will love your book.

Carolyn: Thank you! And I must thank you for suggesting that we speak with Mohandas Gandhi during our first interview—my goodness. [Note: I had spoken with Bush in October 2022, on topics unrelated to this book.]

Bush: Yes, did you do that?

Carolyn: Yes! Oh my gosh, I wish you could have seen it. I had no idea how inspired I'd be, so I can only imagine how the readers are going to feel. It was really something.

Bush: I'm so glad to hear that because Mahatma is someone who is extraordinary. Extraordinary.

Carolyn: You weren't kidding when you talked about his level of wisdom.

Bush: I'm so glad that you got to speak with him. I'll have to look for him and find out how that went for him. But I'm sure he had a wonderful experience as I have had. I'm so very glad that you reached out to him.

Carolyn: Mr. President, when you find Mohandas, can you please relay a simple message from us?

Bush: Yes!

Carolyn: One hundred percent. [Carolyn and John laugh.]

Bush: One hundred percent is the message?

Carolyn: [Laughs.] Yes, and he'll know exactly what we're talking about. He'll laugh, it will be very funny. It kind of became our inside joke.

Bush: [Amused.] Got it. One hundred percent. I just wanted to say, I feel so good about your book. And I'll give you an example: when our dog, Millie, had puppies, she wrote a book. And that book did better than Barbara's book. I know that people will love your book.

John: I think we need Millie's agent. [All laugh.]

Carolyn: On a serious note, thank you so much for talking with us again today. We so appreciate your help with this project, and we would also like to thank you for all your service to this country, in so many ways. And I really enjoy speaking with you. If we have follow-on books, are there any topics that you'd be interested in talking with us about, anything that feels inspiring to talk about?

Bush: Hmmm . . . I think I could be inspired by just about anything, honestly. I think that grief is something I could speak to. Obviously, many people experience this in their lifetime, often many times. I would be happy to help in any way that I can, and thank you for all of your kind words.

Carolyn: Thank you, Mr. President. We look forward to talking again.

CHAPTER 17:

Chico Mendes (1944–1988)

Interview date: January 21, 2023

Chico Mendes was a Brazilian environmental activist who advocated for the protection of the Amazon rainforest and the rights of indigenous peoples. At nine years of age, Mendes began working in rubber tapping, which is the process by which latex is extracted from a rubber tree. At age eighteen, Mendes learned how to read and became aware of the exploitation affecting his home. He organized and led labor unions, and he advocated for peaceful resistance against deforestation, which was occurring at a catastrophic rate in the 1970s and 1980s due to immense economic pressure to clear the rainforest for cattle.

After 130 ranchers ejected 100,000 rubber tappers from the rainforest, Mendes fought back and rallied people to stand in front of and block the bulldozers and chainsaws. Mendes's later efforts led to the establishment of "extractive reserves," areas of land that are protected and allocated to local communities for sustainable use, limiting deforestation and acting as a buffer zone to keep ranching out of the forests. He was able to persuade the World Bank to stop the funding of deforestation and finance nature reserves that function as sustainable rubber plantations. "At first I thought I was fighting to save rubber trees," Mendes said, a year before his death. "Then I thought I was fighting to save the Amazon rainforest. Now I realize I am fighting for humanity."

In 1988, Mendes successfully stopped a rancher from logging

an area designated as a nature reserve. As a result, he and his family received constant death threats. Three days before Christmas, Mendes was fatally shot outside of his home. The then US Vice President and current environmental activist, Al Gore, along with a delegation of US senators and representatives, were on a plane to Brazil to meet with Mendes when he was assassinated.

After his death, the Brazilian government ended subsidies for cattle ranchers and established eight million acres of nature and extraction reserves, including one named after Mendes. Mendes's murder put a spotlight on the hardship faced by environmental activists around the world, as well as the severe threats to the world's largest rainforest and the need for conservation in the Amazon.

Amazon Rainforest Summary

The more than 2.5 million square miles of the Amazon rainforest had been one of the world's greatest buffers against the climate crisis because the trees absorb carbon dioxide, keeping it out of the atmosphere where it would otherwise contribute to global warming. As a result of mass deforestation, the rainforest is now emitting more carbon than it can absorb through decomposition and from fires used to clear the land.

As of 2023, nearly 20 percent of the Amazon rainforest has been lost to deforestation, primarily due to agribusiness and meat consumption. Scientists have indicated that further deforestation could push the Amazon beyond the tipping point of 20 to 25 percent, making it much less efficient at absorbing carbon dioxide from the air, with significant impact on the climate worldwide.

The major challenge now is fighting illegal deforestation and reversing the devastation. Nearly 60 percent of the rainforest lies in Brazil, and deforestation reached historic levels under former President Jair Bolsonaro from 2019 to 2022. Fortunately, saving the Amazon is a top priority for Brazil's recently elected President Luiz Inacio Lula da Silva, who reduced deforestation by nearly 75 percent during his first presidency from 2003 to 2011. Colombia is home to 10 percent of the rainforest, and newly elected President Gustavo Petro has also announced initiatives to protect the Amazon. The remaining 30 percent of the Amazon is shared by seven countries. Amazonian countries must develop and implement a plan to save the Amazon, and countries around the world must support this endeavor. And as consumers of products from deforested areas, the most developed countries have a particular responsibility.

Carolyn: Mr. Mendes, can you please tell me if you agree with my summary of the situation? And then I'd like to get your thoughts on the current state of the Amazon rainforest.

Mendes: Yes, I do agree with you. When I was working as an activist for the indigenous people and for the forest, Brazil was under a military regime. We had very little support from our government at that time. Today, we have the cattle ranchers who are burning the fires and trying to clear the land for the cattle to graze. The fires can burn uncontrollably and burn more [land] than the ranchers planned to burn. With the president that we have now, we expect to have a great deal of support, and the plan is to continue to allow the ranchers to have their parts of the land. The Amazon rainforest is being studied to see how the forest and the indigenous people can cohabitate with the ranchers and prevent damage. What is being studied is how they can all work together as an ecosystem. We've made great advances in studying this.

You see, the plantation owners lost money when rubber was

replaced by synthetic rubber to make tires, so they had to offset that loss, and that's when they started to sell their land to cattle ranchers. We are trying now to work together with them rather than against them so the forest can be preserved and the animals can live in an ecosystem where everyone can thrive. Also, this has to do with replanting as well. But we feel like we have more support today than ever.

Carolyn: With the recent elections of Presidents Lula and Petro in Brazil and Colombia, respectively, where almost 70 percent of the Amazon rainforest is located, do you see us being able to avoid the tipping point, which is when 20 to 25 percent of the forested area is lost to deforestation?

Mendes: Well, it is my hope, of course. It is what I want. So, all I can say is we are working toward that. And for the rainforest in Borneo, there is a funded study group where they are studying, again, how to work together with the ranchers. But they are replanting their rainforest with palm trees for palm oil. The United States does not use a great deal of palm oil, but Asia does. Boycotting the palm oil industry would be a way to help.

Carolyn: And you feel Presidents Lula and Petro are the right leaders to protect the rainforest?

Mendes: I do. There is so much more attention to what is happening with the rainforest than ever before because there is an understanding of how much is at stake—how much we have to lose. The study groups I'm speaking of are being funded by sponsors, and they are looking at how to replenish the forest. They are trying to put in parameters for the cattle ranchers so that they do not infringe on the delicate life within the forest, and we can live peacefully together with the people and the animals and the forest and the ranchers.

Carolyn: Are you feeling that the majority of people in Brazil and Colombia are pro-environment and support protecting the Amazon rainforest?

Mendes: The majority? I feel like they understand ... When you see the devastation, you cannot help but feel that in your body. It is symbolic for what we are doing to our environment, what the world is doing to its environment. I feel that the people of Brazil and Colombia are aware of this, and the recent elections have shown this. They have voted for more support in helping the forest and the forest community as well.

Carolyn: In addition to continuing to vote for pro-environment candidates, what more would you like the people to do?

Mendes: Oh, I would like to see them be more active in helping to fund these study groups. As I said, they [study groups] have sponsors, and I believe the one in Borneo is SAFE. That is the name of the study group. There are ways to help fund the study groups and ways to help the indigenous people as well, so they are not living in poverty and are able to support their community. It helps them to not fall victim to the deforestation and not be in peril.

[Note: The Stability of Altered Forest Ecosystems (SAFE) project is one of the world's largest ecological experiments in terms of size and breadth of ecological processes. The findings of this study are helping scientists to design landscapes that maintain agricultural production at the least cost to biodiversity.]

Carolyn: In addition to supporting study groups, do you recommend any organization or organizations where people can help the indigenous peoples as well as the rainforest?

Mendes: I do not know the name of the organization.

Carolyn: Mr. Mendes, we will do the research and provide names of accredited organizations for the readers.

Mendes: Oh, thank you so much. I think that you have those resources. You have better resources for that than I do.

Carolyn: We recently spoke with conservationist Rachel Carson, on the other side, who was quite instrumental in changing the way the world viewed conservation. We discussed the Amazon rainforest, and she felt the American people, as well as people in other countries for the most part now, do not really understand what is at stake. And I'll be honest, before researching you and the Amazon rainforest, I was not aware of the severity of the situation. What would you like the readers of this book to do, in addition to contributing to study groups and organizations? How can they help? What would you like to see?

Mendes: I would like to see you inform them about why this is happening. I think that people feel powerless because they don't understand why the rainforest is dying off, and they don't fully understand that this is a man-made thing and not a phenomenon.

They don't understand how vital the rainforest is to the world in totality.

Carolyn: Yes, I agree, and I think this interview will help to educate. Since 2002, on average, one activist has been killed in Brazil every week trying to protect further destruction to the rainforest. Most of the killings happen in remote areas of the Amazon. This means that in two decades, over 1,000 activists have been killed in Brazil alone. How quickly do you see President Lula putting regulations in place and ramping up monitoring to crack down on further illegal deforestation to not only protect the forests but also the loss of life?

Mendes: Si. I feel that this is what he ran on. This is his platform—his important platform for becoming president—and the people voted for him on this. This is the work that he had promised he would do, and it is the work that he realizes is so important to put in place as soon as possible. And there just needs to be so much more protection. I had bodyguards, and I was still killed. The ranchers are extremely dangerous because they have money to lose if they don't get their land cleared for the cattle. They hate the activists. They don't *want* to understand, so they don't understand why we are protecting the forest. Even if they understood, they would not care. This is about greed. This is about taking the land and stripping the land for all it has.

John: You've commented that the ranchers are dangerous. Are they dangerous in the same way as the drug cartels, ruthless and willing to kill activists with barely a thought? Is it that kind of problem?

Mendes: Yes, si. It is that [kind of] problem.

John: President Lula is very much supporting the rainforest, but is he strong enough to take on these ranchers who seem to be the biggest part of the problem?

Mendes: I feel yes.

John: Is it your feeling that if the ranchers could be brought under control, they would bring deforestation under control? Is it 100 percent the ranchers?

Mendes: Yes, for the most part. But they want more and more and more. We have designated areas and reserves within the forest where they are not to cross, but there are fires burning as we speak in those areas. I don't know what the plan is with Lula, but there has to be some type of money exchange to keep the forests [as is]. And I hate that, but I don't know how else to do this.

John: It's either done with money, which addresses the greed, or the government has to get very tough to control the ranchers.

Mendes: Yes. With military force.

John: Now, I'd like to shift gears and ask about the kinds of things you might be doing on the other side. Are you working with people on Earth on conservation efforts? Are you working with others on the other side?

Mendes: Yes, I am working [from the other side] with the people who live in the forests, and I help to guide them through this. I am working to try to keep them safe and keep them in their environments. And I meet with the activists when they cross over.

They are giving their lives for this cause, and they know now, with the history of the activists, that they are giving their lives when they become vocal and when they become the peaceful activist. They know they are likely to give their lives. I meet with them when they cross over, and I want them to know their lives have not been in vain—that good will come from this.

John: Do you meet with every activist that crosses over?

Mendes: Yes.

John: Do you see these activists, after they crossover, on a regular basis, and are they also trying to help the people on Earth?

Mendes: Yes, we all have our roles. I am there to greet them and to comfort them when they cross over, and then they move on to their roles.

John: When the activists were still on Earth, were you a guide for them?

Mendes: Yes.

John: Do you think they understood you were their guide?

Mendes: I would like to think so. I think they understood, and I feel they knew. But even if they didn't know, I was there for them.

John: If people understood they have guides, it would make it easier for the guide to do their work. Do you agree?

Mendes: Yes, I would, yes.

John: A good message for people is that you do have help on the other side.

Mendes: That is everything to know, that we are not alone.

John: When you were on Earth, did you feel you had guides?

Mendes: I always felt support from the other side. I did not know who it was coming from at that time, but I knew I had ancestor help from the other side. I always knew that.

John: After you crossed over, what was the entrance like? Were you greeted by family? What was it like?

Mendes: I was greeted by family, and I was greeted by friends. I was enveloped in love and greeted by animals that I had known in my life. It is not an entrance that you walk through. It's a feeling. It is being reunited with those that made you feel loved. It is not everyone you ever knew. It's those you share that connection and love with.

John: Do you have plans to incarnate again at some point?

Mendes: I think I will be incarnating, but I don't know when. I'm feeling more and more prepared to do so.

John: When you come back into a body, do you know what types of things you will want to work on?

Mendes: I want to work to help the people of my country and the people of the world who do not have enough to eat. [For] those in poverty, I want to help to give them hope and light in their life, to be in a place where they do not have constant worry of where their food will come from or where their money will come from. That's what I want to work on.

John: I see. Do you think the project we are working on will be an effective way to spread messages of hope? Are we on the right track?

Mendes: I think you are on the right track; I do. This will be small and grow bigger and reach more people.

John: There are plans to address different topics in a series of books, and we hope that our reach will grow.

Mendes: That is what the plan is—for it to grow.

John: Did you know that we were working on this project and wanted to talk with you? Did you have any advance notification?

Mendes: I did know, but it was very short notice. Very short. I did not know for a long amount of time.

John: I see. Well, I'm very glad that you are available to help us. As Carolyn was saying earlier, when we do the research on the souls that we want to talk with, we are learning so much. And we are finding that everything is connected.

Mendes: Yes! And thank you for the work that you are doing because people need this right now.

Carolyn: Mr. Mendes, is there a message of hope that you would like to give to the people?

Mendes: My message is that we are all connected—with the environment, and the rainforest, and the ecosystem, and the animals, and the trees, and the people living there. It is very symbolic of how we can live together and how we can also take each other down without conscience. We need to live together because we are all connected.

John: Have you met with Saint Francis?

Mendes: No, I have not met with Saint Francis.

John: We spoke with Saint Francis, and he has the exact same message about everything being connected.

Mendes: This is a message that we all need to be reminded of—that we are not separate from each other.

John: Saint Francis also made the point that Earth is our partner. If we respect the Earth, the Earth will respect us. And if we treat the Earth badly, the Earth can actually be angry about that.

Mendes: Yes.

John: The Earth is not here just to give things to man. Man needs to give to the Earth, and then both parties will take care of each other.

Mendes: I believe that your information and your interviews and this education will be, not only helpful but will be like a warm blanket for people. They will get the information, and they will get comfort. We need to know why, and we need to know where, and this is like being wrapped in a warm blanket.

Carolyn: Thank you so much, Mr. Mendes. And thank you for talking with us today and for all the work that you did—and continue to do—to protect the Amazon rainforest. Your efforts and eventual death dramatically focused global attention on the severe threats to one of the most remarkable ecosystems in the world.

Amazon Rainforest Organizations

There are numerous organizations that are working hard to protect the Amazon rainforest and indigenous peoples, as well as other threatened tropical forests around the world. As of 2023, examples of organizations that are highly rated for protecting the Amazon rainforest in terms of overall impact include:

Rainforest Trust (rainforesttrust.org): Founded in 1988, the charity purchases and protects areas of the most threatened tropical forests, including the Amazon. Rainforest Trust focuses on areas that face immediate threats from deforestation and areas that are considered to be permanent refuges for endangered species. Today, the Rainforest Trust protects 43.4 million acres of rainforest around the world, including 15.8 million acres of the Amazon rainforest.

Amazon Conservation (amazonconservation.org): Founded in 1999, Amazon Conservation works to improve conservation efforts in the Amazon rainforest by applying technologies such as their real-time deforestation monitoring system. The charity also works to empower local communities by helping them develop sustainable forest products and protect their land from illegal logging practices. Additionally, the charity brings together government officials and community leaders to advance conservation solutions in the field and transform policy nationally. Amazon Conservation is currently focused on 124 million acres in the Amazon, and has protected over 8.3 million acres and invested $50 million in conservation projects.

Examples of organizations that campaign heavily for the rights of the indigenous Amazon peoples include:

Amazon Conservation Team (amazonteam.org): Founded in 1996, this charity works closely with local communities to monitor and care for their surrounding Amazon ecosystems. Through their land initiatives, the charity works with local governments to secure and expand indigenous reserves. To date, the Amazon Conservation Team has directly assisted with the expansion and creation of over 1.8 million acres of indigenous reserves in South America and has helped secure 193,000 acres of national parklands in the Amazon rainforest.

Survival International (survivalinternational.org): Founded in 1969, this human rights organization campaigns for the rights of tribal peoples around the world. The organization fights for tribal peoples' survival and stops loggers, miners, and oil companies from destroying tribal lands, lives, and livelihoods. Since its inception, this charity has supported approximately thirty-five indigenous tribes in the Amazon rainforest.

CHAPTER 18:

Dr. Stephen Schneider (1945–2010)

Interview date: November 12, 2022

Stephen Schneider was a leading climate scientist, serving as a consultant for the Nixon, Ford, Carter, Reagan, G.H.W. Bush, Clinton, G.W. Bush, and Obama administrations. He was a Stanford University biology professor, author and co-author of numerous climate-related books and scientific publications, and was involved with the Intergovernmental Panel on Climate Change (IPCC), a United Nations scientific body established to assess the science related to climate change. Schneider, along with his colleagues at the IPCC, including Al Gore, was a collective recipient of the 2007 Nobel Peace Prize. Described by the *New York Times* as a "climate warrior", Schneider worked tirelessly to urge political leaders and the public to take immediate action to avoid climate disasters.

Carolyn: Dr. Schneider, before I get started with my questions, I thought I'd open it up to what your thoughts are on the current state of the planet.

Schneider: Well, as a scientist, it's important for me to be honest and truthful. As a human, I also have compassion for the state of the climate and the people, but I'm fearful that we won't make it to the 1.5 Celsius goal in 2030. I feel that we are moving too late on this, and that is something that I feel is important to say.

Carolyn: For clarification, are you saying that you don't think we will meet the 2030 goal [reduce emissions by 45%], but we can still meet the 2050 goal?

Schneider: Yes, 2030. But 2050, we can still meet that goal, but it will be tight, Carolyn, I have to tell you. I'm an optimist, but I'm also a scientist. I feel that we can do it, but it's going to be very tight. We just can't fall asleep anymore.

Carolyn: No, we can't. In the summary, I mentioned the Paris Agreement with the goal of net-zero carbons by 2050 and limiting warming to 1.5 degrees Celsius. I also talked about findings from a report issued very recently by the IPCC, that many countries around the world are failing to live up to their commitments to fight climate change, putting the world on track to reach over 2.5 degrees Celsius by the end of the century, which would be catastrophic. Just twenty-six of the 193 countries that agreed last year to step up their climate actions have followed through with more ambitious plans. China was not one of these countries and is the world's biggest emitter. There is no enforcement mechanism, and the people of the world are relying on these countries to live up to their commitments. What actions can people take to encourage and ensure across-the-board adoption?

Schneider: Well, there needs to be more incentive for China. Obviously, seeing the world in a catastrophic state is not incentive enough for them. There needs to be more incentive. There has to be something, and perhaps it needs to be the same goals that we are working on in the US. They have to be in place with China, as you said, being the biggest polluter of our world at this moment, with the US not that far behind. The incentive should be something that hits them in the economy because their failure to do this is holding us all back tremendously. At least the US has policies and goals, and they are trying to make those goals, but China is not doing a damn thing about it. There has to be some sort of incentive or perhaps the opposite way, punishment, where they are cut off from being able to participate in the US economy and being able to do trading with the US, and shipping goods to the US. It has to be cut off. We have to become more self-sufficient and less reliant on China because that is the only way that I see they will take action.

Carolyn: Can you put into perspective how just 1 degree or even 1.5 degrees Celsius is a huge deal? And that 2 degrees Celsius would be catastrophic?

Schneider: Well, what it boils down to is the greenhouse gas emissions. The heat is being trapped in the Earth. Therefore, it's combating with nature. Nature has its own way of releasing heat during the night and cooling the Earth as well. But these greenhouse gases become entrapped in the Earth and are creating the warming of the oceans and land. When you have the oceans becoming warmer, we are getting more hurricane activity, and we are getting hurricanes that are enormous, and that alone is catastrophic. There is no way to prepare for shelter against these hurricanes that are so large that just hover, and that is because of the oceans that are warming from the greenhouse gas emissions. The drought is because of the emissions being trapped in the Earth. The drought leads to the wildfires. That is how this all becomes catastrophic.

We are in survival mode constantly because there is no battling the Earth when it is angry. There is no competition. We are far, far, far outnumbered. We are defeated because we cannot compete. Our structures cannot compete. The planet cannot compete with itself. That's why it becomes catastrophic. Hunger becomes an enormous problem in third world countries because of the drought. Therefore, you have all of these enormous, enormous issues going on simultaneously.

Carolyn: President Trump pulled the United States out of the Paris Agreement just months after taking office in 2017. And on his first day in office in 2021, President Biden brought the US back into the Agreement. But now, other countries are not convinced the United States can be a stable, reliable partner that can be counted on to commit to the Agreement long-term. Unfortunately, as you know, global warming and climate change have become a partisan issue. From your perspective, do you see the United States remaining in the Paris Agreement for the years to come, even if the next president is Republican?

Schneider: Well, I can't guarantee, but I do see that the awareness now is becoming more out there. And people are realizing, from what they are witnessing, because now it's really reaching them. When we were working on it years ago, there was not the evidence that people are now living with, and it was harder to reach people, convince people. Now people are living in this prediction, and they can no longer deny it. I can understand the other countries seeing us as unstable because we're in or we're out depending on who is in office, but I do not see us pulling out again. It is so critical that even if there is a Republican president, I don't feel that our country would elect another president who is in denial of global warming, especially when it is so prevalent at this time.

Carolyn: We are in the process of a clean energy transition, as agreed to in the Paris Agreement. Fossil fuels currently account for 80 percent of the energy generated worldwide. The top three renewable energy sources are solar, wind, and hydropower. And there is nuclear energy.

As we make this transition to clean energy, many experts agree that nuclear energy will need to play an important role. Nuclear energy can provide a continuous and reliable source of energy, as you know, unlike renewable energy sources, which require sun, wind, and water, which are intermittent. As progress in nuclear power technologies continue, they are leading to innovative next-generation reactor designs that can help make nuclear power a more efficient, affordable, safe, and attractive option for decarbonization. What are your thoughts on nuclear energy and its role in helping us reach the 2050 net-zero carbon goal?

Schneider: Well, I'm not entirely convinced yet that it can be affordable. It's a very expensive process. I'm also not entirely convinced of the safety of it. So, that is something that I'm anxious to see developed. The progression to nuclear energy being affordable and safe—those are the two things that I'm still not completely convinced of—and it has to be safe, and it has to be affordable for us to be able to use this going forward. I'm still a strong believer in solar and wind power. Those are the top two for me at this point. But I never say never. Scientists continue to look into new ways to do things more efficiently, and the inventors and I have great faith. There are a number of people working on this, and they can get there. And I have great faith that if there is a way for nuclear energy to become affordable and safe, they will get there. But at present, we are not close yet.

Carolyn: Can you tell us if there will be beneficial emerging technologies in clean energy that we can expect to see in the near future?

Schneider: Well, I think the entire industry is working on this. Having the universities come into this, and the government is playing its role, and having other components in place, I have great faith because we are going to get there. I just can't say with 100 percent belief that we're going to meet that goal, but I feel that we will do what we need to do. I feel that just now, things are really starting to roll, and if we can keep that going, I'd love to be proven wrong.

I also want to say that being a scientist on climate change is not a very popular position, not a very popular thing to be. Nobody wants to hear it. That's why you are seeing a lot of scary images in the media—it's to get attention. I know that you've been talking about other ways to get attention, and I think that is definitely something that needs to be tried because the media is failing at this. So, I just want to say that I feel that trying to reach out through the media with positive information is definitely something that is a different way to go than what we've tried before, and I'd like to see that happen because the scary images don't seem to be getting the attention we were hoping for as well.

Carolyn: Can you tell me if you are part of a, for lack of a better term, a scientific working group, where you are collaborating with other climate scientists, and researchers, etcetera, on the other side?

Schneider: Uh, yes. I can tell you that. We don't have to use models. And that is an extraordinary gift to be able to go to the source, to be able to study the Earth and not have to use models. I never thought it was possible. At this time, there are about twenty-six of us, which really isn't that many, but we're trying to be there to support those who are still in a body and help them as much as we can with support. If we see something, we try to get their attention.

Carolyn: So, it sounds like there is information being communicated from the working group to scientists, researchers, and others here on Earth?

Schneider: Yes, Carolyn, however, it can be communicated. Sometimes scientists will stumble on something and say, "Oh my gosh, why didn't I think of that before?" And it's because we gave them a nudge. Other times, we are guiding them toward what they need to assess a situation. Just because we are crossed over doesn't mean that we are smarter, but we can see things from a different perspective. It's almost like you're too close when you're working on the same thing all the time. We have a different perspective, and we have a meeting of the minds quite often, and I think that our collaboration is what leads us to a lot of information that we come up with. As a scientist [on Earth], you are not always working in collaboration, and it's very rewarding [on the other side] to be able to discuss discoveries with other scientists and debate. And be introduced to new theories and information. It's a think tank, and we are guiding others in a body who are working on this very same thing.

Carolyn: In your writings, speeches, and interviews, you acknowledged the fierceness of the debate over climate change and environmental policies. You had become a vocal advocate for scientists becoming more assertive in voicing their conclusions in ways that would be clearer to the public and political and governmental leaders worldwide. How do you think the scientists are doing now?

Schneider: Well, they have definitely improved. We could go back to my discussions with Nixon, who thought I was telling him fairy tales. Now I see the politicians are using the scientists as they should to get clear and concise facts as to what is happening with the climate change situation, rather than speculating or saying it will just go away. They are now working more arm and arm with the scientists and realizing they are a vital resource for upholding what they want to do for the country or countries.

We are now getting respect because the evidence is presenting itself on a daily basis with the repercussions of the greenhouse gas emissions and the change, so the scientists are becoming more assertive. I think it's important to be assertive and professional and not aggressive. I think that does not go over well and is something that will backfire. I think we are all working together now in a much better way. There will always be those who can't accept the truth and information. But I will say that I see great progress in this area.

Carolyn: Polls and surveys are all over the place on this one, but most of the American people now believe global warming, caused by human activity, is happening. Republicans in Congress, however, are out of step with the public on climate. Currently, over 50 percent of Republican members of Congress are climate deniers. In fact, President Biden's recent climate legislation passed without a single Republican vote. As I stated earlier, you worked tirelessly, urging political leaders and the public to take action to avoid climate disasters. You were a consultant to seven White House administrations. What message would you like to give to the climate-denying Republican elected officials?

Schneider: Well, the stance is that they don't want to spend the money; they don't want to spend the taxpayer's money. And that is the core of what the Republican Party stands for—they don't want to spend the money, and they are looking out for the taxpayers, protecting the taxpayers.

But the truth is, there is no way out of this unless we spend the money. That stance is starting to wear thin because people are realizing that something has to happen, has to happen now, has to happen yesterday, and we all have to play a role in it.

Those Republican deniers can continue to deny, but the people in this world are living through this climate change and experiencing it, and they realize we have to put money toward this transition, and it has to be done. I don't feel that the Republicans are being taken completely seriously. It's an automatic with them to say no because of the costs. But the more they say no, the more the costs increase because, with anything, it becomes more and more of an expense the longer you wait.

Carolyn: As I mentioned earlier, you served as a consultant to the Reagan administration. In the early years of his presidency, Reagan famously said that trees caused more pollution than automobiles. Reagan removed President Carter's solar panels from the West Wing, he slashed the EPA budget, he reduced environmental enforcement, and he opened public lands for mining and drilling. Many environmentalists insist that the Reagan environmental record will be remembered as one of the worst of any modern presidency along with President Trump. Have you been in contact on the other side with President Reagan, and if so, have his thoughts about global warming changed?

Schneider: I have, and his thoughts about many things have changed. He is, in many ways, a humbled man. When he went through dementia, it's almost like there was a reset, which didn't show itself because of the illness, but it erased so much information. It's like the "tapes" were erased. Now, when I speak with him, he's a humbled man, and it's almost like, in many ways, he is very naive and doesn't understand the things that he did at that time, or didn't do at that time, or said. It's almost like it happened to another person. And I have to say, from my point of view, it all looked very greedy to me, the things that he did not back, the things he cut, all in the name of the taxpayer to save money, but it was very greedy and careless.

Carolyn: Might President Reagan like to talk with me?

Schneider: Do you want to talk with him?

Carolyn: I think it could be important for the climate deniers in the Republican Party to hear his new perspective if it has indeed changed.

Schneider: Well, I think that he would be someone you should seek out then. I really have to say, I'm not sure what you'll get because he is in a bit of a child-like state, and that has nothing to do with his previous illness. He is absorbing more information than sharing. But if you feel like you want to reach out, I don't see the harm in that.

Carolyn: I'd like to get your perspective as to how the shift in the Republican Party went from Theodore Roosevelt, who was one of the most powerful voices in the history of American conservation, and Nixon creating the EPA and protecting the environment, to global warming and climate change being politicized as a bleeding heart, liberal issue in later years. Reagan certainly had a hand in this. However, George H.W. Bush promised he would be the environmental president, and in many ways, he delivered. And we know the battles John McCain stood up for, for the environment, during his time in the Senate. Other than protecting the taxpayers and trying to keep costs down, what are your thoughts on what happened to the Republican Party? Is it simply a matter of elected officials beholden to wealthy donors and corporations?

Schneider: I think that's an enormous part of it. You've answered your own question. I think it's something that also happens on the Democrat side. They are not innocent either. Politics got very corrupt when they started catering to large corporations and following that greed. There is no innocence, but I feel that the Republican Party at this time, the majority, 99 percent, are beholden to large corporations, the NRA, and those huge money machines.

Carolyn: What we can do, as American citizens, to turn this around, especially considering the current gridlock in Congress?

Schneider: Apply a lot of pressure and turn their backs on them [the politicians]. I don't know if we're there yet. There are still a lot of followers who will vote for the party no matter what the party is doing. That is definitely part of the problem. But I feel that people are starting to wake up. I feel there is some comeuppance, and I feel that things are starting to rattle, and they will start to shake, and then they [the politicians] will implode on themselves in many ways. I am just looking at it from my perspective.

Carolyn: Have you had an opportunity to talk with President Nixon?

Schneider: I have not actually spoken with him since I've crossed over. And from what I understand, he's doing a lot of self-reflection, a lot of self-isolation, and that is part of his journey.

Carolyn: As we approach the end of our hour here, is there anything you would like to add?

Schneider: Oh, my goodness, I think that we've talked about a great deal. But if every person does what they can, think of what a difference that would make. Putting in place solar or wind energy for our world, no, but what they can do for their own lives is to make the transition to hybrid or an electric vehicle. You've got an 8,000-pound vehicle that is running on fossil fuel, and all of the greenhouse gas emissions coming from that are pretty impactful. Anything that people can do in that regard will make a difference, and it's important for them to know they can make small differences.

Carolyn: Who else would you recommend that I speak with?

Schneider: I don't know if you have considered Jacques Cousteau.

Carolyn: Actually, no, I have not! That's a great idea, and we will seek him out.

Schneider: He's someone who may be able to help you with what you are working on and someone who is very in touch with the planet and what is going on. It's very important to him also, to be able to reach others, and I think this would be an excellent way for him to do that.

Carolyn: Our next conversation will be with Nikola Tesla. Are there any particular points I should raise with Mr. Tesla?

Schneider: [Laughs.] Don't ask him about pigeons, just don't do that! It's a sensitive subject. He is someone that I sought out when I crossed over because I've always been an admirer of his. He is what you would call an eccentric, but in a beautiful way. Anything you ask him, be prepared because you're not going to get a usual answer. He is an extremely creative individual. I think you'll really enjoy yourself.

Carolyn: Fantastic. And we'll definitely stay away from pigeon talk! Before we part, what message of hope would you like to give to the people?

Schneider: Oh boy, as a human being, you know, keep looking at the positives. Yes, I know most of my life I spent spreading messages of impending doom. Don't take your eye off the positives because the world is full of them.

Carolyn: Thank you so much for joining us today, Dr. Schneider, and thank you for all that you have done and continue to do on behalf of the planet. Thank you!

CHAPTER 19:

Senator Gaylord Nelson (1916–2005)

Interview date: November 19, 2022

Gaylord Nelson was a Wisconsin state senator for ten years until he was elected governor of Wisconsin for two terms. He would go on to serve three terms as a Democratic US senator from 1963 to 1981. During this time, Nelson founded Earth Day, a now annual event first celebrated on April 22, 1970, to raise awareness of the need to preserve the planet's natural resources for future generations. The first Earth Day, celebrated by more than twenty million people, would serve as an impetus for some of the country's most important environmental legislation, such as the Environmental Protection Act, the Clean Air Act, and the Clean Water Act. During his time in the US Senate, Nelson sponsored numerous conservation bills and authored legislation to preserve the Appalachian Trail, create the National Trails System, and ban the harmful pesticide DDT.

Carolyn: Senator, before we get started with questions, I thought I'd open it up to what your thoughts are on the current state of the planet.

Nelson: Alright. Well, I'd like to note that when Earth Day started in 1970, there was five times more air pollution than today, so that is significant progress. Mostly, we are talking about particulate matter that is in the air. We are also talking about ozone issues and other unhealthy pollutants in the air. The levels are much lower now in America, and I'd like to note that progress.

Carolyn: Oh, that is terrific progress. I was not aware of that.

Nelson: As far as the carbon emissions, that is the main crux of what we are dealing with. I know that there is a movement and there has been progress, such as electric cars, but I feel that it is still very expensive at this point. You have to put yourself in the shoes of people who have had the same car for over twenty years because they don't have the finances to move to that type of energy. Electric cars need to become much more affordable. So, not only looking toward new ways to power those cars but ways to make those cars more affordable. We still have far to go.

What I see is there are more and more people populating the Earth and using the Earth's resources. But this Earth is over five billion years old, and I really don't think that it can be terminated by the human race at this point. But sometimes I think we are trying really hard!

Carolyn: Isn't that the truth!

Nelson: Still, I think there is quite a bit of hope. The environment is something that people have so much more awareness of than they ever did. It starts in small ways, but we have to keep doing what we can. It starts at home. We need to remove the plastics that we see outside from the environment. We need to cut down or remove pesticides from our gardens and look toward natural ways.

And there are many small things that we can all be doing, such as swapping out kitchen and household products that are not environmentally friendly and reduce, reuse, and recycle. People are doing that more than ever. When I started campaigning about environmental protection and talking about Earth Day, no one recycled. Everyone threw everything away, no matter what it was. There was no regard to what it would do to the Earth. Now, little children grow up learning how to do that.

Also, conserving water, of course, not doing as much, laundry and wearing things more often than one time. We've become phobic about our own body smells, and I don't want anyone to become offensive [laughs], but you can get away with wearing things more than one time. Just those small things make such an impact.

Carolyn: In the summary, I mentioned the Paris Agreement, with the goal of net-zero carbon emissions by 2050 and limiting warming to 1.5 degrees Celsius. Unfortunately, in a report issued very recently by the United Nations, many countries around the world are failing to live up to their commitments to fight climate change, putting the world on track to reach over 2.5 degrees Celsius by the end of the century, which would be catastrophic. Very few of the 193 countries that agreed to step up their climate actions have followed through with more ambitious plans. China was not one of these countries and is the world's biggest emitter. There is no enforcement mechanism, and people around the world are relying on all of these countries to live up to their commitments.

Relations between China and the US have been more than frosty until recently. President Biden and President Xi are finally back on speaking terms, and the White House recently announced the two countries would resume their climate talks. Do you see China taking steps in the very near future to finally get on board to meet their Paris Agreement commitments?

Nelson: I do, but not until they are pushed into a corner. And that could be fees and embargoes, but the line has to be drawn. They are dragging their heels, which I don't understand. Who wouldn't want to live in a safer, healthier world? Economically, they would take a hit, and they realize this by making these changes.

Carolyn: What actions, in addition to embargoes and fees, should governments and even people around the world take to ensure or encourage commitments are being met by the largest emitters, and not only from China?

Nelson: Well, limit trading with these countries, limit the purchase of goods from these countries, and I think that would be very effective. We would take a hit by limiting goods for sure, especially since America no longer produces as it once did. But I think it would need to be prioritized, and it certainly can. Have medical needs at the top of the list and plastic dolls at the bottom of the list. That list is quite large and vast, and it would still limit them in a way that would make them rethink their plan of action.

Carolyn: Ultimately, do you see the world being able to meet the net-zero goal by 2050 and not exceed 1.5 degrees Celsius?

Nelson: Well, I believe we can do it. I don't have a crystal ball, but I believe we can do it. And that's not just about good old-fashioned faith. I believe we can do this, especially as it begins to have more and more impact on us. It is not an illusion; it is reality. With our climate and our weather systems, it is affecting everyone. There is no one who will not be affected.

Carolyn: We are in the process of a clean energy transition, as agreed to in the Paris Agreement. As I stated in the summary, fossil fuels currently account for 80 percent of the energy generated worldwide. The top three renewable energy sources are solar, wind turbines, and hydropower. And there is nuclear energy. As we make this transition to clean energy, many experts agree that nuclear energy will need to play an important role. As progress in nuclear power technologies continues, they are leading to next-generation reactor designs that can help make nuclear power a more efficient, affordable, safe, and attractive option for decarbonization. What are your thoughts on nuclear energy and its role in helping us reach the 2050 net-zero carbon goal?

Nelson: Well, I think it will play an important role. What I believe is part of the current conundrum is that we need to devise a way to clean up radioactive uranium. There are scientists working on that, and I believe it's something they will be able to solve. I also want to mention geothermal energy. I see where it could possibly be changing. It's very expensive to build, but it has almost no negative effects. And it actually may have a positive effect in removing the heat from the water to create the steam. My concern is that it will not be available to enough people. It's a work in progress.

But I feel very positive about solar because it's very cheap and very effective, and I feel very positive about nuclear energy. I think that these methods could accelerate our progress quite a bit, and I hope to see them come to fruition so they are in play very soon. I'm mostly speaking about nuclear energy. I feel that would be a way to give us some time.

Carolyn: Let me switch gears a bit here, and I'm sorry if I'm being nosy.

Nelson: [Laughs.]

Carolyn: Can you tell me if you are part of a working group or think tank where you are collaborating with other political leaders, scientists, etc., where you are at?

Nelson: I am. And I don't feel like you are being nosy.

Carolyn: Are you able to share who else is in your working group?

Nelson: No, I'm not. I'm so sorry.

Carolyn: That's okay. Is information being communicated from the working group to people here on Earth, and if so, are the messages being received and applied?

Nelson: You can guarantee it. Why else would we be doing this if not to help? That's what I like most about what we do. We are able to make a difference.

Carolyn: Can you share if there will be emerging technologies in clean energy coming from this group or other groups, and if so, what the innovations might look like?

Nelson: Let me think about this ... We have, as you say, a think tank where we consult with each other, and then those ideas are passed on to those on Earth. It becomes their ideas. It's very much like a whisper in their ear, but we do not claim that we create technology.

Carolyn: Most of the American people now believe human-caused global warming is happening. Republicans in Congress, however, are out of step with the public on climate. Currently, over 50 percent of Republican members of Congress are climate deniers. In fact, President Biden's recent climate legislation passed without a single Republican vote. What message would you like to give to the climate-denying Republican elected officials?

Nelson: Wake up and smell the coffee. Wake up and smell the planet. Wake up!

Carolyn: You were a senator for nearly twenty years. In 1969, you came up with a plan to raise awareness and put pressure on politicians to enact environmental legislation. You proposed a day when citizens nationwide could host teach-ins to raise awareness of environmental issues and send a message to Washington that the public supported a bold political agenda on the environment. The media provided coverage of the plans, and your office was inundated with overwhelming support. Your idea became Earth Day, and twenty million Americans gathered on April 22, 1970, to address the ecological problems in their communities, country, and planet—and to demand action from elected officials.

What actions do you suggest the American public take to make their voices heard by these members of Congress that would be meaningful and impactful enough for them to want to act?

Nelson: Ahh, well, I don't think we have to wait for Earth Day, but if the American people staged their own improv Earth Day outside of April in front of the [government] offices and buildings, I feel that just being there and seeing that would make an impact. That's very simple compared to other ways we have to reach the politicians today.

Carolyn: And why not fly an Earth Day flag every single day?

Nelson: Of course. Small things have such an impact, especially when they are done by many people. I feel that we still have that American spirit, where when we are passionate, we can get things done. We can make an impact on these brick walls. Meaning the politicians that are denying climate change is real, denying that things need to be put into action immediately—yesterday. And if there is a way that we can all do things simultaneously to promote awareness, I think that could be very positive. It could be about displaying the flag. And there could even be an incentive attached to that. I'm not sure yet what that would be, but some type of incentive.

Carolyn: My next question is centered around actions the American public can take to further support environmental awakening and increase awareness amongst their fellow citizens. For example, I had an idea to write my elected officials to suggest the creation of a program where special interest license plates featuring the Earth, along with some sort of "green" tagline, are offered free of charge with no annual renewal fee to hybrid and electric vehicle drivers. Do actions such as this make a difference, from your perspective?

Nelson: Yes, I think that would make a difference. Earth Day—it came about as a way to spread the word of awareness and remind us about the human race and the effect it has on the planet and also to prevent the human race from wreaking further damage to the planet. We didn't have all of the information at the time, but it made a tremendous impact, and it became global. It is still happening. More and more people are coming together for Earth

Day, and they do good things for the Earth on that day. If there is any way that awareness can be promoted, I'm all for it, and I believe that it has a positive impact.

Carolyn: Do you have additional ideas that could increase public awareness to inspire people to get on board and take action on behalf of our planet?

Nelson: I know that there's been talk of positivity, a campaign of positivity of good things that have happened. I support that 100 percent, just as I was saying that air pollution was five times more than in the 1970s than it is today. Who knows that? People don't have that information out there.

I don't like the idea of people living in fear. I like the idea of people feeling encouraged and inspired to do more good for the planet because they see how it can have a positive impact. I appreciate the campaign of positivity about what is happening with the planet.

Carolyn: How can we encourage those individuals who have the financial resources and are strong supporters of the environment, such as Bill Gates and Michael Bloomberg, to help drive a positivity campaign?

Nelson: Perhaps that's something that you can discuss with them [Gates and Bloomberg] prior to the publishing of your book, about creating a website, or something where messages can be sent to them in support of this. People tend to not write letters, but if it takes just a few seconds to send an email, they are there.

Carolyn: On Earth Day 1970, you said we should outlaw the internal combustion engine unless pollution from it could be reduced to near zero. Well, this will finally be happening in a handful of states starting in 2035 in terms of banning the sale of new gas-powered cars. Do you see this ban gaining in popularity, becoming more widespread across the states, along with a robust electric vehicle charging infrastructure to support such a shift?

Nelson: Initially, I don't see a lot of followers, but then, as it grows, I see more and more of the states getting on board with this. I don't see it happening overnight. As far as the infrastructure, I feel that we are slow to embrace change in this country, but we will realize that we have no choice. Again, if it [electric vehicles] can be made in a way where it is more affordable for families and individuals to make this transition, the transition will be more popular.

Carolyn: I was wondering if you've watched any of my interviews, and if so if you had any comments.

Nelson: Yes, I have, and I do. I think that what you are doing is fantastic and so thought-provoking, and I thank you. One thing that I ask is that you look toward the women. I don't see women on your list. There are hundreds and thousands of indigenous people who were environmental activists who have been murdered for protecting the rainforest, their land, from being encroached upon by people who wanted to profit through illegal poaching and hunting.

I will say that Rachel Carson is a very important person to speak with. If you speak with no other women, she would be at the top of the list. And I do want to say that the work you are doing is going to be very inspiring, and I thank you.

Carolyn: Oh, thank you so much. Rachel Carson is on our list to speak with, but I will also look into speaking with indigenous peoples who were environmental activists. As we wrap things up, Senator, is there anything you would like to add?

Nelson: I would like to add that I am honored to have been a part of this today. I apologize for not fully understanding some of your questions, but I feel that we still got there. I feel that you are extremely passionate about this project, and I am very proud of you personally, and I thank you for what you are doing. I also want you to know this makes me feel quite proud to know that you know who I am and that you know some of the things I have accomplished. It's not because my ego needs stroking as much as it makes me feel proud that I have helped influence others to protect our planet.

Carolyn: Well, that you did. And, you know, I have the best "job" in the world to be able to talk with souls such as yourself, who have made such an impact on this planet. I thank you, truly, for all that you have done and continue to do. Senator, who else would you recommend that I speak with, in addition to indigenous peoples who were environmental activists?

Nelson: Are you talking with Einstein?

Carolyn: He's not on my list, but that's a fantastic idea.

Nelson: Well, if we're talking about nuclear energy, he might be someone who could give some insight on that. But he is also funny and nice to talk to. It wouldn't be a wasted day; let's put it that way.

Carolyn: Lastly, what message of hope would you like to give to the people?

Nelson: My message is that I believe in the people. I know we all have our differences on Earth right now. But I believe that we can do this. And I believe that the information to make this happen—to meet our goals in protecting this planet and protecting the human race—that information is out there. There are many souls working on this, and I think that is something very hopeful to know. People are dedicating their lives and careers to bettering our world.

Afterword

As I sit on a bench at the end of a little street on a bluff overlooking the ocean in Northern California, I reflect on the last fifteen months since this journey began. I take in my surroundings and feel a strong heart connection, that didn't exist before, with the ocean as well as the sandy earth beneath my feet. I feel a sense of peace and comfort for the future. I can breathe. The conversations transcribed in this book are responsible for this shift in the quality of my thoughts and the feeling of interconnectedness with not only the planet but with people as well. My awareness has been raised, and I see the changes in my own actions in response to how I care for our planet.

I think more about my carbon footprint now. I know that a roundtrip flight from San Francisco to New York City will generate 1.5 metric tons of carbon dioxide per passenger. But I also know that many souls are working diligently on the other side to help people on Earth develop future solutions to make travel more environmentally friendly.

I look forward to taking another cruise when zero-emission ships are commonplace, and marine wildlife safety is a priority.

This year alone, John and I have visited seven California state parks and natural reserves. Inspired by Theodore Roosevelt and John Muir, we've twice taken in the beauty of a massive redwood tree grove, walked scenic trails that led to pristine and secluded beaches, and delighted in sea otters, elephant seals, and monarch butterfly sanctuaries.

I think of Gandhi's motto, "simple living, high thinking." I've stopped buying so much stuff. I don't need more things. Instead, I've been freeing up physical and mental space around my house by finding a second life for unnecessary items. I'm more aware of product packaging, the amount of waste I am generating, and the impact on the landfills. I can no longer ignore a piece of litter on the ground, especially when I'm near the coast. Instead, I hear the calls to action from Charles Keeling and Jacques Cousteau. Because of Rachel Carson, greater consideration is given to our household cleaning products and garden insecticide choices and their impact on the environment. And now my thoughts go to Gaylord Nelson after I've worn an article of clothing and am tempted to toss it in the hamper. Is it really dirty or can I wear it one more time?

When there's breaking news of yet another mass shooting, my first thought is to send love to Samuel Clemens and the other souls who are busy on the front lines on the other side, meeting these victims as they cross over and working so hard to quell the gun violence epidemic in the US. At this point, I keep a photo of Clemens on my wall. And, as encouraged by so many of the souls, I've been writing to my elected officials. I also send cards of gratitude to US representatives and senators in other states when they do good things for the environment or for the country.

I ask The Council for their assistance with things that are bothering me. I talk to my guides more frequently and ask for their help. As I recover from a stubborn case of pneumonia, I connect a lot with Theodore Roosevelt these days. I know he had struggled with asthma and that he is well-equipped to support me with my breathing challenges. I try to keep negative emotions out of my heart. I am much quicker to forgive others and just move on. I think of John Muir's words to me, "Let that go. Let that go. It's just garbage."

I now have a very special connection with Saint Francis and have placed my two-foot-tall garden statue of him with the wolf in my office/meditation room. I don't want the statue outside—I want Saint Francis closer to me. Sometimes, after a meditation, I give Saint Francis a big kiss on the side of his head. I have adorned the statue with a rose quartz necklace and my childhood rosary beads, and I place items that need healing at the foot of the statue.

And every day, I reflect on Saint Francis's powerful words. "We must treat Earth as family, as a loved one. The lesson is we need to come together; we need to be kind to each other and honor each other; we need to love each other as best we can and love everything in our world. That kindness needs to be shared with our planet, and that kindness needs to be shared with the animals. I have hope that humanity can start to love and heal the Earth. I feel that once that is in place, once that is genuine and coming from the heart, that things will begin to turn around. Earth will begin to heal. Together, we are all One, and we need to have mercy and compassion for each other and for all living things."

Yes, indeed, Saint Francis. We *are* all One.

Carolyn Thomas, Santa Cruz, CA
December 2023

Carolyn Thomas lives in Northern California with her husband John and has been on a spiritual path since the 1980s. With a BS degree in marketing, she worked for many years at high tech companies in Silicon Valley and is now retired. Carolyn has an agreement with a group of ascended master beings on the other side known as The Council to put forth messages of hope from inspirational souls to people on Earth. The Council initiates contact with these noteworthy souls, facilitating the interviews conducted through Sam. Carolyn looks forward to her role as messenger for future books on a variety of topics that can provide messages of hope and healing to many people on Earth.

John Thomas is a classic Silicon Valley "tech guy." After receiving his chemical engineering degree, John worked for many years in various technical fields including software, semiconductors, and advanced battery technologies. Along the way, he was able to see the environmental impact of these technologies, and he developed a deep appreciation for those companies that were serious about creating sustainable practices and protecting the environment. In *Channeled Messages of Hope*, John led the more technical interviews and participated with Carolyn in most others. John is currently the CEO of a start-up developing highly sustainable technologies in the food and agriculture industries.

Sam Larkin holds a master's degree and works in financial services in the Bay Area. She is highly clairvoyant and clairsentient, and for many years shared her psychic and animal communication gifts with others by offering readings on weekends. With an intention to take her intuitive gifts to the next step, Sam began channeling notable spirits with Carolyn. Sam is able to "step away" from her body, surrender control, and allow the essence of the soul to inhabit her body, utilize her vocal cords, and converse one-on-one with Carolyn. Her incredibly rare gift enables Carolyn to have a conversational dialogue with souls that can be humorous at times, as well as more serious, and makes for highly compelling content with much depth and richness.

Made in the USA
Middletown, DE
18 September 2024